What Others Are Saying

I've always believed in the motto, "Work smarter, not harder". Drs. Duckworth and Langworthy have shown how this can be accomplished in their latest installment of the "Shifting Gears" series. This book provides mountains of valuable information on assessing if a shift to a career working online is for you and how to go about achieving it. Both pre- & post-retirement aged people will gain greater insights and knowledge from this terrific book that will have you feeling better about yourself and more energized in your potential future work structure from home. Buy it, read it, act on it and then, pass it on!

Larry Dasilva—*Host/Producer, "Studio 411", Talk Program, Stars & Legends CT/NutmegTV*

Having worked remotely for the better part of seven years, I know the significance of having access to these resources. Even more importantly -- know yourself well enough to assess if working online is for you. This book has invaluable advice and provides a treasure chest of resources for working and being employed remotely.

Kirsten E. Hoyt—*Academic Dean, College of Information Systems and Technology, University of Phoenix*

What a piece of work! This is one stop shopping for anyone who has ever dreamed of ditching the traffic jams and office politics of the modern workplace. I simply can't say enough. It changed my life!

Sam Cook—*Online Owner and Manager of Mastery Tutors, Inc.*

Shifting Gears to Your Career Working Online

Your Guide to Successfully Finding & Claiming Your Place in the Cyber-Workplace

Carolee Duckworth & Marie Langworthy

ISBN-13: 978-0-9845136-5-9

Library of Congress Cataloging-in-Publication Data

Duckworth, Carolee, & Langworthy, Marie

      Shifting Gears to Your Career Working Online / Carolee Duckworth and Marie Langworthy, New Cabady Press.

Included Index, References.

ISBN-13: 978-0-9845136-5-9

1. Personal Living 1.a) Self-Actualization 1.b) Finance—Personal
   646.79
2. Career Change 2.a) Technology   650.14
3. Career Development   370.113
4. Home Based Businesses   658.041
5. Internet Marketing 5.a) Electronic Commerce 5.b) Success in
   Business   658.8

I.   Duckworth, Carolee & Langworthy, Marie
II.   Title

DEDICATION

To Barry and Bob, who patiently and supportively endure us, their writer wives, and who in their wisdom and love, know that, yes, there is life beyond the book.

About the Authors

Dr. Carolee Duckworth is a curriculum designer specializing in applied learning theory and optimum use of technology. As *Director of Instructional Computing* for a community college, she was project leader in 1996 for the design and start-up of a thriving Online College—*www.college-online.com*.

Carolee has worked online as a full-time teleworker ever since, first as a professor in the online college she created, then as an author and publisher when she "shifted gears" herself. She co-authored a highly successful guide to retirement, *Shifting Gears To Your Life & Work After Retirement* (with Marie Langworthy, available through all online booksellers, including www.amazon.com, both in paperback and e-book versions). She also is co-author of the *Your Great Trip* series (with her son, Brian Lane), including *"Your Great Trip to France," "Your Great Trip to Italy," "Your Great Trip to Canada"* and *"Your Great Trip to the Pacific Coast."* Her writing focus is on career empowerment and independent travel.

Carolee has degrees and certificates that include a BA in Psychology from Duke University, an MA in *Instructional Systems Design* from UNC, Chapel Hill, an EdD in *Instructional Technology and Distance Education* from Nova Southeastern University, and a Certificate in *Expert Systems Design* from Georgia Tech.

Dr. Marie Langworthy, in her former career as an educator and administrator, was a cyber-pioneer and "early adapter" of technology. As *Director of Instructional Technology* in several school districts, she introduced the entire range of then current and emerging technologies to staff and students.

While earning a doctorate in *Instructional Technology and Distance Education* in the late 1990s, she predicted that: "Satellite and online systems, wireless networks, and use of relevant software and courseware will become the norm, providing anytime, anywhere learning and working, with unlimited opportunity for forming international learning and career alliances." And so it has transpired, as we all now know.

As a member of the first wave of Baby Boomers, Marie "shifted gears" herself, co-authoring *Shifting Gears To Your Life & Work After Retirement*. As final editor for New Cabady Press, she specializes in the "spit and polish" process of word-smithing the next potential "great American literary piece"... or future NY Times bestseller.

Not one to shy away from multitasking, Marie has started her own web-based business, *Super Writing Services,* where she exercises her passion to "write it right" (*www.SuperWritingServices.com*), providing her clients with a spectrum of business, professional and personal writing services.

She admits that she's still "a work in progress"—trying to determine what new horizons she'll follow if and when she ever "grows up"or "grows old," whichever happens first. In the meantime, she continues to welcome the adventure of each new day.

Table of Contents

INTRODUCTION

"For me, working from home is the best thing I have ever done. It has allowed me to purchase my home and buy my dream car. I make more money now than I ever would have working outside my home."
—Anonymous Home Worker

Why is the idea of working at home growing more enticing to an increasing portion of the population? This interest seems to cross all demographics. And fascinating demographics they are!

Working online may once have been the realm of improbable get-rich-quick schemes. But within the past decade, cyberspace has become not only a viable workplace, offering a full spectrum of career options, but has grown to supplant a significant proportion of the total marketplace of employment. The "cheese" has been moved. Do you know where to find it now?

Why has work been moving to the Web? Why have employers shifted to outsourcing many of the job functions for which they once hired on-site employees? Why are storefront businesses falling behind their online competitors? Why has on-site work declined while online work has thrived?

These are important—even essential—questions. For a start, "listen" to the numbers.

What the Data Shows: How Many? How Much?

The community of "teleworkers" (individuals who work primarily from home) has grown steadily to become more mainstream. Showing its greatest growth spurt between 2005 and 2006, telework gained a phenomenal 26% in that year alone (*Global Workplace Analytics American Community Survey—www.GlobalWorkplaceAnalytics.com*). This dramatic growth was followed by another 22% growth within the next two years, 2006 to 2008.

Predictions were that telework would decline during the recession, following the pattern of dramatic decreases in total employment.

In actuality, while total workforce numbers declined from 2008 to 2012, telework continued to grow, although at the more modest pace of around 4% per year. So telework actually grew nearly 16% during the recession.

Overall, the total growth in telework has equated to a stunning composite leap of 64% between 2005 and 2012. This represents an increase that is nine times that of the total workforce, which showed only a 7% growth rate during the same time period.

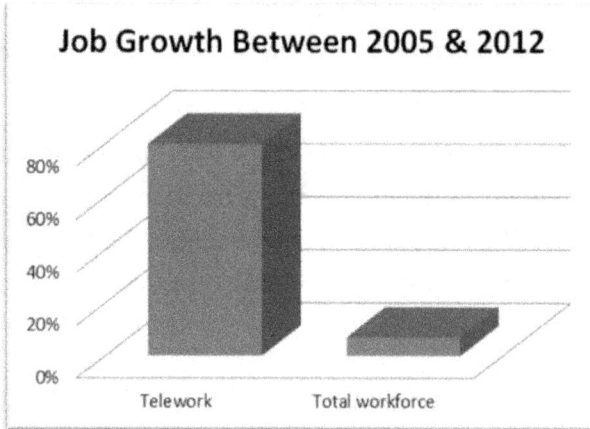

Job Growth Between 2005 & 2012

Add In the Millions of Self-Employed Teleworkers

Perhaps even more significant, these dramatic growth figures *do not* include the considerable additional numbers of the self-employed.

With self-employed teleworkers factored in, the overall growth figures for telework would be substantially higher.

The *United States Department of Labor* estimated in its 2004 survey that *7+ million people* were self-employed and worked from home. Of these 7+ million, two-thirds were operating home-based businesses. Surveys indicate that *nearly half* of home-based workers are self-employed (SIPP).

How Does All This Add Up, and What Does It Mean?

The percentage of the total workforce who work exclusively from home increased from 4.8% *of all workers* to 6.6% between 1997 and 2010 (according to the *U.S. Department of Commerce Survey of Income and Program Participation—SIPP).*

These percentages confirm a pattern of steady migration of the workforce in the direction of the tele-workplace. Extrapolating from these various telework estimates based on growth rates, and translating this into an approximate total for all teleworkers, including the self-employed, by 2015 almost 37 million members of the total workforce made the shift to telework.

This estimate of 37 million online workers is supported by Forester Research projections that by the year 2016, upwards of 63 million people will be working remotely.

In the 60's we asked: "Where have all the flowers gone?" Now it is time to ask: *Where have all the jobs gone? Clearly, they have gone online.*

Who Are the Teleworkers & For Whom Do They Work?

The patterns in *who* has shifted to the tele-workplace, doing *what* work, and *for whom*, are in themselves interesting. In terms of percentages, the highest proportions work for "For Profit" businesses, live in metropolitan areas, are mature and experienced, are engaged in contract employment, and work in management, professional, sales or technical positions. Here are some figures that support this emerging picture of who has already made the move to the world of online work.

The Majority Work at "For Profit" Companies

More than three out of every four (76%) teleworkers who are not self-employed, are employed by "For Profit" companies (according to *Global Workplace Analytics)*. Another 10% work for Non-Profits, and the remaining 14% are employed by local, state and federal employers.

Most Live in Metropolitan Areas

Regionally, the highest five-year growth in teleworkers who are not self-employed has been in metropolitan areas. In a quarter of the nation's 20 largest metro areas, *more people now telecommute than use public transportation* to get to work (*Global Workplace Analytics*).

Metropolitan areas in the Southeast, Southwest, and West have the largest percentage of workers who work from home (SIPP).

Most are Mature and Experienced

As we look at telework numbers by age group, based on the SIPP findings, the shift to working remotely is clearly more pronounced for mature workers than for young, entry-level employees.

- On-site work predominates for younger workers in the 15–24 and 25–34 years age groups.
- By age 35-44, the number of teleworkers is roughly equivalent to that of on-site workers.
- For the 45-54, 55-64 and 65+ groups, online work predominates over on-site work.

The table below vividly illustrates this data. About one in ten workers who worked exclusively from home are over the age of 65.

Age of Worker by Work-At-Home Status: Survey of Income and Program Participation, 2010

■ Total workers   ▨ Onsite workers   ▨ Mixed workers   ▢ Home workers

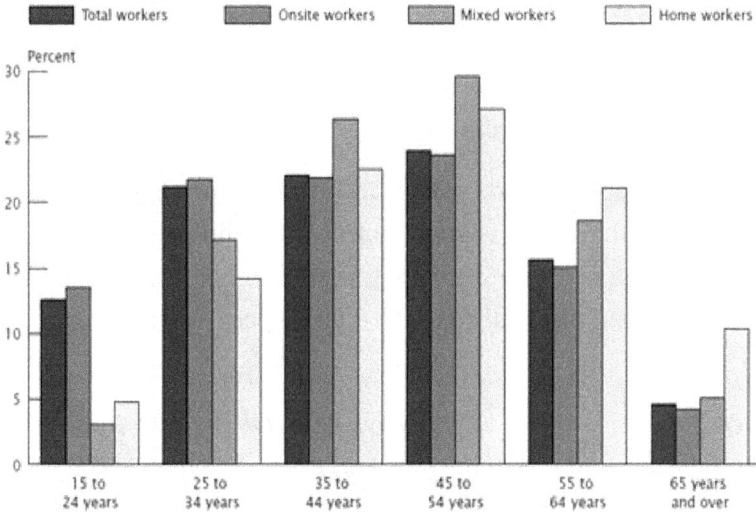

Source: U.S. Census Bureau, Survey of Income and Program Participation, 2008 Panel, wave 5.

Many Are Engaged in Contract Employment

The stats cited above coincide with dramatic data about online contract employment. One of the most illuminating sets of findings was reported in the *Online Employment Situation Summary* issued by oDesk (_www.oDesk.com_), a major online contracting agency that matches freelance online workers to companies seeking services.

ODesk reported that non-traditional contract workers make up more than one third of the US workforce. Furthermore, according to their research, this contract-employment segment is growing at twice the rate of the standard workforce.

ODesk stated that more than 90% of US firms now use contract talent on a regular basis. These companies approached $1 billion jointly in contract spending in 2014, employing remote independent workers from around the globe. Of that total, around half, $500 million, was earned by American freelancers.

Odesk alone works with over 1.5 million business clients seeking contract employees, long-term or short-term, paid hourly or by the project, from entry level to expert.

According to Fabio Rosati, *oDesk* CEO, these stunning figures are a clear indicator that work is steadily moving online. He compares this online relocation of work to the migration of other significant parts of the economy from physical space to digital space—namely commerce. Rosati says:

> *"Work [online] started primitively, with job boards that were essentially translations of your newspaper's classifieds section put on the Web. Then came the next phase: the résumé went online, and people started becoming professional "friends" on LinkedIn. Now, with platforms like Elance and oDesk, organizations can directly [employ and] work with individuals... The relationship is mutually beneficial" (www.businessinsider.com/).*

Most Are Engaged in Management, Professional, Sales or Technical Positions

Relative to the total population, a disproportionate share of management, professional, and sales workers telecommute ("*State of Telework in the US*"). The *Survey of Income and Program Participation (SIPP)*, confirms this pattern, reporting that about *one-fourth* of workers who are home-based are in management, business, and financial occupations.

Technical careers also feature a strong online component. Home-based work in computer, engineering, and science occupations are on the increase, up 69% between 2000 and 2010 (SIPP).

The *Top 10* areas of online job opportunities through *oDesk* include:

Top 10 Areas of Online Job Opportunities	
Web Development	Administrative Support
Software Development	Design & Multimedia
Networking	Customer Service
Information Systems	Sales & Marketing
Writing & Translation	Business Services

What About You?

So ask yourself whichever of the following two significant questions best fits your own situation:

1) *If online job and work opportunities are on the increase, and if many workers have already moved to the online workplace, is it time for me to consider going cyber too?*

2) *If I already work part-time online, either as part of or in addition to my job in the brick-and-mortar workplace, am I ready to consider moving online completely?*

The Mission of This Book

The purpose of this book is to take you into the world of online work and help you find yourself there, then to guide you as you prepare yourself well, establish your own starting point as a webworker, and become highly successful working online.

Here you will find a wealth of useful information and a sense of the scope of the opportunities available to the 21st century webworker.

Regardless of what work you do now or plan to do in the future, read through Chapters 1, 2, and 3 to determine if the cyber-workplace is for you, and, if your answer is "yes," to prepare your home-based office, then prepare yourself for the cyber-workplace by moving through a *7-Step Process*. These first three chapters answer questions such as:

- What are the pros and cons of working from home?
- Based on these advantages and disadvantages, does telework match my career goals, personality and lifestyle?
- What physical realities do I need to resolve and establish before I begin the process of job searching for online work?
- What knowledge and understanding do I need to acquire about the world of cyberwork before I embark on an online job search?
- What tasks do I need to accomplish to establish and promote my professionalism in the cyber-work environment?
- What specific skills and learning do I need to master in order to prepare and present myself as an authentic, credible, value-adding online worker?
- Where and how do I begin my job-hunting journey?

From Chapter 4 on, feel free to explore according to your particular interests and talents.

- *Chapter 4* is for you if you plan to find on online job—"work for hire."
- *Chapter 5* speaks primarily to those of you who have always wanted to write, and know that you do it fairly well.
- *Chapter 6* is meant for those whose talents lie in the visual arts.
- *Chapter 7* focuses on those who are interested in pursuing an online career in business or business support services.

- *Chapter 8* highlights opportunities for online teaching, investigation and research.
- *Chapter 9* is your guide to creating products, artistic or artisan, to meet the escalating demands of online commerce.
- *Chapter 10* focuses on some diverse career choices and ideas available to you if you want to go entrepreneurial and start your own business.

Later you may want to return to the chapters you initially skipped. Don't underestimate your abilities and talents to succeed in areas that you heretofore may have dismissed as "not for you."

Take every opportunity to explore even those career territories and options that are less familiar to you. Many online careers and jobs did not even *exist* before the advent and pervasiveness of the Web. You may surprise yourself to discover that work options you have never even *heard* of actually require just those skills and talents you may already possess, albeit in their pre-web format. In other words, you may have more to offer than you initially thought.

This book invites you to come and discover for yourself that the world of cyberwork, almost infinite in its prospects and choices, awaits you to engage and thrive.

Chapter 1:
Is the Cyber-Workplace for You?

"After having two children, I found myself becoming weary of the corporate world. I wanted the opportunity to spend more time with my children AND make decisions impacting my life. When I want to work, I work. When I don't want to work, I don't. If I want to go on a field trip with one of my children, I don't have to "get permission" from my boss. I AM MY BOSS."

—TAH, New Mexico

Cyberspace has become the emerging workplace for millions. But will it be your choice of workplace? Let's consider some pros and cons before you decide. Then, if your answer is "yes," read on to explore some of the many new options available, and to think through what you might want to pursue, as well as where and how. These steps are important to discovering what telework, if any, will work for you.

Reasons *TO* Work from Home

Reasons to shift to working online are varied, with as many stories as there are people who cyber commute. Your own story will be unique. But certain themes emerge that lead people to shift their work and career to the online world. Here are some of the primary reasons...

I Want More Flexibility

Yes, there was a time when location determined the success of a business. And location is still a determining factor in any brick-and-mortar enterprises. But for many who work from home, the key factor determining their work environment is: "Where is the closest Wi-Fi hot spot?"

Today, the local coffee shop, many restaurants and even fast-food establishments provide Wi-Fi. And I challenge you to find a motel, hotel, resort, or rental condo that doesn't provide this feature. You can even work online via satellite from the middle of the Atlantic Ocean on a transatlantic cruise to Europe. And now airlines are providing online resources and services even while you're in the air!

These establishments know that, in order to compete for their clients' business, they need to provide the latest and greatest in technology connections and telecommunications options. The result—for many individuals, doing business online is ubiquitous—anytime, anywhere, with anyone!

Many people who work online would not consider returning to a job "out there" because now that they have experienced the flexibility of online work, they are not willing to relinquish the freedom and independence that this new work style affords.

SNAPSHOT

Barry shifted to working online when his industry, construction contracting, entered difficult times. He now works from his home office, running *Mastery Tutors* (www.masterytutors.com), a one-on-one, in-home tutoring business. The tutors he hires work face-to-face with students. But Barry's workday is spent completely online and on the phone, recruiting, matching, interviewing, and coordinating tutors. Initially his business focused within a 60-mile radius of his home outside of Charlotte NC. Now he has expanded to two new locations, Baltimore and Raleigh/Durham/Chapel Hill.

One of the major benefits he has enjoyed since making this shift to working online is the flexibility to work anytime and anyplace,

> while also sharing travel adventures with his wife, who is a travel writer. In the recent past, he has worked from the balcony of a condo on the Mediterranean French Riviera, from a canal house in Amsterdam, and from a castle on a hill high above the Rhine River in Germany.

I Want to End My Daily Commute

You may be considering online work to end the 5 to 10 (or even 15 to 20) *unpaid* hours per week you now spend on your own daily commute. And that's on a "good" week, with no road construction, auto accidents or adverse weather conditions.

And then you need to factor in the *costs*. The cost of gas. The wear and tear on your vehicle. The erosion of your nervous system! While you can easily compute the material, physical costs of commuting, how does one quantify the damage done to your mental and physical health—the nerve-fraying hours you spend on the road, sometimes unnecessarily, because of chronic road construction, unpredictable accidents, inclement weather, and commuter-hour traffic jams?

Over time, Marie's daily commute cost her an outrageous amount of time, energy and money. For most of her career, depending upon her various job locations, she travelled anywhere from 76 to 87 miles *each* way every day, adding an exhausting 3 hours per day to her already long workday. This *added 15 hours to her work week*, almost the equivalent of *two* extra workdays! Her lament was that she never saw spring arrive, nor did she ever experience the beautiful New England fall foliage, since she left for work before daylight and returned home after dark!

Then factor in the wear and tear on her mental wellbeing, as well as her vehicle, battling inclement weather, witnessing horrendous car accidents, enduring the perennial road work projects, and experiencing the mental stress created by all these situations.

I Want and Need Broader Options for Employment

Another major reason for working online is to expand your options beyond your own local employment area. You can live in the country and work in the city—or live in the city and work abroad—or live abroad and work in the US.

SNAPSHOT

Carolee provides a typical example, living across from a lovely lake in a North Carolina town that is really only a crossroad with a gas station, a country store, and a post office. By making the shift to working online, she was able to move to the lake, yet continue working for her college in the neighboring state of South Carolina, although the campus was over two hours away.

Carolee has worked totally online since 1998, teaching classes from her sun-drenched home office, and making the trip back to her college's campus only for faculty meetings, the annual Christmas party and graduation. Since her retirement from the college in 2010, she has continued to work online, now as an author and publisher.

She says: "By working online, I have had the best of both worlds! I can work where I want to work, yet live where I want to live!"

You, too, may be considering working online because options are limited in your local area. Or your current job has been phased out and you now find it necessary to broaden your work options. Or you need to find work, yet your personal family situation prohibits you from relocating.

I Want More Money from the Work I Do

Many work at home because they have discovered a niche that makes it more *profitable and cost effective* for them to work from home with an Internet hookup than to make the drive to work for someone else. While flexibility is nice, increased profits are even more appealing. Artists and freelance writers certainly are among this group, but so are many business people and other former commuters.

Focusing purely on the math of earnings versus expenses, and depending on various factors such as commuting costs, dress codes, lunch expenses, and perhaps childcare, a 40-hour, $20-an-hour, in-town job can quickly be reduced to actual take-home earnings closer to $12, or even a $10, per hour.

Nearly 50% of surveyed online workers reported that they were able to make *more* money working from home than they did at their former traditional jobs. Of those who stated that they made more money working from home, 25% added they made *significantly* more money working from home than they would otherwise. That's encouraging news for anyone seeking the opportunity to stay at home and work!

I Need to Resolve Childcare or Eldercare Issues

For those who are parents, the idea of spending the day closer to their family may be what draws them to the telecommuting work lifestyle. Fifty-six percent of those working from their home offices reported that doing so solved their issues with daycare—such concerns as the cost, quality, and convenience of finding and utilizing satisfactory daycare services and facilities.

The problems and concerns that families face vis-a-vis daycare issues include:

- Cost,
- Quality,

- Flexibility, and
- Peace of mind.

Let's take a look at the *cost* of daycare. These costs, when combined with the expense of gas for your daily commute, can begin to make you question just how profitable your on-site job really is. This is even more the case if you have more than one child, with additional money needed to pay the daycare expenses for multiple siblings.

Furthermore, parents often agonize over the *quality* of the daycare program, staff, and facility. Finding the ideal daycare situation can, in itself, become a stressful ordeal, especially in communities where quality certified daycare programs are limited.

Finally, take into account the *flexibility* and *convenience* aspects (or lack thereof) of some daycare programs. Many dictate strict child drop-off and retrieval time limits. Such restrictions can create angst and inconvenience for parents whose work schedules may be unpredictable and demanding.

Conversely, in a dual-parent family, if one parent works at home, he has the flexibility to shuttle children to and from points A and B throughout the day. This convenience is especially necessary when several siblings have different schedules as well as in single parent households, where the burden of child-rearing falls upon one person.

And whether we want to admit it or not, in spite of what "conventional wisdom" may dictate, parents often deal with feelings of *guilt* when they are not able to spend more time with their children... Not able to be at home when their children get home from school... Not available to help their children with homework... Not able to attend school-day functions and after-school activities.

SNAPSHOT

For years, Kevin managed a major record store chain, long before the existence of Napster, Amazon, and the explosion of universal online access to the entire range of digital audio, video, and film media. As a manager, he received scads of free LP's, and, later, music CD's, sent to him by music vendors.

A musician himself, Kevin was immersed in the music industry. He witnessed first-hand the growth of the 70's and 80's genres, artists and groups that would eventually become successful brands. And so he was in a position to amass a huge collection of what later would become valuable music collector's items.

As brick-and-mortar music stores began to decline, Kevin found himself jobless, while, fortunately, his wife's career as a nurse was still flourishing. Their dilemma—the new jobs now available to Kevin would barely cover daycare costs for their three small children, all still in diapers.

With time on his hands, Kevin began dabbling in Internet commerce, especially on eBay, then in its early stages. There he noticed that there was a market for classic albums, and he just happened to have a basement full of now valuable "first editions," rare LP's, and early albums of once-unknown musicians who now had become music icons. Using his knowledge of the music industry as powerful leverage, Kevin was, before long, making money on eBay, buying, selling, and reselling music collectors' items. He had found his "dream job"!

Kevin boasts that the most unexpected and best outcome of his newfound online career has been his role as the classic stay-at-home dad. "How lucky I have been," says Kevin, "to have the

> opportunity to watch my kids grow up, to make their school lunches, and to chauffer them to sports and school activities."

You, too, may be considering working online to resolve childcare or eldercare issues, and thereby to bring work and family demands back into balance.

I Want to Combine Work with School

There are so many life situations where, as a matter of necessity or of choice, earning a living needs to be combined with furthering one's education in order to earn a *better* living. Let's take a look at several such scenarios.

Traditional Students Who Need to Work

First, consider the typical newly graduated high school student who is trying to further her education by attending a community college or university. Many such students find themselves overwhelmed with the thought of prospective student loans and daily cost-of-living expenses.

Because a college student's course schedule generally does not fit into a traditional 9-to-5 job model, it can become almost impossible to hold down a brick-and-mortar job. Members of this cyber generation, comfortable as they are with playing and working online, may opt to earn at least part of their college expenses by seeking online employment.

SNAPSHOT

Katie, who recently completed her BA degree, and is now enrolled in a Master's Program, has worked in various part-time jobs throughout her undergraduate life, from waitressing to clothing boutique sales associate to dance instructor. In grad school, she secured a work-study job in the registrar's office. She was so successful in recruiting new students to the school's graduate programs, that the administration decided to provide her with a dedicated phone line so that she could work from her apartment for a designated number of hours per week.

Katie is so grateful that she now can work efficiently from home, regaining precious commuting time that she now can put to much better use on her academics.

Single Parents

Now let's consider the plight of a single parent, newly divorced or widowed, possibly lacking formal education beyond high school. To make attending school a viable option, especially if this parent works as an unskilled or semi-skilled laborer, she may find it not only advantageous, but even necessary to find online work. While working online he will be readily able to pursue some type of formal training, or to learn a marketable skill, through the many online learning programs that offer certifications and degrees.

Picture the almost ideal situation of a single parent who is able to earn money working online, while pursuing a degree or skill, also online, while fulfilling her role as parent.

SNAPSHOT

At age 18, Monica found herself alone and pregnant. Determined to raise her child on her own, she aggressively pursued job opportunities available to those with only a high school diploma. Financially, Monica was in no position to be able to afford any type of additional formal training. But her tenacity earned her an entry-level position working online with a major telecommunications company just at the time when many corporations were experimenting with employee telecommuting options.

Not only was the company willing to invest in training employees who were receptive to the idea of working from home, they provided their online staff with all necessary telecommunications, hardware and software, including a high-end computer. Monica, who was smart, determined, and hard-working, soon found herself working from home full time, with company benefits and no childcare worries. One day a month she was required to travel to a major nearby city for a full day of meetings—a small price to pay for what she considered to be an ideal work environment.

As young as she was, Monica realized the importance of self-discipline and of setting work boundaries for herself, as well as for her family and friends. As she continued to demonstrate competence, and showed her eagerness and willingness to master the company's latest software applications, Monica began to earn one promotion after another, assuming more and more responsibility, all as she continued to work from the comfort of her home.

A few years into her career, Monica had a second child. Still a single parent, she continued to be able to rear both of her children while engaging in a demanding career. Fast forward to today. Monica is now a grandmother, and guess what? She now occasionally takes care of her grandchild while continuing to carry out her job responsibilities from her home-based office.

I Want to Shift to a More Entrepreneurial Career

Then we have the scenario of full-time, successful professionals who are interested in making career changes, but who are encumbered with the financial responsibilities of raising a family, carrying a mortgage, and dealing with all the trappings of sustaining a middle class lifestyle. Particularly if they are highly successful in their current day jobs, but want, over time, to make a shift to work that is more entrepreneurial or more suited to them, their only option initially may be to pursue their hoped for "future career" on a part-time basis.

Possibly these individuals hope to convert a hobby-type interest into a small, part-time online business, with the intention that this endeavor eventually will grow into a full-fledged career. Many a successful online entrepreneurial venture has developed in exactly this way.

The convenience and timeliness of working online opens the way for these and other *career changers* to "dip a metaphorical toe" into entrepreneurial waters, while keeping their "day job," at least initially. This allows them to transform their overall work lives gradually, while limiting the associated risks.

I Have Been or Will Be Impacted by Downsizing

Another very realistic scenario in contemporary society is the down-sizing phenomenon. Many a middle-aged, middle-class person has found herself jobless, possibly with antiquated skills, in a not-so-promising job market.

Hence a two-fold urgency becomes clear. How is it possible to find work and to upgrade one's skill set simultaneously? Options for both of these—work and training—may be found in abundance online. In the cyber-work world, the opportunities to seek out and network with potential employers, past colleagues, and new contacts are enhanced, while new doors, once unheard of in the traditional limited physical work environment, are now opened wide.

I Have Retired, but Want or Need to Continue Working

For some, working online is the perfect opportunity to continue to be engaged and productive, while also earning money, after retiring from demanding on-site careers.

You may be among the retired or semi-retired. Retirement may have come a bit earlier than you had anticipated, and you now may find that you want and/or need to work to maintain your lifestyle—or even just to give meaning to your life. But you really like the idea of protecting some of your flexibility too.

It may seem unsettling even to contemplate taking on another day job like the one you just left, particularly if your past work consumed all your time and emotional energy. But you still may want to work, and you still may want to earn money. These and other considerations can make working online start to look like a very attractive alternative. Perhaps it is the only type of "next work" you would even consider at this point.

If you fall into this category of early or late Baby Boomers, and are making the shift to your "retirement career," we highly recommend that you read *"Shifting Gears to Your Life & Work After Retirement"* (Duckworth & Langworthy). This book provides a comprehensive, compelling road map to *seven different pathways* and an in-depth *five-step process* through which retirees can find a meaningful, productive, profitable strategy to reinvent their third and possibly most fulfilling life's passage. And it discusses the special viability of entering the cyber-work world as an optimum choice for retirement work that can be combined with other retirement objectives such as travel.

SNAPSHOT

Marie, a recently retired educator and administrator, had always known that she had a talent for and a love of writing. She also knew that, in retirement, a life of sedentary leisure would not be "her cup of tea." Moreover, her retirement income would not sustain her desire to travel and to pursue other cultural and social interests. And so she *needed* to work. She also *wanted* to work.

Not one to shy away from multi-tasking, in addition to supervising student teachers and teacher interns as an adjunct within a local university, Marie decided to test the waters of embarking on a writing career. Fast forward four years. Marie has co-authored two books, started her own web-based writing business (*www.SuperWritingServices.com*), and serves as an editor for *New Cabady Press*.

If you ask Marie how her current life suits her, she'll say: "I don't have to deal with commuting in bad weather and in horrific traffic conditions; I don't have to endure sitting through long, boring, unproductive night meetings; I don't have to deal with difficult personalities; I select my own hours, my own tasks, in and from the cozy comfort of my own home. And I'm learning so much in, on, and through online resources. It doesn't get much better than that."

What's Your Story?

Are you a student attempting to work part-time in order to finance your way through school? Are you in a career or profession where the opportunities have diminished and you are ready to move on? Do you want to shift towards another type of work, but need to continue using your existing skills while you attend school to develop new ones?

Perhaps you have a health issue that makes working from home the best option for you. Or maybe you want a broader horizon of opportunity than exists in the town where you live. Perhaps you just want to eliminate the hour you spend sitting in traffic on the interstate every morning. *Whatever your reasons, the time has come when you can be confident and determined to pursue your goal of shifting to an online career.*

Reasons _NOT_ To Work from Home: A Few Challenges

Keep in mind that no matter what route you take to work—the highway or the hallway—you will discover that each alternative carries with it some disadvantages. Although for some individuals working in the cyber-workplace is ideal, for others this option holds little or no appeal. A full 20% of those surveyed—one out of every five people—reported that they were completely satisfied with working from home and did not cite any disadvantages, while others saw some down sides. And for some, the disadvantages of working online even outweighed the good points.

Statistics show that over 33% of those who work from home cite lack of healthcare as a major disadvantage. Almost as many—nearly 30%—said the biggest disadvantage was the anxiety and uncertainty they experienced of not knowing where their next work, and by extension, their next paycheck, would come from. Another 26% said that the feeling of being isolated was a down side of the at-home workplace.

Why would anyone *not* want to work at home? Here are several reasons...

No Work Means No Pay

Let's look first at the financial aspect of working from home. Unless you are working from home at a job for an employer, online work often is pay for product, *not* pay for attendance. This means no work, no pay. When you take the week off... When you're plagued by the flu, or beset with your annual cold... When a family member passes away... In all these instances that may once have been handled through vacation days, sick days or bereavement pay, you will need to bear the expense yourself. When you are paid only for hours worked, your budget will feel the impact of every hour you are not working.

Many individuals simply do not have the personality type to deal with the uncertainty and personal responsibility that comes with the online, work-for-yourself scenario. For some, the security of knowing that, no matter what, on Friday afternoon, or on the first of the month, someone will be handing them a paycheck, brings them back to work every Monday morning. It's important that you acknowledge this need about yourself before you quit your day job.

I Would Have Too Many Interruptions

Although some parents love the flexibility of working from home because it keeps them closer to their families, this proximity can be a two-edged sword. For many people, being constantly accessible to their families is a reason they would choose *not to* work from home.

It can be very difficult to concentrate on entering critical data, or operating a call center, or writing the next chapter of an eBook, when your five-year old interrupts you every half hour demanding your attention. Or when the TV is blaring in the background. Or when the dog needs feeding or walking. Or when a family member unexpectedly announces that she needs a ride to the airport.

Also there are those adults you know with too much time on their hands who will try to squeeze as much time as possible from your workday. Your aging parent, or your book club friend, or your next-door neighbor, may assume that since you are at home, and you don't have a boss looking over your shoulder, you are free to take time out to chat with them socially whenever they call or appear at your door.

If you elect to work from home, you will need to adopt a proactive and self-disciplined stance of establishing work guidelines and declaring these limits to family and friends. And you will need to adhere to these practices yourself as a condition of your success. Time-management skills and a diligent work ethic become "must have" traits for anyone who plans to work from home.

I Would Have the Sense That I Was Always "At Work"

This brings us to yet another potential disadvantage of working from home—not knowing when to walk away. With your work living right there with you in your home, will you know when you have worked enough for the day and it's time to turn off the computer and "come home"? And, for that matter, how exactly *will* you "come home" from work at the end of the day when you already *are* home?!

Just because you will be able to work all day and also into the night, doesn't mean that you *should.* In fact, you *should not!* Why not? Because of the law of diminishing returns. Conventional wisdom indicates that we all have a built-in productivity meter that dictates when we've reached the point of maximum return on our investment of time and energy. In a word, you need to know "when to hold 'em, when to fold 'em, and when to walk away."

My Family Won't Know If I'm "At Work" or "At Home"

The challenges of living with your work in your home go both ways. As well as knowing when to stop, you will need to be your own boss in terms of getting yourself to work, staying focused, and otherwise taking your own work as seriously as you did when you worked "out there."

Although working online will give you lots of flexibility, work still needs to be work, and play needs to be play—with clear boundaries between the two. When you work from home, time can be diverted and consumed by the "just"s. I'll *just* put in a few loads of wash... I'll *just* check my Facebook page... I'll *just* make a grocery list, then run to the store for a few things... Will you have the self-discipline to keep the "just"s at bay?

As we mentioned earlier, balancing your work life and your home life when your work is *in* your home, requires a combination of management skills—both managing yourself and managing others. It also requires good communication skills. You will need to establish firm, consistent parameters with the people in your life concerning your work and non-work schedule.

It is no accident that some online employers specify requirements in order to ensure that their work-at-home staff does, in fact, put in uninterrupted work time. Some require that your home office has a door as well as a dedicated phone.

Other online employers use systems that monitor your focus and productivity electronically. Some online work teams use Skype throughout their work day to simulate working side-by-side in an office, readily available to each other for back-and-forth consulting, as needed.

Cloud 10 Corp (*www.cloud10corp.com*), an online agency that hires customer service professionals to support some of the nation's most well-known brands, enforces a requirement that the at-home professionals they hire have no conflicting responsibilities during their work shifts. Their list of potential threats to productivity includes disruptive pets or being the primary caregiver for a young child or an elderly parent.

In fact, if you have a young child or a parent whose needs are demanding, or any other extenuating personal circumstance, even though you will be physically present yourself when you work from home, you still may need to enlist the services of a backup caregiver during your work day.

I Would Miss the "Water Cooler Gang"

Some people have a difficult time making the adjustment to working at home simply because they are effectively separated from their circle of work friends. Your gregarious persona may never have realized until now how much you looked forward to hearing about the usual weekend escapades when you arrived at work Monday morning.

Working alone in your home office, you will find yourself, for better or for worse, out of the loop of all that savory office gossip. You will have no one, at least no one who is there physically, with whom to swap recipes, talk about the weekend's sports scores, or share the latest fashion trends. And all those solitary coffee breaks and lunches can quickly start to seem *very* quiet.

When you start working from home, you will need to engage in specific tactics to ward off feelings of social and professional isolation. You may need to develop a new set of "work buddies," possibly other online workers who live nearby, with whom you can band together and occasionally meet for lunch.

What About the Challenges of Constant Togetherness?

If you and your spouse both work from home, whether in separate home offices or side by side, and then "come home" together, this proximity can begin to constitute *too much togetherness!* You both will need breathing room from time to time, with probably at least some time apart. Planning an occasional lunch out with other friends may become essential to your productivity as well as your sanity.

That said, as part of a couple where both work full time from home offices, this arrangement can have its perks, too. Barry and Carolee especially enjoy their morning break doing the crossword puzzle together, and their afternoon break playing three rousing games of ping pong to "get the blood flowing back into our brains."

And So...

You have just spent some serious introspective time determining whether the cyberspace work environment is where you want to earn a substantial portion of your living from now on... or *not!* If you're still vacillating about whether you want to leap ahead into this ubiquitous online work world, then we suggest you continue to read on.

Initially, you may be feeling somewhat overwhelmed by what you perceive to be a daunting mental and physical paradigm shift when you think about working online.

Before you make a final decision, the upcoming two chapters will take you mentally through the steps of making the transition to the cyber-workplace, envisioning yourself working there, preparing your workplace and then preparing yourself.

As you continue to learn about the variety of work opportunities the Web offers, you may discover that you are not only open to exploring a new career direction, but also starting to feel excited, committed, and even eager to get started.

If you already fall into this latter category and are determined to forge ahead, kudos to you. In the next chapter we will tackle the tangible business of taking some immediate preparatory steps. Also you will have the chance to set into motion several necessary decisions as you prepare to prove to your potential future employers or clients that you are professionally capable of serving their needs better than anyone else.

And here's the good news. If you enjoy shopping for bargains and spending money... If you like to design creative and conducive environments... If you love to organize... Or to repurpose spaces... Or to toy with technology... Or to master new skills... In all these instances, Chapter 2 will be sheer, unadulterated fun for you, as you set out to design, furnish, equip and otherwise to prepare for yourself an ideal work space to which you will "commute" up the stairs or down the hall!

Chapter 2:
Prepare Your Workplace

"I know the price of success: dedication, hard work and an unremitting devotion to the things you want to see happen."

—Frank Lloyd Wright

A key consideration about working from home is planning how you will establish your home office. You will need a place that is dedicated to your work, equipped with current equipment and software, with storage areas to organize the professional resources, files and supplies you need to work efficiently. Office facilities and capabilities that were provided by your employer when you worked "out there," now will be your own responsibility, and of your own design.

This does not necessarily mean you will need to look for a new house in order to work from home. But you *will* need to establish for yourself a place to work productively within your home by specifically designating your space, then redesigning it to serve this new purpose.

Mark Your Territory

With some creative thought and planning, an infrequently used dining room, a guest room, or even a large closet can be transformed into a small office, rearranged and refurnished with a desk, office equipment and supplies.

At a Minimum, Designate and Redesign a Space

If your plan is to use a large closet for your home office, accomplish this transformation by redesigning the space to look and function like an office. Remove the closet doors. Add power strips and good lighting. Install a functional desk, work station and office chair. Purchase ample file cabinets and shelving.

Marie has implemented this strategy of converting a closet in her home den into an office. Since space in her "office" is limited, she goes through her entire inventory of materials and resources once a year, removing those items she hasn't used and relegating them to another less accessible place in her home. Through this strategy, she refreshes her awareness of what she actually does own, what refurbishments she needs to add, and what she needs to keep on hand to continue her work. Through this process, she rids herself of obsolete material, and forces herself to "get organized—again!"

In addition to a workstation, Marie uses a laptop, which gives her geographical flexibility when needed. Since her office also functions as the family den, Marie is sensitive to the social needs of others, moving to the guest bedroom when her work involves lengthy phone conferences, interviews or discussions. At times like this, privacy, concentration, portability and flexibility are key.

Optimally, Create a Full Office for Yourself

At the other end of the spectrum, you may decide to go beyond a closet or corner, and dedicate a full bedroom to become your home office. If you and your partner both will be working from home, you may even opt to take over two bedrooms. One advantage of repurposing a full room or rooms as dedicated office space is that your home office then becomes a tax deduction based on what percentage of the total floor space of your home has been so assigned.

Carolee and her husband, Barry, have transformed two of the four bedrooms in their home into dedicated home offices. Each office is lined with wall-to-wall, floor-to-ceiling shelves to hold work-related books, manuals and resources, as well as manuscripts, presentation products, marketing materials and publications now in progress or already completed. They also have converted an oversized walk-in closet to become their on-site "Staples," fully stocked with office supplies—paper, file folders, mailing materials, printer toner, and notebooks.

These home offices are dedicated to office use, and so meet the IRS requirements for space to be deducted as a business expense. Since the two offices equate to 28% of the total floor space of their home, they thus have the advantage of being able to deduct as business expenses 28% of all costs associated with their home—electricity, gas, upkeep, insurance, WiFi, phone.

Find Home Office "Models" to Imitate

If you know someone who has an established home office, offer to treat her to lunch in exchange for visiting her home office to gather some ideas. Ask her to give you some "do and don't" startup tips, as well as to share her purchase contacts and sources.

Spend Some Money (The Fun Part!)

Remember the saying, "In order to make money, you need to spend money"? Learn early on that in order to reap future financial rewards you need first to invest in and establish an authentic, practical office environment. This is the fun part. What will you need to buy to prepare your home-based workplace? And where will you buy it?

Fortunately, there are lots of online as well as human resources to help you determine what to purchase to get started. For now, think "less is more." You can always add to your hardware, software, supplies inventories as you grow, and as you realize what additional resources you need.

For starters, scan space planning, home office planning, and office storage websites and catalogues such as:

IKEA	Amazon	
http://www.ikea.com/	http://amazon.com	
Staples	Best	Buy
http://www.staples.com/	http://www.bestbuy.com	
HGTV	Home	Offices
http://www.hgtv.com/designers-portfolio/home-offices/index.html		

These businesses, and others, provide great ideas for carving out your own workspace and creating for yourself a work environment where you can be a productive (and happy!) home worker.

Ikea offers clever multipurpose furnishings, such as shelves that also function as room dividers. HGTV allows you to search by style and/or by designer. Staples and Best Buy provide all the hardware and software options you'll ever need. Amazon offers books, but also much more, including electronics and supplies. And by subscribing to Amazon Prime, everything you order will be express shipped for free and will arrive within days.

Do a search using the terms "home office design" to find more sites and strategies. With a reasonable outlay of money, you will be able to establish a functional, productive, inviting home office space.

Don't overlook your local bargain outlets. It's amazing, for example, what you can discover on a trip down the office supplies aisle of your town's *Dollar Store*. All types of practical, necessary clerical treasures that you'll need to launch your new venture—pens and highlighters, folders and index cards, mailers and envelopes—all yours for $1 each.

Don't Be Tempted to Temporize

What will *not* work is temporizing. Are you thinking that you could just spread out on the kitchen table, and then push everything aside at dinner time? Or maybe just stack up all your books and files on the coffee table, and take over the sofa with your laptop? Think again! Learn from the pros. This type of make-do, half-baked strategy will only result in frustration for both you and your family. And you will most certainly not be able to function at your focused, most productive best.

Rather, from the very beginning, think and act like the well-organized, goal-oriented professional you are now or intend to become. Your at-home office space needs to support your work, not thwart it. Serious work requires a serious workplace.

Reapply These Office Set-up Skills When You Are Working Elsewhere

These same steps you used to set up your at-home workspace will serve you well when you need or want to carry your work elsewhere, and find yourself working from a hotel room or a vacation condo. Again you will need to carve out for yourself an efficient, productive mobile work area.

Transforming a section of a hotel room or apartment into a practical, comfortable work niche may require that you rearrange the lighting and the furniture, run drop cords and surge protectors, and make other needed adjustments. Fortunately, most major hotel/motel chains have become increasingly attuned to the needs of the business traveler, who now expects his "home away from home" to provide a workdesk, high-speed Wi-Fi, and possibly a business center equipped with computers, printers and fax capability.

Planning & Set Up: Appeal, Style & Functionality

Once you choose a space that you can claim, and redesign it as your dedicated work area, plan how to make that workspace appealing and comfortable. You will be spending a lot of time here, so make this niche your very own, complete with your favorite photos or even an indoor plant!

Think Light

Pay close attention to light, both natural and electric. Light can be stimulating, but glare is tiring. If you can, arrange a window view. This is a healthy strategy for your mind as well as your eyes. It can't hurt to sit adjacent to a window where you can watch birds feeding or look out onto a flower garden, or, if you're lucky enough, face a body of water.

Office design experts stress that when you spend hours looking at a computer screen, looking up regularly from your monitor, and focusing on a more distant point, prevents eye strain. This also reduces stress by providing a temporary respite from work.

Think Decor

Treat yourself to a décor that matches your taste and style. Furnishings need not be high-ticket items. You can buy reasonably-priced work stations from the websites listed earlier, or from your local Staples or Office Max. Ikea features lots of trendy, stylish and appealing furnishings, such as computer desks, at affordable prices.

Think Functionality

Think functionality first, not just good looks. For starters, select a work station with a keyboard tray where your hands will be at an ergonomically correct level when you type. This will prevent strain to your wrists. Do not attempt to make do with a standard desk or card table, where the height is wrong for comfortable long-term use of a keyboard. It is essential that you protect your back and wrists for the long haul.

Second, find an arrangement that will provide you ample space to spread out your current project to the right or left of your work station.

Third, set up places to keep materials you access frequently close at hand, and organize items you use less often out of the way.

Think Organization

Be sure to plan for shelf space, file drawers, and storage room for supplies, so that your immediate workspace will not become cluttered with books and notebooks, files and papers, printer cartridges and cables, when you are trying to work.

If your online work requires multitasking, then consider how you are going to seamlessly switch gears between projects. In particular, how will you "clear the decks," setting aside one project to make room for another? Whether you prefer baskets or shelves or cubbies, find a way to keep your projects separate and distinct.

It's very important to think through your filing system, even at this early point. An efficient filing system contributes to your productivity. Your ability to locate quickly the essential information and materials for current as well as past projects is essential, especially when you have a client waiting on the phone!

Think Work Comfort

When selecting your office furniture, do not underestimate the need for work comfort and correct ergonomics. Even if finances are limited, give special priority to purchasing the right office chair! Your office chair is *not* the place to try to save money.

That said, there's no reason to go over the top when selecting your "work throne." Prices for an excellent chair can range from $250 to as much as $3000! But you will find many viable options within a budget of around $300–$400.

Consider how many hours you are going to spend sitting in this chair. It is imperative that it be ergonomically suited to your body. A conservative estimate is that you will spend around 2000 hours per year sitting in this chair. So if you spend $300 to buy a comfortable chair, you will be paying around 15¢/hour to sit in it for the first year. After that, you will be sitting in it for free.

Many office chairs are not even slightly comfortable. Anyone who has worked from home for a while will attest that if you scrimp on your chair, or buy one based on looks rather than comfort, you will be replacing it sooner rather than later. To save money (and pain) in the long run, invest in an excellent chair from the start.

Select a chair that is adjustable and that supports your arms at the proper height for typing. Some of the qualifications for a chair that will serve you well over time are:

- Knee tilt
- Adjustable seat height
- Adjustable arm height
- Adjustable tilt tension
- Lower back support

If possible, take a "sit test" before you buy any chair to make certain that it is comfortable and that it properly supports your lower back. If you purchase your chair online, make certain that it can be returned if it doesn't suit you.

Here is a viable $319 option (discounted from $595) from the OfficeChairs.com website (*http://www.officechairs.com*):

WorkSmart Ergonomic Faux Leather

Think Manageability

There are other needs you should consider early on as you establish your home-based office. These requirements dictate that you attend to how you will control noise, schedule, policies and procedures, and the demands (and possible stress) of performing multiple roles.

Noise Management

How will you achieve and maintain the quiet you need in order to get your work done and make and receive phone calls without any background noise. What office setup will you need to be able to concentrate and do the high quality work you were able to accomplish from an office outside your home?

Work Schedule

What will your normal work schedule be? To determine this, you will first need to answer two underlying questions that address your time versus money balance.

1) What are your goals in terms of the number of hours you can or want to work in order to "get the job done"? and

2) What are your goals for the amount of money you want to or need to earn?

If your driving force is the amount of money you need or want to earn, you may need to adjust your number of work hours. And if your intention is to have more time free, you may need to adjust your expectations as to how much money you will earn. Also, as you take on online work projects, and learn the specifics of what each job, contract or assignment will pay, you may decide to readjust your adjustments.

Multiple Roles

When you assume the multiple roles of boss, work staff, purchasing department, accountant, and quality control, you will need to establish some realistic guidelines. It might even be a good idea to develop a set of brief job descriptions for the roles that were once performed by someone else but now will be yours to accomplish.

As the CEO and also the sole employee of your online office, you will need to take charge of the work as well as to do the work. The "boss" who will be "looking over your shoulder" will now be *you*.

Policies and Procedures

Every workplace has its *Policies and Procedures* for a reason. Work processes that are covered by your *Policies and Procedures* do not need to be reinvented every day, or every month. Establishing guidelines and parameters for your home office will help maintain efficiency, provide consistency, and facilitate your success.

As well as protecting your time, this "written rulebook" will maximize productivity and provide you with ready responses to outside, unrelated demands and interruptions. Enforcing your *Policies and Procedures* with yourself, your family and others, carries more weight than just saying "I don't want to do this" or "I can't do that." When you receive an interrupting solicitation phone call, you will be able to say that your company's policy is "No solicitation or personal calls during the workday." No contest there. Your interrupter generally will apologize and hang up.

What will your office's *"Policies and Procedures"* be? Will you answer emails after lunch? Allow calls to revert to voicemail during your writing time? Place orders for critical supplies biweekly, and well in advance of when they're needed? Process payments twice a month, on the 15th and 30th?

Will you begin seeking new contracts when you reach the half-way mark on current contracts? Limit the work you accept to 30 hours a week? Or 40? Or 20?

What specific duration, place and time will you designate for lunch? Will you take or not take coffee breaks? Fill out daily or weekly timesheets? Take off 4-weeks of vacation a year plus holidays?

It might even be a good idea to put your *Policies and Procedures* in written form. For a model to follow to develop your own *Policies & Procedures Manual,* do an online search, or adapt one from your previous work environment.

Your "Corporate Capabilities"—Hardware & Software, Abilities & Skills

Your "Corporate Capabilities"—what your home-based enterprise is capable of producing and at what quality level—will combine with your personal and professional efforts to produce earnings. Are your capabilities adequate to ensure efficiency, effectiveness, productivity and professionalism?

If not, what do you need to upgrade, update or add? Budget for these improvements, and implement them as early as you can. As an online worker, your hardware and software capabilities, as well as your skill in using them, are valid components of your ultimate success.

You already know that you will need a fairly current PC and an Internet connection in order to work online. To be productive, and to qualify for many of the online positions available, your Internet connection must have high speed capacity. Additional functional capabilities and needs are:

- High speed, high quality printing;
- Dual screens for accurate and efficient input;
- Capacity for visual "meetings" and interviews;
- Ongoing security protection;
- Regular backup of all critical files; and
- Clear phone lines.

Be Prepared to Print Efficiently: High-speed, High Quality

While you are equipping yourself for productivity, consider acquiring that high-speed printer you have been wanting. As an example, a *Konica Minolta Magicolor 5850EN* color laser printer reliably churns out 31 perfect color pages a minute, and costs less than $500. When time is money, wasting time waiting for your printer to crawl along for 15-20 minutes to print out a 20-page document will cost you precious time that you could and should be using for more productive tasks.

A quick check online will indicate that current prices for high-speed color printers start at $250–$350 or less, depending on the features you need. Many high-quality printers today include fax, copy, and scanning capabilities. Don't underestimate your need for these additional features as your home office business develops and expands. Think about the convenience and time you'll save if and when you need to send a fax, make copies, or scan documents.

And here's a piece of earnest advice. Whatever printer you choose, always make it a rule to purchase your next set of toner cartridges well in advance of when you will need them to avoid "down time" if and when you run out of ink at a critical moment.

Be Prepared to Work Effectively and Accurately: Dual Monitors

Consider purchasing a second monitor to enable you to view two screens at once. For about $150, you will in essence double your productivity. A second monitor will allow you to dedicate one screen to viewing the sources you are referencing, while using the other screen for input.

Working with dual monitors decreases the tedious need to click back and forth repeatedly between windows several times a minute. View your search results on one screen, and the article you are writing on the other. Access live online data on one screen, while developing your spreadsheet analysis on the other. Use your website design software to update your web pages on one screen and view a refresh of your live website on the other.

After a day of working with two screens, you will wonder how—or why—you ever managed to work with just one.

Be Prepared to Interface LIVE: Webcam & Microphone

It is highly advisable to include a headset with microphone, and possibly a Webcam, as part of your home office equipment. Some interviews for online work are now done via *Skype*, a service that supports online audio and video transmissions at very low costs, even for international calls.

Skype enables people to communicate with each other in real time as though they were face-to-face. In fact, most new, high end computers feature built-in live video and *Skype* capability.

Be Prepared to Communicate Professionally: Phone Line & FAX

At a minimum you will need a clear phone line and a way to capture voice messages. This might entail installing a second phone line in your home, especially if other family members share your only home line while you are working. Some online employers also require that you secure your own toll-free number.

By installing a separate business phone, you will alleviate the problems inherent in attempting to receive business calls on a personal family phone line. It is essential that you set up your work voicemail using your name and title, and the name of your business, thereby creating and reinforcing your own professional footprint.

FAX capability is another absolute necessity. Although some organizations now prefer to do business by exchanging documents attached to emails, or by using electronic signature features, some official documents still require an official signature. These are likely to include employment contracts that still may need to be signed by hand. If you add a printer/scanner/copier/FAX combo to your home office-equipment arsenal, you will be ready to exchange FAXes when the occasion so requires.

Be Prepared to Write, Compute, Present & Visualize

Software for your home office begins with the latest version of the Microsoft Office Suite, including Word (word processing), Excel (spreadsheet), PowerPoint (presentation), Outlook (email) and possibly Access (database).

A word of warning—beware of download sites where the cost of *MS Office* seems to be too low. Counterfeit products are a big problem in the software industry, so it is essential to purchase from a company that takes the issue of pirated software very seriously, and guarantees that you will receive authentic and legal full-version software. If a price seems too low, the authenticity of the product may be suspect.

One excellent option is to subscribe to *Microsoft Office 365* through the MS "cloud" for a set monthly fee. This ensures that you will have access to the latest versions of Office software, with automatic upgrades included, and one Terabyte of online storage in *OneDrive* (in the Cloud) for anywhere access to your files and documents.

The "Pro" option of *Microsoft Office 365* also allows you to assign up to five users, each of whom will be able to install all of the software in the Office suite and have use of their own individual Terabyte of storage in "the cloud."

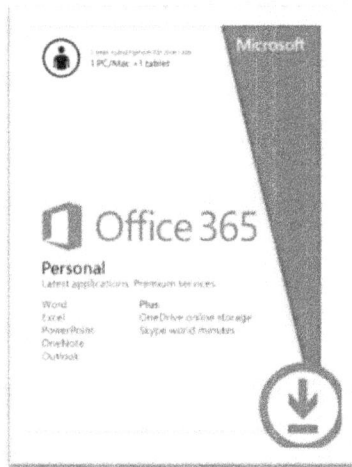

Other software tools you may need will be those programs that are specific to your particular trade, such as:

- *Dreamweaver, Fireworks*, and *Flash* for Web designers;
- *Photoshop* and *Illustrator* for graphic artists;
- *Dragon, In Design, SnagIt, PDF Converter* and *NovaMind* for writers;
- *AutoCad* for drafters.

Future chapters elaborate on these specialized software programs, each targeting a specific digital profession.

Some companies that hire services online will provide you with their own custom software programs, and require that you load and install them to your computer. In these instances, you are, of course, also expected to master these programs, sometimes at the company's expense, but possibly on your own time.

Be Prepared to Keep Track of the Money

While you are equipping yourself with hardware and software, you will thank yourself many times over if, early on, you purchase and learn the basics of *QuickBooks*, (*http://quickbooks.intuit.com/*) or another accounting program that is sufficiently robust to handle all the invoicing, billing, ordering, payroll, and other accounting functions of your business. And, no, *Excel* will not serve the same functions as efficiently, particularly if you plan to start your own business.

QuickBooks

QuickBooks, currently considered to be the standard operational accounting program for small businesses, sells at around $200, depending on the version you choose. The features of *QuickBooks* provide you the "services" of a bookkeeper, billing clerk and accounts payable/receivable assistant without paying their associated salaries.

After you input your clients, vendors and contractors *once*, all you will need to do monthly (or weekly or biweekly, according to your billing and payroll cycles), will be to input ongoing sales or services to clients (to be billed), and payments due to vendors or contractors (to be paid).

QuickBooks will keep track of every dollar in and dollar out, and will provide you with any report you need, on demand, including the *Year End Report* needed for filing your taxes.

If you start using *QuickBooks* now, you will avoid playing catch up later. It is much easier to establish your accounting processes and procedures from the outset, and maintain them as you go along, than it is to delay this task until later, when you are submerged in the daily demands and operations of your business.

Initially, you may be overwhelmed by *QuickBooks*, especially if you begin to look through one of the 600-page instruction manuals available for purchase. Just remember that at first you will need to master only a few of its components. You can learn more of its features in the months ahead if and when you actually need them to run your business.

To simplify your accounting process, and later the filing of your taxes, set up a dedicated bank account to receive payments and pay expenses for your online work. This account then can be tied to your *QuickBooks* files so that transactions, updates and transfers are recorded back and forth. *QuickBooks* is even capable of emailing invoices, and processing deposits, transfers and credit card payments on the dates you specify in advance.

FreshBooks

Another option is *FreshBooks* (*http://www.FreshBooks.com*). Called "incredibly user friendly" by *Forbes Magazine*, this cloud-based alternative to *QuickBooks* is built to support the needs of small and growing businesses.

FreshBooks can be accessed via either iOS (Apple) or android mobile devices, enabling small businesses to check in and process invoices and payments from the road. According to *TechCrunch*, a leading source for breaking technology news and analysis, "The *FreshBooks* iPad app enables all the features that one might expect from the cloud-based accounting platform, including the ability to create and manage invoices, estimates, expenses, and projects all in one place."

This accounting software service is designed for owners of the types of small client-service businesses that send out invoices to clients to be paid for their products, time and expertise. *FreshBooks* allows businesses to invoice clients from their desks or on the go. According to company claims, customers receive payment an average of 5 days sooner than they would with competing accounting programs.

Software features include the ability to:

- Create professional-looking invoices with your own logo;
- Bill clients by sending invoices via email that they can download as PDFs or print;
- Capture expenses from your desk or on the go;
- Log time from your computer, tablet or phone to invoice clients directly from your timesheets;
- Instantly track earning and spending with *Profit & Loss*, *Payments Collected*, and *Expense Reports*;
- Choose from dozens of standard business reports;
- Bill in any currency for extra flexibility;
- Interface with and export data into Quickbooks.

If you are a fledgling start-up, with a limited budget, and are perhaps a bit daunted by the complexity of *Quickbooks*, *FreshBooks* might be a practical beginning alternative.

Be Prepared to Use Dictation to Increase Efficiency

Another valuable software tool that is worth its weight in gold is *Dragon Naturally Speaking*, by Nuance, costing around $100–$200 (for

Home or Premium Edition). After you install *Dragon*, and train it by reading stories to enable it to learn your natural way of speaking, you will be able to dictate your work instead of typing it. This will save you time and energy. It also will preserve your wrists. Using Dragon provides you the benefits of hiring a secretary without the associated expense.

Dictation is a fast and painless way to facilitate most kinds of computer-based work. The caveat—you will need to be very careful to edit everything that you dictate. Although the developers claim Dragon to be 99.9% accurate, it can and does make errors—some of them potentially embarrassing.

Minimum Computer Technology Requirements

Whether you purchase a new computer or already own one, desk model or laptop, your system ideally should be three years old or less. And then expect to purchase a new computer system every 2–3 years.

The key principle once again is that "time is money." Your technology should never limit or hinder your capabilities and the quality of work you are able to provide your employer or clients.

Here are some initial guidelines for minimum capabilities for computer and networking hardware and software, based on the *"Minimum Technology Requirements"* specifications published by the University of Denver.

HARDWARE

Computer System: Desk model, Laptop or Notebook

Note: a netbook or tablet is suitable for basic web browsing and word processing, but is *not* adequate as a primary computer.

Processor: MINIMUM: Core i5 Processor. RECOMMENDED: Core i7 Processor.

Memory: 8 GB RAM or higher. For best performance, install as much memory as you can afford at the time of purchase.

Primary Hard Drive: MINIMUM: 250 GB. RECOMMENDED: 500 GB hard disk drive or larger.

Graphics Card: MINIMUM: 256 MB Video Memory. RECOMMENDED: 512 MB Video Memory or higher

Sound Card with speakers or USB speakers.

Backup Device or Service: For local backup, an external hard drive with double the size of the internal hard drive or a subscription to a cloud-based backup solution is needed.

Note: A quality backup service, running continuously as you work, is vital. If your PC becomes unavailable due to loss, theft, or physical failure, the backed-up files will be fully recoverable, and accessible from any computer with an internet connection.

SOFTWARE

- *Operating System*: Windows 7 (64-bit) or newer.
- *Anti-Virus Software*, Anti-Spyware & Firewall—current and regularly updated.
- *MS Office 2010* or better.
- *Web Browser.*

Minimum Communications Capabilities

The logistics of working at home include creating both a professional and a family identity. Your phone greeting for your professional identity will need to include your job title and company name, followed by your offer to be of assistance. Your personal greeting will be much less formal.

At a minimum, according to one online employment agency, the communications capabilities required to work from home include:

Telephone

- Analog (not digital),
- Corded phone (not cordless),
- Key pad on the base (not on handset),
- Removable handset (cord from jack),
- Established, recognized brand.

Headset

- Corded, able to connect to telephone base,
- Noise cancelling, and of a quality brand.

Telephone Access

- Dedicated work phone line (land line only). Analog or *Fiber Optic Digital* (no VoIP—e.g., Vonage).

Fax Capability

Prepare to Take the Tax Advantages

Remember that your preparations and expenses as you set up and operate your home office will be tax deductible if you establish some or all of your enterprise as a business. Give your business a name, and keep accurate records.

Do you need to buy technology equipment, supplies, furniture or software? Do you need to take a class to improve your Microsoft Office skills, or to learn *QuickBooks*? Do you need books or an online subscription or an online course, or even an online certification or degree, to increase your knowledge and/or your credibility? Do you need to travel for training or to attend a conference? All these activities and materials will save you major money at tax time, because all these expenses are tax deductible.

Another major benefit to you tax wise if you establish a home business is the opportunity you have to deduct as a business expense whatever space in your home you have dedicated to office use *only*. For example, if the room you dedicate constitutes 15% of the total square footage in your home, then 15% of all expenses for your home will be tax deductible. This means that 15% of your heat, water, gas, electric, phone, housekeeping, and grounds care bills can be deducted, too!

Talk to your tax preparer about what records and receipts you will need to retain to take advantage of these deductions. It's also a good idea to begin recording financial expenses within a spreadsheet, where your accountant can easily access all expense details, such as date of purchase, item purchased, vendor, cost, and expense category.

And So...

So far you have considered the yes/no question and have decided "yes", you do want to shift your career to working online. And you have planned your home office and established your "corporate capabilities" in preparation.

Before we consider Chapter 3, stop to appreciate how far you've come and what you have accomplished thus far. Even if you haven't yet taken the tangible steps to set up your work environment, think about how much you have learned in terms of knowledge, understanding, and realization of what's required in order to establish a home office. You now are aware not only of the tangible material costs of what you need to purchase and to learn about, but more importantly, you have an appreciation for all the intangible components that must be considered to establish an effective work environment.

With your *workspace* now prepared, you will learn in the next chapter to prepare *yourself* by following a seven-step process that will facilitate your transition to working online for full or part-time income. This will include learning about the seven trends that define the current online workplace, and exploring the four types of online work. These explorations will combine to broaden your awareness of your range of possibilities.

Chapter 3:
Prepare *Yourself* for Cyberwork:
A 7-Step Process

"To find out what one is fitted to do, and to secure an opportunity to do it, is the key to happiness and success."
—John Dewey

"Working from home may be ideal," you say. "But how will customers or employers ever find me out there? And how will I locate them? Where exactly will my next job, client or commission, come from? Where in the *Worldwide Web* will I find customers who will pay me for what I do?"

These are undoubtedly the most common questions and concerns posed by anyone contemplating a decision to hang up those car keys, or cash in those subway tokens, for a morning walk into the den.

The idea of shifting totally to online work can initially seem overwhelming. This will be much more than just a job change. It will require a full shift in mindset. After all, consider the almost infinite breadth and depth of the Web, perking along out there, with or without you, with a seeming life of its own.

Instead of allowing the enormous size and anonymity of the Web to intimidate you, plan to use its vastness to your advantage by preparing yourself and your thinking to grasp and comprehend the world of cyber work you will be entering. This new world of work will be boundless in ways that you have not experienced. Many constraints you have come to accept as givens will drop away.

Think about how you searched for and located your past jobs "out there" in the brick-and-mortar work world. As you shift to your online career, you will follow through with many of the same tasks and activities, but translate these traditional job-hunt tasks to the online environment.

Unbounded Opportunities

But you will not stop there. Once you have prepared your preliminary action list, plan how you will expand your search to go beyond the constraints of job hunting in the brick-and-mortar work world. Now you will not be bound by location. And you will not be limited by physical traits or challenges.

Not Bound by Location

In the past, when you were seeking on-site employment, you were limited to your own surrounding geographic area, and forced to make time and cost compromises based on how far you were willing to commute. Or you needed to factor in whether or not you were willing and able to make a potentially costly move.

These constraints rose exponentially if you were married—even more so if you had growing children. In this 21st century work environment, where it is likely that both members of a couple have demanding, challenging, high-powered careers to which they are committed, making the decision to re-locate becomes doubly complicated.

Traditionally, if you aspired to start a business, you scouted your local area for a site that could generate enough local traffic and commerce to be profitable. Depending upon where you lived, you may have eliminated otherwise attractive business startup options because you knew that your locale was not a suitable location for that, or perhaps any, sort of business. Opening a gallery that sells Dr. Seuss sculptures or Norman Rockwell limited edition prints clearly will not work well in a small remote town, where boating, fishing and car races are the major pastimes.

When you move to a career online, these constraints no longer apply. Ironically, when your commute shrinks to a walk up the stairs or down the hall, your customer base expands to the entire world! How's that for increasing the size of your target market?

SNAPSHOT

Frank, who has a dual Master's Degree in Physics and Computer Science, is a bright, creative computer programer who earns a comfortable living creating and delivering software systems and designing sophisticated websites for major companies in the state of Texas. His limitations—he decries and shuns the hassles involved in travelling, especially any travel that requires him to deal with the airlines. Because of his reluctance to put up with what he perceives to be the inconvenience of airline inefficiency and unreliability, as well as the high cost of flying, he has placed severe limits on his opportunities to find work "out there."

But because of Frank's reputation for reliability, content competence, and trustworthiness, he has, for more than 20 years, developed an online customer base that continues to grow and provide new clients. And so he is able to work steadily while seldom leaving his home.

As an added bonus—his wife's profession as a pharmacist demands that she work erratic hours. Frank's ability to work from home provides them as a couple with all the flexibility they need to cart their two tween children to karate, the dentist, gymnastics. And one parent is always available to attend those very special school day functions.

Not Bound by Physical Traits or Challenges

When you enter the online work world, your success or failure will not be contingent upon your age, sex, how much you weigh, how you're dressed, or any other physical imperfection or limitation. Unless you select a phone-based career, you will not be limited by having an accent, a lisp, or a stammer.

The world of cyber work is physicality neutral. It's all about your ability to provide your client with that competitive edge. Your challenge will be: "How can I make this product or provide this service, better, faster, with more features and options, at less cost than the competition?"

Making the Mindset Shift: A 7-Step Process

Shifting to online work is a transformation of mindset. In this chapter we will carry out a *7-Step Process* to accomplish this transition:

Step #1: Recognize the seven trends that define the current online workplace.

Step #2: Define yourself— ask "what value can I offer?"

Step #3: Upskill yourself—master the learning curve.

Step #4: Select from the four categories of online work.

Step #5: Translate yourself—do you speak "cyber"?

Step #6: Present yourself—accomplishments and show-and-tell.

Step #7: Plan your trajectory and launch

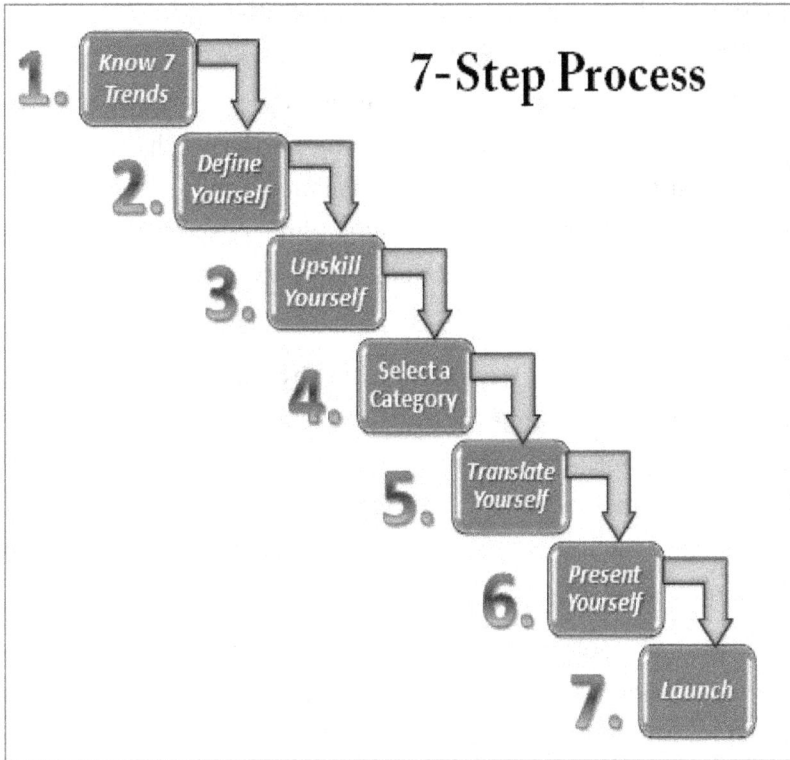

7-Step Process

1. Know 7 Trends
2. Define Yourself
3. Upskill Yourself
4. Select a Category
5. Translate Yourself
6. Present Yourself
7. Launch

Step 1: Know and Understand the Seven Trends that Define the Current Online Workplace

The Internet has affected and altered the world of work as we once knew it. Seven important trends have both resulted from and fueled the penetration of the Internet into every corner of the world.

To understand these trends will significantly increase your awareness of what new kinds of online and telecommuting work have come into existence as a result. These trends have produced whole new work categories—jobs that did not exist ten, or even two, years ago—some of which were not even possible before.

Trend #1: The Changing Economy Has Caused Increased Outsourcing

Given the challenges of the current economy, many companies have determined that online outsourcing some portion of their work leads to significant savings and better performance, while allowing them to focus on their "core business." Through online outsourcing, businesses can gain access to skills, knowledge and expertise that would be expensive or time-consuming to develop in-house.

Additionally, companies have found that by taking advantage of the added capabilities of online talent that are available to them through online outsourcing, they are able to increase their innovation and reduce their time-to-market. This can significantly accelerate their market responsiveness through the design, development and production of new products.

The movement towards ever-increasing outsourcing by businesses has created a flood of new online work opportunities. There are many types of online outsourcing services—call centers, customer support providers, customer relation management firms, data processing services, virtual assistant agencies, and telesales specialists, to list a few. *This trend has resulted in the need for and the proliferation of increasingly large contractor databases offering online outsourcing services.*

Trend #2: *Globalization* of Business Has Created New Online Work

Now that the *world* is the marketplace, many new jobs have been created based on increased needs for people to bridge the previous cultural, monetary and language divisions, and the limitations this dividedness formerly imposed. If you are bilingual or multicultural, your employment possibilities abound.

Companies like *abGlobal* (*http://abglobal.net/*) hire bilingual translators to serve hundreds of clients, from large government agencies and law firms to nonprofit organizations and private individuals. There are many other agencies that enlist expert freelance translators to handle the deluge of translation needs the Internet has generated.

Without a doubt, the ability to speak English is also a significant asset for finding work in this global world of business. Because the Internet is primarily an English-speaking medium, small businesses, as well as mega-corporations, realize that they need to acquire or improve their English writing and speaking ability. In order to compete, they need to be able to communicate clearly and precisely in English. Moreover, their Webpages, emails, articles, sales materials and customer support documents must reflect mastery of standard English.

Companies like *ISpeakUSpeak* (*http://www.ispeakuspeak.com*) hire native English speakers to work one-on-one as English language trainers with students worldwide through a series of English conversations with their trainers, and then receive immediate feedback in order to improve. We'll explore this profession in depth in Chapter 8.

This language-related example is just one of the many job functions that have emerged *because* the Web has globalized business.

Trend #3: *Glocalization* of Business also Has Created New Online Work

To understand the term "glocalization," think about the two words it combines... *global* and *local*. Glocalization describes a product or service that is developed globally, but adapted locally in order to accommodate the consumers particular to each local market. The products or services of an online business are tailored to conform to local laws, customs, culture, and consumer preferences. Services that are effectively "glocalized" are of much greater interest and utility to local customers, and as such, are significantly more marketable.

Yahoo! is an example of a company that practices glocalization. It markets a portal that is viewed worldwide. But it offers multiple distinct versions of its website and services, customizing content and language to appeal to individuals who live in some 25 different countries, including China, Russia and Canada.

An ever-increasing number of businesses are developing their own version of glocalization in an effort to build their customer bases and increase sales. To cite *VIPdesk.com* (*http://www.vipdesk.com*) as an example, the "glocalization" of their services are described as *"international* coverage and presence combined with *local* expertise."

For example, *VIP Desk* hires a local home-based professionals to perform web-based *Concierge Services* for clients who are visiting the area. The local expert aids with requests for local information, guidance, or assistance with everyday tasks such as making restaurant reservations, scheduling transportation services or purchasing tickets to shows or events.

VIP Desk currently offers a customized local version of global services in 20 market areas: Atlanta, Baltimore, Boston, Charlotte, Dallas, Denver, Detroit, Houston, Los Angeles, Miami, New York, Philadelphia, Phoenix, Portland, Salt Lake City, San Diego, San Francisco, Seattle, St. Louis and Toronto, Canada.

Trend #4: The Internet has Significantly Expanded Shopper Expectations

Shoppers now expect knowledge along with their products—condensed and useful information through which they can become fully educated and savvy before they make a buying decision. They are not so much looking for recommendations as they are seeking a basis for making their own intelligent choices.

Consumers also want more options—a fuller selection of choices than they generally can find in a brick-and-mortar store. And they expect convenience while making their purchases, with full support afterwards.

This trend of expanded customer expectations and demands has generated new categories of jobs that are designed to address these needs. Increased customer requirements have changed the landscape for all businesses—traditional as well as online—if they want to thrive, or even if they just want to survive.

As an example of the types of jobs this trend has generated, *VIP Desk* (*http://www.vipdesk.com*) hires at-home "*Brand Ambassadors*" to help companies differentiate their company "from the crowd" in order to build customer loyalty. *Brand Ambassador* services help companies to:

- attract and retain their best customers,
- increase customer engagement,
- extend their brand into the daily lives of their customers,
- capture lifestyle and behavior data of their customers,
- differentiate their brand from competitors, and
- increase customer satisfaction scores and lifetime customer value.

Trend #5: Social Media Has Changed the Needs & Challenges of Business

Companies know that social media is now a critical component of their customers' decision-making processes. Consumers are more likely to make buying decisions based on what they read from people they trust on social networks such as Facebook, Twitter, forums, blogs, Wikipedia, and Yahoo!Answers.

Here are some market statistics:

- 72% of customers use social media to research customer care reputation before making a purchase.
- 92% expect companies to have a social media presence for customer service.
- 66% want companies to increase the use of social media for customer service.

This new phenomenon creates online jobs that were never even contemplated before—jobs that involve interesting tasks, such as:

- capturing data from across the social media landscape,
- analyzing and identifying trends,
- actively listening to social media conversations,
- responding to customers through social media channels,
- participating in and understanding global conversations,
- merging social media data with other data sources, and
- integrating social media when generating contact lists.

One category of work that has been generated by this trend is "social media intelligence and analytics." What new tasks and services are needed to maintain and maximize a company's brand presence in the world of tweets, blog posts, and hashtags? In Chapter 8 we'll talk more about what talents, skills, and strategies you need to put into play to be successful, to find employment, and to establish a career in the world of social media.

Trend #6: Ubiquitous Access to Online Education Has Removed Former Barriers to Learning

What degrees and/or credentials do you already have? What additional certifications, degrees or credentials do you need? The Internet has significantly shifted the playing field for those who need or want to know and learn more.

The goalpost for what you need to know and be able to do is advancing constantly. On the other hand, you now have ready access to whatever degrees, credentials, certifications or training you need or want, simply by locating a school or program online.

Where once an education was an event, it is now an ongoing and continuing process. And where once you may have been forced to choose between going to school and taking a job, now you can have a job and go to school at the same time.

This ubiquitous access we now have to learn what we need to learn, when and where we want to learn it, means that it is now possible for you to enter areas of work you may once have thought to be beyond your reach. By attending school, you can prepare yourself to acquire that better job you always wished you could acquire.

As well as opening up opportunities to learn anything, anytime, from anywhere, the online education movement has generated many new types of jobs in its own right. There are positions for online college faculty, online high school teachers, online tutors, online trainers, and online training materials producers, including online training videos.

Now that access to learning has, thanks to the Web, become ubiquitous, the hunger for learning—learning throughout life—has created its own ever-escalating set of demands.

Trend #7: Access to Information Has Made Us Want to Control Our Own Physical and Mental Welfare

The Internet has made us advocates for our own health, and active participants in everything related to it. Where we once may have been completely dependent and reliant on local health facilities and personnel, we now want to assume more responsibility for our own physical and mental wellbeing. Instead of feeling helpless about a symptom or diagnosis, we actively seek and have access to quality information on that topic, including alternative treatments, health maintenance practices that could make a difference, and even possible alternative diagnoses.

This trend to want to take control of our minds and bodies has been fed by the increase in available accurate information, and, in turn, has created an online market demand for information, consulting, and interaction with professionals.

Step 2: Define Yourself—Ask "What Value Can I Offer?"

Now that you have the seven trends in mind, the second step of the 7-Step Process is *Self-Definition*. Do not be tempted to skip this one! Start by clarifying what you have done in your career so far. What are you particularly good at? What are you enthusiastic about doing? What else would you like to learn to do? And how do these combine to define what you want to do... *really*. In order to define yourself fully, invest some time and effort. You may not know yourself as well as you think you do, at least in terms of what career would suit you best and would make optimum use of your talents.

Assess Your Interests, Skills and Work Values

One excellent tool that is based on the most respected and widely used career theory, *Holland's Theory of Career Choice*, is *Kuder Journey* (*www.Kuder.com*). This is an online career exploration system that assesses your:

- *Interests* (what you like to do; what engages you),
- *Skills* (what you're confident in doing), and
- *Work values* (what is important to you in your work).

Career assessment is the first and most critical step in effective career exploration and planning. While career assessment will not fully determine who you are, or answer the question of what your career should be, it can be extremely valuable in helping you to narrow your search, and guiding you towards discovering your optimal career possibilities. These prospects may include some that you have not previously considered. Also important, career assessnent can preserve you from moving in a direction that is not suited to you and where you will not be happy or engaged.

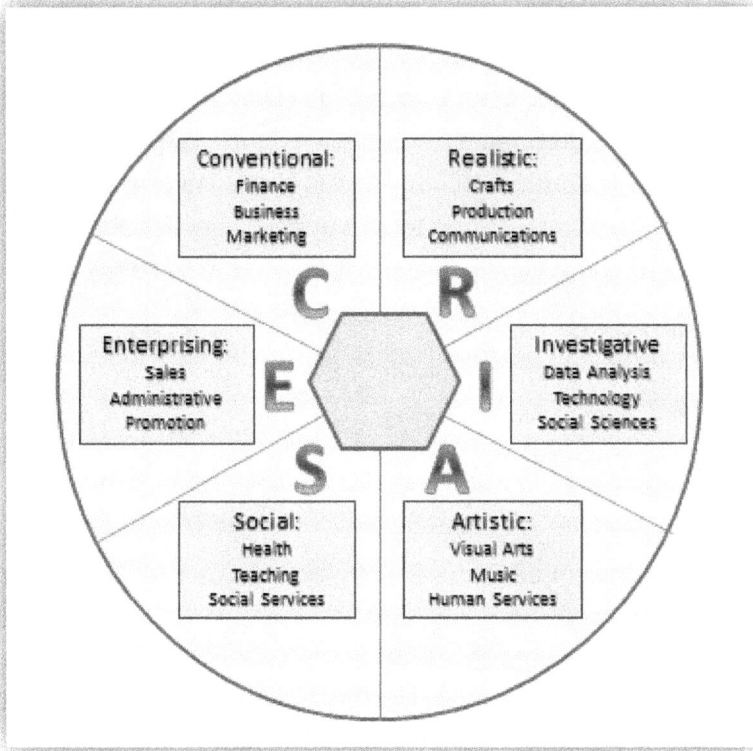

Completing this set of scientifically validated career assessments will take 20 minutes or less, and will cost $35. After you have answered all the questions, your results will be "mapped" to the *6 Holland Career Clusters* that include:

- *Realistic*: Crafts, Production, Communications;

- *Investigative*: Data Analysis, Technology, Social Sciences;
- *Artistic*: Visual Arts, Music, Human Services;
- *Social*: Health, Teaching, Social Services;
- *Enterprising*: Sales, Administrative, Promotion;
- *Conventional*: Finance, Business, Marketing.

Pause now to determine what cluster defines you, based on your *interests*, *skills*, and *work values*. Knowing this will enable you to proceed more clearly in your transition to your new online career.

Another resource that also is based on *Holland's Theory of Career Choice* is available on the *Career Key* site (*http://www.careerkey.org*). This test uses a scientific matching system that enables you to identify careers that match your set of interests, traits, skills and abilities.

You will be able to take the *Career Key* test in 10–15 minutes. The cost is $12.95 to take the Career Key Test or $17.95 to take the test and also receive an eBook entitled *"What Job is Best for Me?: How to Make a Decision You Won't Regret"* written by the nationally recognized counseling psychologist Dr. Lawrence K. Jones.

Determine the Extent of Career Change You Intend

An additional element of your self-definition is to determine the *extent* of career change you intend to make as you shift to working online. Are you in the process of making a full career shift? Or are you just shifting your current career to an online version of the same? Would you want to combine work for pay with something more entrepreneurial? Do you have a talent that you've always wished you had pursued, such as art or graphic design or writing? Are you mechanically inclined? Have others told you that you are a natural organizer or communicator or negotiator or leader?

Before you begin to present yourself for employment online, you need to decide what *self* you want to present. You certainly can present yourself as you are now, and work at something similar to what you already are doing. But why stop at that?

Since you already will be making the significant life change of shifting your career online, this also is an opportune time to expand your horizons beyond where you are and what you do now. Include new skills and abilities you have acquired or would like to pursue. Then repackage yourself accordingly.

To increase your work options by reconsidering and broadening what you have to offer professionally, follow these five strategies:

1) Write your own *Job Description* (or descriptions) and keep a printed copy close at hand.

   Helpful Hint: If you need assistance on how to write your job description, go to the *Bureau of Labor Statistics Occupational Handbook* (*http://www.bls.gov/ooh*). There you'll find thousands of model job descriptions, arranged by category.

2) Develop your own *Strategic Plan.* What will be your focus and goals for the upcoming year?

   Helpful Hint: Create a realistic timeline for yourself, indicating specifically what you expect and need to accomplish, by when.

3) Create your own *Professional Development Plan.* What will you need to learn? What capabilities could you add to your arsenal in order to advance yourself in your intended direction?

   Helpful Hint: Get online and search through the current course catalogs of local Community Colleges. Here you'll find two-year degree programs, certification options, non-credit courses, and single- or multiple-session workshops on a wide variety of topics and skills.

4) Plan for your next *"Promotion"* and do what it takes both to deserve it and to make it happen.

   Helpful Hint: Try job shadowing. Seek out someone among your family, friends, professional acquaintances who currently is engaged in precisely your future "dream job." Offer them your services gratis for a period of time. What better way to obtain a "front row center" view of what that potential career entails?

5) Give yourself your own *Annual Performance Review.*

   Helpful Hint: Be your own hardest yet most inspiring boss. Be ruthlessly objective and honest in assessing your progress toward your goals, and making specific, positive plans and adjustments to improve.

Step 3: Upskill Yourself—Master the Learning Curve

Now that you have defined yourself as you are now, it is time to look at what else you need or want to be capable of doing as part of making this shift to your online career. Many of the skills you will need to add will be technical ones. As you enter the cyber-workplace, you will want to be confident that you know what you'll need to know and can do what you'll need to do.

"How can I be expected to learn all this technology in a short time, while simultaneously attempting to launch an online work presence?" you ask. "How can I become at least somewhat competent at using all these essential technology tools? And where do I go to learn them?"

In terms of what you do and do not know how to do so far, online or otherwise, there are two primary categories: "can do now" and "cannot do yet, but can and will learn."

To work online, you need to learn how to use technology as a communication interface, as a research medium and as a productivity tool to accomplish your work efficiently and effectively. Take heart. Help is available in many venues, including:

- Vendor product training;
- Community College offerings;
- Cyber-learning.

Vendor Product Training

For starters, many commercial companies, chain store outlets and small independent computer, telecommunications or video businesses offer free courses in how to use the technology—hardware or software—you just purchased." They do this because it's sound business practice to do so. Their marketing staff knows that such a strategy creates customer loyalty and acts as free advertising.

Don't be in a hurry to dismiss these free training opportunities as "sales pitches." On the contrary, these workshops are often taught by a certified member of the parent manufacturer, a highly competent trainer whose expertise is product knowledge, not sales.

Marie is proof positive that taking advantage of these free resources really work. When she purchased an iPad from Best Buy, she was lucky enough to be helped by a young techie who was more than willing to give her a jump start in using her new tool. But further, the sales associate told her about free Monday evening classes taught by a certified Apple trainer and open to any iPad owner. Each Monday the instructor focuses on a different iPad App, or on its various system setup options, rotating through the device's major features. The workshop is hands-on. Participants bring their own iPad to custom configure, while the trainer answers individual questions and patiently reviews topics previously addressed. Each week 20–30 eager tech learners gather for this invaluable *free* training.

Marie also happens to live near a major university with an ATT/Apple authorized store that employs lots of tech-savvy college students who are more than willing to spend time helping new users become comfortable with the latest current and emerging technologies. She is now on a first-name basis with several of these employees who always seem ready, willing, and able to answer her litany of "how do you do" questions.

Community College Offerings

Another great source of technology training is the Community College network in your town. A quick glance at the latest catalog yields multiple options for hardware and software workshops and courses that are available for a modest, affordable fee, ranging from a single workshop to sessions that last several weeks.

For example, just a quick glance at the technology courses and workshops offered by a nearby community college during Spring session provides detailed descriptions of more than 70 topics, ranging from graphic design, Web design, business/office skills, programming, multimedia, manufacturing, and social media. Many of these programs are certification-based; others result in a two-year Associate's Degree.

Some offerings focus on a particular software or technology skill and are much less demanding in terms of time commitment and cost. These skill-focused offerings go by a variety of names—adult education, continuing education, enrichment, credit-free, life-long learning. But they all share similar goals—to provide training opportunities for participants to learn a new skill within a pressure-free, relaxed, affordable environment.

As both an instructor and a student within the community college system, Marie can personally and professionally attest to how cost-effective and productive these workshops, courses, and formal programs can be.

Community College offerings provide not only the opportunity to become a lifelong learner, and to master the specific skill you need to launch your new online work, but, as an added, unexpected benefit, these programs and sessions also open up doors to network with other professionals who are there to learn, just as you are.

In fact, you'll often find that, as an added benefit of participation, you'll connect with several others who are more than willing to share their experience, knowledge, tips, tricks and shortcuts, as well as their contacts. In a word, you might find that you have become a member of an informal "users' group" that agrees to meet periodically for a "working lunch" or to share leads and contacts for potential online work.

Another advantage—actually enrolling in a school for some or all of your learning projects generally qualifies you for "student pricing" on many of the software products and programs you're learning to use and will eventually need to purchase. These discounts can be fairly substantive.

Cyber Learning

There is another very effective technology training tool available to you 24-7. What about using technology to learn technology? When you are comfortable using the Internet, you'll find countless online opportunities to learn for free at your own convenience from home. Just think—you won't need to worry about the weather, the hour, the traffic, the way you're dressed. And because these tutorials are self-paced, you can repeat a task at your own speed, until you've reached a comfortable level of mastery.

To discover what is readily available, just do a Google search combining the term "training" with the name or phrase for the technology tool or topic you want to learn. Using this method, you will find multiple user-friendly tutorials, many with step-by-step video components. Some of these programs may require a small fee, while others have been posted gratuitously by the product developer, who knows that his best advertising asset is customer satisfaction and expertise in using the product.

Let's look at a few of the free (or for a modest fee) online tutorial tools available to you as you increase your base of technology skills.

Microsoft Office Online—*https://office.com/start/default.aspx*

Office Online tutors commonly-used features of Word (word processor), Excel (spreadsheet), and PowerPoint (presentations).

Lynda.com—*http://www.lynda.com/*

An online learning company that helps students and users learn software, graphic design, and business skills to achieve their personal and professional goals. For a reasonable monthly subscription fee, members receive unlimited access to a vast library of high quality, current, and engaging video tutorials.

New courses and topics are added every week at no additional cost. Instructors number among the world's top experts who are among the best in their fields, passionate about their subject matter, and who know how to teach.

GCF Learn Free—*http://www.gcflearnfree.org/*

Creates and provides quality, innovative online learning opportunities to anyone who wants to improve the technology, literacy and math skills they need to be successful in both work and life.

By delivering over 750 different lessons to millions of people in over 200 countries and territories absolutely free, GCFLearnFree.org is a worldwide leader in online education. This site also provides a free app, so that learners can access the program anywhere, anytime.

EXCEL Central—*http://www.excelcentral.com/*

Entirely video-based, this site is outstanding for those who want and need to learn Excel. For a very modest annual fee, this series of lessons in two categories (Essential & Expert) walks the user through each specific Excel command, in a user-friendly interface. Highly recommended for both the beginner and advanced Excel user.

QuickBooks—*http://www.quickbooks-training.net/free-quickbooks-videos/*

Features more than 100 short videos from different sources, each focusing on a specific function of the QuickBooks program. Since the videos are not sequential in any way, and are topic based, users can pick and choose a topic, based on whatever aspects of the program they need and want to learn.

ADOBE Suite—*http://www.lynda.com/*

Again, this amazing site offers courses and video tutorials in each of the *Adobe* programs. With 1,111 *Adobe* courses and 54,336 video tutorials on offer, the site can be searched by *Adobe* software version, title, skill level, subject, or tutorial author. Photo editing, illustration, layout design, Web development, video production—all these skills are explained and demonstrated. Membership fees start at $25 monthly, and allow unlimited access to the entire library of 3,408 lynda.com video courses.

Even for more expensive online training courses, there are frequent coupon offers that can bring these prices within reach. For example, a recent groupon offered a 99% discount on the *Microsoft Office Certification Career Advancement Bundle* through *SimpliLearn.com*, reducing the price for nine courses, 100 e-learning chapters, seven simulation exams, 200 demos, 30 chapter in quizzes and eight certification exams, from $2799 to a one-time cost of $29.

Shifting Gears to Your Career Working Online

Step 4: Select from the Four Categories of Online Work

Using your career self-definition, now upgraded in terms of technology or other strategic learning, the next step is actually to begin the process of finding the online job or work you think you want to do. We'll begin by thinking about the four primary ways to work and earn money online.

These four possible categories are:

4 Categories of Online Work

Find an Employer

Start Your Own Business

Online Work

Find Contract Work

Promote & Sell Your Services

Type 1: Find an Employer (Company-Based)

A major category of online work is work-for-hire for employers, performing tasks, producing products or providing services at their direction. This type of work will require that you interview and go through the hiring process, then work according to the standards and processes that are determined by the company.

There are three ways to find *work for hire* online:

- *Look* for existing direct employment,
- *List* yourself with outsourcing agencies,
- *Define* work that needs to be done and offer to do it.

We will discuss these options in more detail in future chapters. For now, here are two samples of actual online job listings of work-for-hire.

SAMPLE 1: Content Writer with Fitness Background

Work at home: TeleCommuting.

We are looking for a candidate to write content for an online company selling nutritional supplements. Candidate should:

- Have a working knowledge of fitness and supplement practices.
- Be able to produce high quality content & maintain social network sites.
- Be highly creative.

This job will require the candidate to create content for new products and post blogs/twitter/facebook updates to help increase product awareness and boost page rankings.

This candidate will need to have a broad knowledge of general fitness, popular supplements and their ingredients, while being able to transfer this understanding into quality online content. We are looking to hire someone to work 20-40 hrs per week.

SAMPLE 2: Customer Service Representative

Virtual (Anywhere)

Shift availability: must be flexible to work at least 8 hours between the hours of 7:00AM to 2:00AM, as schedules will be based on performance

---

and tenure. Shifts may not include weekend days off.

Purpose: To represent *American Support* and their clients by ensuring cable entertainment satisfaction through excellent customer service. The *American Support Customer Service Representative* will offer courteous problem solving, provide quality information and promote additional services in response to customer needs.

Major Duties and Responsibilities:

- Sign in and out for scheduled shifts at appointed times.
- Use a computer terminal to access customer information and convey necessary information to customers.
- Answer customer questions with appropriate and accurate information.
- Communicate effectively, both verbally and in writing, face-to-face, on the radio, and over the telephone, with customers and co-workers.
- Resolve basic customer problems/complaints promptly and refer complex issues and concerned customers to appropriate lead representative or supervisor.
- Acquire and maintain up-to-date cable product knowledge.
- Contact customers concerning scheduled service calls.

Type 2: Find Contract Work (Project-Based)

Whereas *work for hire* focuses on a company and job description, *contract and freelance* work is generally assigned on a project-by-project basis. You likely will be completing contracts for multiple company employers.

There are three primary ways to find *contract work* online:

- *Look* for contract work listed on the freelance boards and other sites where large and small employers post their needs,
- *List* yourself with outsourcing agencies, and
- *Define* work that needs to be done and offer to do it.

Here are two sample postings for contract work.

Sample 1: Instructional Designer (Contractor)

We are looking for an *Instructional Designer* to work on two e-learning modules. The position requires working with Subject Matter Experts (SMEs) to understand the project and add e-learning components to the final product. PowerPoint material will be provided to input into *Articulate Storyline*. The process may involve edits and conceptualizing final product. About 80 hours to complete with flexible timelines.

Job Description: We are looking for a talented *Instructional Designer* who will be responsible for creating compelling and innovative e-learning modules.

Your responsibilities: Understand business and user requirements. Translate requirements into highly engaging and compelling e-learning course. Effectively conceptualize, design and create high-quality e-learning course. Work with SME's to make edits and finalize e-learning courses.

Skills: *Microsoft PowerPoint, Articulate, Articulate Storyline*

Preferred Location: United States

Sample 2: Part-time bookkeeper - Chicago

We are a small company that needs help with monthly bookkeeping.

Job Description: I have the receipts; you have the time and patience to enter the data into QuickBooks.

Initial Tasks

- I have consolidated the current tax year into what should be journal entries.
- We need our local install of QB set-up correctly and the general ledger entries completed based on last tax year's QB trial balance.
- We have an accounting firm that files our taxes. Your results will be reviewed once the books are set up and current year journal entries are

made.

Monthly

- Import your work into my local copy of QB.
- You must have monthly financial statements available by the 10th of the following month.
- We will meet monthly for 30–60 minutes to review the books.
- Initially, I would prefer to meet in person. Once we are comfortable with each other, we can meet in person quarterly and online the other months.

Requirements

Strong written and verbal communication skills. Bookkeeping, Intuit QuickBooks.

Preferred Location: United States

Pros and Cons of Contract Employment

Contract work has both pros and cons to be considered. Recognizing these from the outset will allow you to balance them and achieve the type of outcome you desire.

Eight *pro's* for contract employment include that it generally pays more per hour, and is competence-based, tax deductible and free of office politics. Also it allows for sampling multiple employers, enables a self-controlled schedule, provides for a self-managed income and offers diversified security.

- *Pays more.* According to *The Wall Street Journal*, independent contractors are usually paid 20% to 40% more per hour than permanent employees who perform the same work. Hiring firms can afford to pay independent contractors more because they generally *do not* pay for their Social Security, unemployment insurance or workmans' comp. They also are saved the expenses of providing sick leave, paid vacation time, health insurance or a retirement plan.

- *Competence-based.* You gain the opportunity to establish your reputation for competence, reliability, and maturity—all qualities that contribute to the potential for earning on-going, permanent work.
- *Tax deductible.* Since you are being paid as an independent contractor, at tax time you may be eligible to deduct a portion of your work-related expenses, such as travel, home office space, equipment, meals and office supplies.
- *Free of office politics.* You have the luxury avoiding office politics and what often can be a toxic competitive work environment.
- *Allows for sampling multiple employers.* You have an opportunity to sample a variety of employers, industries, and different types of work, to determine which venues you prefer to accept, based on your interests, skills, and potential income.
- *Enables a self-controlled schedule.* You have the independence to determine how, when, where, and for whom you will work, for as much or little time as you choose. Freedom and flexibility in time management and work environment are yours.
- *Provides for a self-managed income.* You are in control of how much potential income you generate, based on how much work you solicit and complete, and what pay rate you can demand for your skills. You negotiate your salary with your client, who is fully aware that the greater your skill level, the more marketable you are, and the more you can justifiably charge for your services.
- *Offers diversified security.* Your job security is not dependent upon the good or bad performance of a specific organization. Since, over time, you will probably acquire several companies as

clients, you are, to some degree, protected against and not affected by the economic misfortune of a single entity.

Six *con's* for contract employment include: professional isolation, being responsible for your own taxes, absence of benefits, limited in duration.

- *Professional isolation.* As an "outsider" in the organization, you may experience feelings of professional isolation. Although you may be marginally affiliated with several work groups, you are never truly an integral member of any of these groups.

- *Responsible for your own taxes.* Since you are being paid as a contractor, the employer generally will not deduct for taxes. At tax time you will be responsible for reporting and paying appropriate federal (and, if applicable, state) income taxes.

- *Absence of benefits.* As an independent contractor, you will forfeit traditional employment perks such as vacation pay, sick leave benefits, training and travel allowances, and employer-paid pension contributions, unemployment insurance and workmans' compensation.

- *Limited in duration.* You will continually need to be on the lookout for that next lucrative contract job. And you may experience weeks, perhaps months, without work, at least initially, requiring that you plan ahead for such "dry" periods. But as you develop a reputation for quality, reliable work, you might find that you have more work than you can handle. Your balancing act will consist of simultaneously seeking future work while producing quality current work.

- *Delayed cash flow.* Unless you negotiate a financial portion of your fee up front, you may find yourself waiting for 30, 60, or even 90 days before you receive payment. In order to avoid being scammed by deadbeat employers or clients, it's important that you negotiate payment arrangements *in writing and with at least partial payment in advance* before you sign any project contract.

Type 3: Promote & Sell Your Services (Skill-Based)

Offering your services online can be based on what you already know how to do and have experience doing or on what you want to do next. This type of online work differs from both *work for hire* and *contract work* in terms of who initiates and defines the work. In w*ork for hire* and *contract work* scenarios, the prospective employer defines the work and oversees the outcome. They are the seeker, you are the responder.

When you select the direction of promoting and selling your services, you are the definer and the initiator, seeking out clients to engage your services.

Here is a sample of a posting by a self-employed *graphic designer* from San Antonio.

Sample post with service offering, San Antonio Craigslist

Paul Corrado: Graphic Designer

I am a freelance graphic designer working with clients all over the US. I have 10 years of professional design experience ranging from package design for clients such as Rubbermaid and Ace Hardware, to web design for small businesses around the country and logo design for every type of business imaginable.

My wide range of experience will bring insight and creativity to your next graphics project. Design experience includes: Web design. Logo design. Newsletters. Advertisements. Postcards. Brochures. Flyers. Posters. Marketing materials. Web banner ads. Book covers.

Please contact me if you are interested in my services. Call or email today! 414.431.6595. paulcorrado.com. paul@paulcorrado.info.

Type 4: Start Your Own Business (Independent)

A fourth way to work online is to set up a business of your own. Establishing an online business mirrors the process you would pursue in the brick-and-mortar workplace.

Your venture of providing services or products, or both, can exist solely online, or it can combine online and local offline elements. If you already have an established local business, your online business can both complement and supplement it. For instance, you may set up an online business selling products to supplement cash flow from your offline service business, or vice versa.

Steps to Take to Set Up Your Own Business

For starters, before you decide to take the plunge into the deep, dark, unknown waters of business entrepreneurship, we suggest that you spend some time on the *Small Business Administration* (SBA) website (*http://www.sba.gov*). This site offers key information, beginning with "*Is Entrepreneurship for You?*" and "*20 Questions Before Starting.*" Other critical articles include: "*Understand Your Market*" and "*Business Types: Green Businesses, Startups & High Growth Businesses and Home-Based Business.*"

There is a lot to know about starting a business, but this site will walk you through the process, including these action items:

- Register a domain name;
- Select a web host;
- Design your website;
- Begin to advertise and market;
- Comply with online business regulations;
- Find state and local compliance information;
- Learn federal, state and local tax requirements;
- Understand international trade laws; and

- Strategies for growth.

Another excellent resource is Alyssa Gregory's *Small Business Information* website (*http://sbinformation.about.com*), where you will find an entire range of practical, helpful articles on this topic, such as:

- Starting a business or online business;
- Writing a *Business Plan;*
- Legal issues & tax ramifications;
- Marketing & sales strategies;
- Ways to be a happier small business owner;
- Ways to avoid small business owner burnout; and
- Applying for a small business loan.

The *Small Business Information Site* also provides readers with access to a free newsletter that deals with the many aspects of setting up and operating your own online venture.

If you do start your own business, even though you will be working primarily from home and online, you will need to create and distribute promotional materials for your business. An excellent resource site for this is *VistaPrint (www.VistaPrint.com),* where you can readily design brochures, flyers, postcards, and business cards, using a wide selection of templates.

The design process on *VistaPrint* involves choosing a template that best fits your business, then filling in the blanks with key contact and promotional information. After previewing and reworking your materials until they suit your purpose, you will be asked to approve the final result, after which your materials will be printed and shipped to you for distribution.

Another option for distributing your materials is to use *VistaPrint's* targeted mailing list service. This allows you to appropriately target your market according to demographics, household makeup, income, and location, then decide how many addresses from the total available you wish to purchase at a time. Once you've purchased addresses, they are yours to keep and reuse as you plan and conduct future ad campaigns for your business. Another option is to use *VistaPrint's* mailing services to mail out your marketing materials for you to the names and addresses on your mailing list.

Consider Combining Options

Think in terms of combos, too. You may want to find work for hire and also do contract work. You may decide to find contract work, but also to set up a business through which you do that contract work (think tax benefits). Or you may decide to offer your services via self-employment and then establish an entirely different business of your own, perhaps an online shop of some kind.

You have a really good reason to add your own business to whatever mix you decide on, even if your main income will be from working for hire or contract work. Why? Because of the advantageous tax benefits that ensue.

Or Even a "Family Business"

As you initially consider what you could do online, the scope of work you plan to accomplish may begin to exceed what you are realistically able to do by yourself. If this is the case, it may make sense to "think larger" in order to "work smarter."

Would you want to entertain the possibility of a family business? Imagine how combining the collective capabilities of several family members or friends and associates would increase your options to provide multiple services and products. What if you added your son to the mix? And his wife? And your daughter? What if you went beyond family and included your best friend or a professional associate with whom you always enjoyed working?

Carolee can personally speak from experience that, under the right conditions, and with the right mix of personalities, incorporating multiple family members and friends into an operational entity can work quite well. When she established her own publishing company, she elicited the expertise of her son, Brian, whose professional background is in Internet marketing. Brian not only plays a pivotal role in teaching her current marketing strategies, including SEO (Search Engine Optimization), he also happens to be very tech savvy. She continues to take advantage of his expertise on how to use current and emerging technologies to establish her business presence on the Web. And she has relied heavily on her daughter-in-law's graphic design skills to provide her with logos, covers, and layouts for her publishing company, *New Cabady Press.*

Also, as author of two book series, *"Shifting Gears"* and *"Your Great Trip,"* Carolee elicited co-authors, starting with her long-time professional and personal friend, Marie Langworthy, who is also a writer as well as owner of her own web-based writing and editing business, *Super Writing Services* (_www.superwritingservices.com_). Together, Duckworth and Langworthy co-authored and published their successful book, *Shifting Gears to Your Life & Work After Retirement,* and co-authored this current work, *Shifting Gears to Your Career Working Online.*

The second of Carolee's co-authorship partners is, again, her son, Brian. Both seasoned travelers, Carolee and Brian are co-authoring the *"Your Great Trip"* series of travel books, targeted at travelers who want to fully experience the countries and cultures they visit abroad—to become more than tourists on the run—on the bus, off the bus, and follow the leader like a herd of cattle. Instead, *"Your Great Trip"* travelers will be guided through immersive, independent experiences, where they enjoy a sense of adventure and connection—with ample time to explore, to be surprised by the unexpected, and to savor each and every destination.

Carolee is living proof that a business collaboration with family members and close friends *can* work *if* the right dynamics exist—that magic complementary combination of talents, personalities, skills, and mutual goals!

Step 5: Translate Yourself—Do You Speak "Cyber"?

As you know, the Web has its own language. In order to shift yourself to the cyber-work world, it will be essential that you learn to "communicate with the natives." And then you will need to translate yourself, as well as your skills and abilities, using the terms and needs that are particular to this current and emerging world of cyberspace.

This new lexicon of words and concepts—terms that you will need both to understand and to use with ease—constitutes the "native language" of the Web. And so you must become fluent in it. These techno-terms will become your means to bridge the gap between what you can do and want to do, and the world of online work that needs the use of your skills and talents.

For example, you may know that you are an excellent writer—creative, articulate, relevant. This talent could open doors for you online. But first you will need to learn the terms and the particular style and requirements for online writing, and then translate your own skills into these terms. If you can write logically, clearly and well, you could be a future "SEO writer" or "eBook ghostwriter" or "blog writer" or "article marketer." But first you will need to know what these activities *are*, exactly.

We will talk at length about working as an online writer in Chapter 5. For now, just be aware that you will need to prepare yourself to make knowledgeable use of the language of cyberspace in your own writing.

Then create samples that showcase your writing abilities in these particular formats.

Other areas of online work also have their own technical lingo and requirements. For example, if you are experienced as an administrative assistant, you might translate yourself into a *"virtual assistant"* in order to find work performing administrative tasks remotely. As part of your translation task, address issues such as:

- What *cyber-speak words* will my potential clients use to determine my capabilities?
- What portfolio pieces will they ask to see?
- What *cyber-speak words* will they use to specify how they want my portfolio pieces to be uploaded and shared?
- What essential skills, including software skills, will I need to be ready and able to discuss coherently and to demonstrate?

Your new lexicon will need to include all of the key terms relating to online connection and collaboration. Some examples are:

- *Mindmapping*—to capture and organize collaborative thoughts and ideas.
- *Google docs*—to jointly input and revise shared files stored online.
- *Skype*—both audio and video—to enable you and your coworkers to work "together" as though you were sitting in a room side by side.
- *Microsoft OneNote*—to collaborate on and synthesize research.
- *Microsoft Project*—to plan and assign the tasks and timelines for joint efforts, where schedules and deliverables need to be coordinated, timely and efficient.
- *The Cloud* cyber-speak— from which you will download software updates and to which you will backup all critical files.

The list goes on... "File attaching." "Version control." "Revision tracking." "Screen sharing." "Digital signatures." These are the types of additional words and phrases you will need in your lexicon to demonstrate your ability to collaborate as part of a virtual work team.

These terms (as well as the associated online skills) will need to become part of your vocabulary. So take some time to look them up (online), learn their definitions, and prepare to use them in a sentence, just as you did before the spelling tests you took in the third grade.

Step 6: Present Yourself: Your Résumé & Portfolio

With your awareness of trends honed, your work path defined and updated, your decision made about what type of online work you will engage in, and your cyber-speak ready, it now is time for you to present yourself. To this end, you will call upon two tried-and-true standards—your résumé (evidence of your accomplishments and capabilities) and your portfolio (show-and-tell of your work).

The time and energy you spend preparing an outstanding résumé and portfolio will yield you returns that are well beyond your highest expectations. For every hour spent, you will reap substantial benefits, both in terms of dollars as well as the quality level and sheer volume of the work you will attract.

Your Résumé: Summary of Accomplishments & Skills

Start by turning your attention to your résumé and cover letter, both of which will need critical updating and creative revision. Crafting an excellent résumé is hard work, but you are well advised to resist the temptation to cut corners or to rush through this process.

Remember that your résumé is your professional self-portrait. It is your potential client or employer's first introduction to who you are and what you can do. As the door opener to future connections, your résumé is going to make you money, and it's going to keep on making you money for a very long time.

You will *never* earn more money per word than you will by writing an *awesome* résumé. If your 400 word résumé gains you $40,000 a year in work, then over the course of 10 years this will equal $400,000. That's like being paid $1000 per word!

Résumé Content: Functional or Chronological?

The task that your résumé and cover letter need to accomplish is to provide evidence to your potential employers and customers of what you are capable of doing, highlighting those types of accomplishments you can apply to the benefit of their business.

When you plan your résumé, *think match-making, not autobiography*. You may have the notion that the purpose of your résumé is to tell the world all about you. But, to be effective, the focus of your résumé needs to be more about *them*, your potential clients, customers, or employers. It needs to answer *their* question: "What can this individual do to help me and my organization beat the competition and succeed?"

Create a résumé that stands out from the mundane crowd and lands at the top of the competitive pile. Be your client's first phone call. But, at the same time, in no way sacrifice professionalism by using trendy or gimmicky visual or text devices. No pink paper or funky fonts, please.

A *Functional Résumé* (based on tasks you have accomplished) will serve you much better than a *Chronological Résumé* (based on your job description). A *Functional Résumé* communicates more effectively *what you can do*, and enables potential clients and employers to translate from what you have done to address the all-important question of *what you can do for them*.

An effective résumé says to employers and clients—"As you can see, I have these skills and expertise, and with them I have successfully accomplished these specific types of results. And so, I can accomplish the same types of results for you."

Where to start? Complete these *Five Tasks to Create a Powerful Functional Résumé.* These tasks will yield effective *content* for your résumé. Later you will input this content into a professional-looking *format.*

Five Tasks to Create a Powerful Functional Résumé

Task 1: Brainstorm

Take a blank sheet of paper and brainstorm every task you have ever accomplished at work or elsewhere. Include anything relevant from past jobs, volunteer activities, and work you have done for yourself or your family and friends, even when it was for social occasions or family events.

Also include substantive projects you completed as part of your education and training, or even those you produced recently while participating in technology workshops, tutorials and classes. As you continue to add the many types of tasks you have successfully accomplished, you may surprise yourself by how extensive and even impressive your list turns out to be.

Task 2: Expand Your List

Is that everything? Really? Don't be humble. Ferret out the hidden accomplishments and qualities you have missed. Increase your list by one third, adding to it all the writing, research, training, relating, leading, coordinating, organizing, computing, analyzing, negotiating, arranging, budgeting, troubleshooting and problem solving in which you have been involved.

- Have you conducted web research and pulled that research together into clearly written form, or used it to create a PowerPoint presentation?
- Are you the "go to person" when something needs fixing, from a piece of jewelry to a broken mailbox?
- Did you single-handedly plan and guide a recent trip to Europe?
- Have you resolved client problems with either external or internal clients, family members or friends?
- Did you rank #1 this year in car, cookie, or cyberspace sales?
- When family, friends, or work colleagues want to plan any type of social function, do they always appoint you "head honcho"?
- Were you the first one to master and apply the new software program adopted at work?
- Did you then help others to do likewise?

Task 3: Seek Input

Next, seek input, and don't be shy about it. Approach key family members, friends, and professional colleagues, and ask this question: "What are the three things that you think I do best?"

Again, it's always surprising to see how others perceive you! You might find yourself adding unexpected skills and talents to your already extensive list of accomplishments.

Task 4: Turn Your Lists into Bullet Points, Sorted into Categories

It is now time to turn your litany of "can-do's" into bullets points, stated in action terms. Then you will sort these points into functional categories, with a heading for each major section. As an example, your three main categories could be: *Administrative Support*, *Customer Service*, and *Management & Supervision.*

This bullet point activity will be generative in nature. As you continue to add bullet points, you may see that you need to create an additional category. And once you've arrived at your categories, you may think of additional bullet points.

Under each category, your bullet lists will cross over and combine all your past jobs, plus volunteer tasks and even school projects. The goal is to paint a strong and complete picture of how your experience and accomplishments of this type have accumulated and been demonstrated across the years.

Start each bullet item with an action word! The stronger the bullets, the stronger the résumé. Use action words such as:

- *Coordinated* projects...
- *Registered* incoming patients...
- *Conducted* patient interviews...
- *Orchestrated* events...
- *Oversaw* operations...
- *Resolved* problems...
- *Mediated* staff disputes...
- *Handled* customer complaints...
- *Received* corporate visitors...

Task 5: Compile Remaining Sections

Four main sections of your résumé remain to be developed:

1) *Header*: Name, Address, Phone, Email (photo optional).
2) *Qualifications Summary & Goals:* Insert this at the top of your résumé, clustered within categories.
3) *Chronology of Jobs:* List in reverse order, starting with the most recent. Include only the dates, company names and job titles.
4) *Academic Background:* Cite all academic and training credentials, with dates and institutions, again in reverse order.

If you have had a varied career and realize that your résumé is too long, too broad, and too fragmented, don't hesitate to break it apart to create multiple versions of your résumé, each highlighting your experience in a different way. Then use these varying professional self-portraits, as appropriate, to target specific job opportunities.

Select and Apply a Résumé Format

Now that you have focused on your résumé's content, let's turn our attention to format. Content constitutes the "meat" of your résumé, but format is part of that all-important first impression, and determines, to a degree, whether or not your résumé will be read.

Follow the 6 C's

The format of your résumé needs to follow the 6 C's: Consistent, Clean, Concise, Correct, Contemporary and Comprehensive:

- *Consistent:* Uniform use of headings, capitalization, and text formatting.
- *Clean*: Uncluttered, free of distracting icons, images, graphics.
- *Concise*: Less is more. Use economy of terminology; avoid unnecessary or redundant wording.
- *Correct*: Free from spelling, grammar, and usage errors. Use parallel structure.
- *Contemporary*: Modern, readable and efficient style; pleasing appearance.
- *Comprehensive*: Include all essential contact information.

Use a Template

Why invent the wheel, when you can rely on professional help? MS Word has an extensive library of free, professionally designed, downloadable résumé templates, arranged by job category. Each template can be customized and adapted to fit your needs and goals.

Your Portfolio—Show & Tell What You Can Do

Your next task in preparing to present yourself online is to create a solid portfolio. Portfolios are not just for writers or artists. No matter what your eventual business, you need to be ready to showcase samples of your work.

Focus your energies on creating a respectable, even dynamic, portfolio of what you can do. Your online portfolio should include several references or testimonials from past employers or clients, as well as samples of your best work.

Extend Your Portfolio

Extend your portfolio items beyond the types of work you have done in the past, to include samples of work you learned to create more recently, even work you are producing in current training classes.

If you used the Kuder system (_www.Kuder.com_) to focus a renewed spotlight on who you are and what you can do, you will have the option of uploading your portfolio items there. Otherwise, you will need to make arrangements to have your portfolio and résumé hosted on another site that is available for this purpose and offers this service. Again, Chapter 11 contains several ideas and strategies for publishing your résumé and portfolio online.

Update Your Résumé and Portfolio Regularly

Lastly, remember this: every time you add an additional work experience or learn something new, update your résumé with additional bullet points, or even a new category of bullet points, and refresh your portfolio with a sample of that type of work.

Think of yourself, your résumé and your portfolio as continual "works in progress." Because these documents and materials represent your best current persona, they will need to be updated and revised continuously. Also, they will need to be adjusted to custom match each potential job opportunity. These are your faithful "agents"—declaring your talents and value to the world. Attend to them regularly, as you would a paid agent.

Throughout this process, practice the 5 "B"s:

- Be all that you are and hope to be.
- Be the one who knows.
- Be the one who can.
- Be the one who will.
- Be the one they need.

Three Things _NOT_ to Do

Keep in mind that you will be represented by your portfolio, and also through any interaction you have via online applications, phone conversations, email and social networking outlets. Your potential employer will not meet you in person, but rather, through your mutual written and verbal communication, as well as your work samples. So here are three things _not_ to do…

First—Do not represent yourself in vague terms, such as "I am interested in any kind of work" or "I will do anything" or "I just want a job." If you yourself do not know what you are able to accomplish or contribute, then a potential employer will not know either.

Second—Do not allow errors into your communications, oral or written. Make sure that all your communications and exchanges are 100% error free. Your written text and spoken communication must represent your best face forward, since these exchanges will be the only "face" your future potential employers and clients will "see."

Third—Do not commit the error of being unprepared, or even underprepared. In fact, it is better to be over-prepared. Allow for nervousness or time constraints on either your or your potential employer's part. Be ready for any unexpected directions that an interview or communication may take.

Step 7: Plan Your Trajectory & Launch

Now that you are ready to present yourself, after having defined, up-skilled, and translated yourself... And after you have observed and understood the seven trends, and considered the full range of the types of online work you can pursue... Now, and not before, you are closer to being ready to plan the action steps towards your online career.

But first, read on... In order to plan your trajectory and launch, consider the areas of opportunity in the chapters ahead. What aspect of the world of online work will engage you? Where will you apply your talents and skills? What best suits your personality type and temperament?

The Web is "word hungry." Will you write for it? The Web is visual. Will you design graphics for it, or take photographs, or produce videos? The Web is global and "glocal." Will you support businesses as they evolve to meet its increasingly diverse customer base and demands?

The Web is a vast font of information. Will you harness it, synthesize it and communicate it? The Web joins production to demand. Will you create arts and crafts of your own design to sell through it? Will you sew, assemble woodcrafts or hand craft artistic products designed by others? The Web connects the providers of goods and services with their clients and customers. Will you go entrepreneurial?

Before you narrow your selection, begin by broadening it briefly to visualize yourself traveling along one or several career routes on the *"Information Highway."* As you read and consider, bookmark whatever looks interesting to you in order to return to it later. By making your selection from a significantly broader base of possibilities, you may surprise yourself when you make your choice of what to pursue first.

And So...

The level of effort you have put forth so far to prepare yourself for the online work world will benefit you as you move forward. We have just spent time drilling down from the macro (world view) to the micro (your view) in order for you to gain a full understanding of the emerging world-wide career and job trends that have taken place, thanks to advances in telecommunications technology—namely, the World Wide Web.

With this appreciation of the opportunities and challenges that the Web provides, we then turned attention to *you*, and the professional portrait you will project to find your niche in the 21st century cyber market.

In our next chapter, we begin the nuts and bolts of finding a job online by exploring the *Eight Major Job Hunting Resources* to help you focus in on a starting point. These resources will be valuable to you if you elect to pursue either or both of the first two types of online work— *Type 1: Find an Employer*, or *Type 2: Find Contract Work*.

We will talk about the more than 20 ways to boost your search for employers and customers and to promote yourself, depending on your choice of work. These explorations will prepare you well to make the decisions and take the actions you need to launch your new online career.

Keep in mind that once you discover your career niche (and where is it written that you should tackle only one?), only some of these search strategies may apply to you at the outset. However, as you develop a more comprehensive understanding of what's available and possible, you later may want to return to some of the ideas and options that did not seem relevant to you initially.

Don't be surprised to learn how broad your options are, or how you'll find yourself wanting to explore more than one area of job searching. That's the exciting aspect of looking for online work—you often will find that your search leads you to unforeseen opportunities, resources, and connections.

Chapter 4:
Work for Hire: Where & How to Find Your Cyber Job

"The most successful businessman is the man who holds onto the old just as long as it is good and grabs the new just as soon as it is better."

— Lee Iacocca

Now you have done your due diligence in preparing to present yourself online. You are prepared to demonstrate to employers in the cyber workplace who you are, what you can do, and how they may reach you. And you are ready to present yourself as a professional entity to be reckoned with. Now your hour of decision making is at hand.

Hopefully you have confidence that you are ready to begin your new job search. "But," you ask, "*where* do I begin? *What* are the actual tasks I need to accomplish? *How* will customers or employers locate me, and how will I find them?"

Other essential questions follow close behind. "Since my potential employers will not know me and will not meet me face to face, how will they know that I am the one they should hire to accomplish the work they need done? How will they be assured of the quality level of the products I will create and the tasks I will perform? What skills and accomplishments will I need to demonstrate for them to trust that my work will enhance and maintain their reputation, and foster the growth of their business? How will I earn their confidence that the work I produce will be at a level they will be able to use without their needing to redo it themselves?"

Another question is: "*How much* searching is enough? How much time should I expect to expend to find my new career niche? *How long* will it take to secure the job I want, and will it be worth the effort?" Lastly, "*How* will I discern real opportunities from those that will result in costing me money and wasting my time, instead of generating income?

The purpose and focus of this chapter is to help make sense of, to analyze and to synthesize, the various online methods and vehicles available to you to help you "find your road to Oz."

Because this journey can seem overwhelming and confusing at first, our goal is to remove some of the angst and anxiety about where to start, how to separate "the wheat from the chaff," and how to maximize the productive use of your time.

Before You Begin: Some Initial Advice

As you begin this process, four principles will go a long way towards determining your success: 1) take action, 2) stay focused, 3) request feedback, and 4) beware of bait and switch.

Take Action: How Much Search and Action Is Enough?

Plan to commit a significant amount of time and action to the task of locating your online work. How much activity is enough? The magic number cited in job hunting workshops is 100. Assume that it will take 100 actions on your part to yield 8 to 10 responses that will turn into four to five serious possibilities that will lead to two or three offers that will yield that one perfect job.

What constitutes an action? Doing a job search, posting a résumé, applying for a job, presenting yourself and your portfolio to someone who needs your skills ... these are all legitimate actions.

To determine how many actions to take each week, think of how many weeks you will have available to locate work. Then do the math. If you complete 1 action per week, for example, it will take two years to complete 100 actions. Five actions per week will accelerate the process to 20 weeks. To shorten the process to five weeks will require 20 actions per week. And if you hope to complete your goal in two weeks, 50 actions per week will be what it takes to make that happen.

TOTAL ACTIONS	ACTIONS PER WEEK	HOW LONG TO COMPLETE
100	1	2 years
100	5	20 weeks
100	20	5 weeks
100	50	2 weeks

These guidelines will help you plan whatever actions you need to take to meet your goals within your current time constraints. Job hunting is an action sport. There are 100 yards to a football field. And it takes 100 actions to locate and land the right job. Play ball!

Stay Focused & Organized While Searching

Throughout the search process, keep detailed notes, and create bookmarks for sites to which you plan to return. Organize these bookmarks into folders that make sense to you. Otherwise you will find yourself wasting time pouring through a profusion of sites you have saved for one reason or another, many of which no longer have any immediate relevance to you.

Keep a log of when and where you have posted your résumé and portfolio, or applied for a job. Leave space to record results when you receive responses. Use a journal, a table, or a spreadsheet to keep track of what you are sending to whom, when, and with what outcomes.

Request Feedback

When you receive any negative response, request specific feedback on why your application was rejected. Sometimes slight changes to your résumé or cover letter can make all the difference. Often one academic class, hands-on workshop, or certification is the only temporary obstacle you need to address.

Adding one piece of equipment to your home office, installing a dedicated phone line, or expanding the hours you are able to work can become the key that changes a "no" to a "yes" response. Knowing how to improve your game and become more marketable is a valuable lesson in itself as you go through the job hunting process.

Beware of Bait-and-Switch

Beware of so-called "jobs" that turn out to be sales hype for "business opportunities," multilevel marketing, or products that you will need to purchase. Remember, you are in the market to *make* money, not to *spend* it.

If you do happen upon an entity that seems like it could be helpful but costs a modest amount of money, take one simple precaution before you pull out your credit card. Check out the vendor by doing a Google search using the company name. This will quickly reveal any problems or complaints about this enterprise, and will ensure that you avoid being conned into purchasing something you do not want or need.

Small registration fees may be legitimate for software or equipment that is necessary for a particular type of job. However, never write a check or submit your credit card information until you have totally investigated a company's background and what they promise versus what they deliver. Also, how does their product or service align with your business needs or career goals?

The operative term in this process is "due diligence." In other words, invest the effort and time up front to do what you need to do to learn as much as you can about a particular online promise of employment, product, or service *before* you make any financial commitment or sign any contract.

Prepping Your Mindset to Find Online Work

As you carry out your search for work, start by focusing on your tasks at hand. You know that you are capable and have valuable skills, abilities, experience, and knowledge to offer. And you know that you can make a positive contribution. So how will the people who could benefit from what you have to offer, learn enough about you to trust you to represent them and their business? How in the world wide Web will you ever find each other? And how will these matches between you and your employers and/or clients be made?

Now you will be presenting yourself and your skills to people who do not know you or your capabilities—people who likely will never meet you face to face. Your potential clients or employers will go through a process of determining whether or not to trust you with important work, knowing that if you do not produce as promised, they may jeopardize their own professional and business reputations. And so you can and will be judged totally on your ability to deliver the goods and services that your potential client or employer expects and demands.

To establish the mindset you need to address these search-and-find employer-employee-matchup questions, proceed from the known to the unknown. Start by reviewing the types of actions you took to "see and be seen" by potential employers when you were seeking jobs in the brick-and-mortar workplace. Your action list likely included:

- Knock on doors;
- Scan the classifieds;
- Network with business people;
- Watch for new start-up ventures;
- Search out work tasks that need to be done and offer to do them better than anyone else;
- Translate yourself in terms specific to each potential employer's needs.

As you begin to seek out your new online career, you again will be working through the same action list. But this time as you watch and network, knock on doors and scan classifieds, search out work tasks and translate yourself, you will accomplish each of these actions online. And then you will go beyond them, adding other activities that will make you even more effective at finding work.

Eight Types of Places to Find Online Jobs

While it might be interesting to explore the entire spectrum of "what's out there," let's not lose sight of your immediate mission—to find meaningful employment. With these determinations in mind, we have segmented the resources for seeking online employment into eight major categories:

Outsourcing services	**Freelancer networks**
Job consolidation sites	**Google searches**
Online Classifieds	**"Careers" links**
Job boards	**Newsletter Subscriptions**

1. Access Outsourcing Service Sites

A rich source for work-at home job opportunities are the online:

- outsourcing services,
- employment services, and
- virtual staffing services

A list of sites follows. One example from this list, *ClickNWork* (*http://www.clicknwork.com*), engages online workers from a wide range backgrounds and skills. Partnering with companies to determine what work home-based workforces can complete for them remotely, *ClickNWork* matches up experienced and home-based professionals with companies worldwide who need their services.

Companies that have tried online *"homesourcing"* as an alternative to moving jobs offshore in order to increase profits, realize that it not only can be as cost effective as *offshoring*, but can also provide quality gains and much more flexible staffing options. Through online employment service agencies like *ClickNWork,* companies are able to make strategic use of the "vast and largely untapped resource of skilled and experienced people who want to work from home."

A partial list showing the types of virtual workers *ClickNWork's* client companies regularly hire includes:

- *Analysts/consultants*—with specific analytic, consulting and reporting skills who want to work from home;
- *Information professionals/specialists*—with strong track records and proficiency at a range of information sources (Factiva, Lexis Nexus, Profound);
- *Writers/editors*—with experience at high quality business writing;
- *Web searchers*—proficient at quickly finding information on the Web to answer business questions;

- *Data entry specialists*—skilled at rapid and accurate data entry;
- *Shoppers, trend spotters, social observers*—avid shoppers who are adept at seeing trends, drawing parallels and generating valuable commercial insight regarding specific product lines;
- *Telephone interviewers*—proficient at interviewing senior business people, discussing business issues and eliciting opinions on often-sensitive business questions;
- *Photographers*—professionals to take photos of buildings, store interiors and products on shelves;
- *Translators*—people qualified to translate between languages commonly used for business.

Most companies have work tasks that can be accomplished remotely, including research, report preparation, data entry, writing, analysis, and graphic design. These organizations value and utilize the cost savings as well as the greater flexibility they experience by outsourcing staffing tasks that traditionally had been done in house.

On a project-by-project basis, *ClickNWork* identifies from within its network those who are capable of completing a client request accurately and reliably. These assignments might be permanent, temporary, full-time, part-time or *ad hoc*. Sometimes clients require that people be in the same country or time zone; otherwise, contractors can complete their work from anywhere.

Some assigned contractors work by accessing the client's server through a secure remote connection, and complete the work without the data ever leaving the client's server. Other companies provide laptops to individuals to give them access to internal systems and to integrate them more seamlessly into the organization's culture.

To become part of the *ClickNWork* network, you first must pass rigorous tests and submit references for a background check. All applicants must have a reliable broadband-connected PC and excellent

English skills. Experienced managers perform quality checks on all work. If an individual fails to meet the company's high quality standards, he is quickly replaced.

Other primary outsourcing services agencies, employment agencies and virtual staffing services include:

Outsourcing Services	
Prime Outsource http://Prime-Outsource.com	**VIPDesk** http://VIPDesk.com
AccounTemps http://AccounTemps.com	**BalanceYourBooks** http://BalanceYourBooks.com
ABGlobal Translations http://abglobal.net/joining.htm	**OutSource Your Books** http://osyb.com
oDesk http://www.oDesk.com/	**ClickNWork** http://clicknwork.com/

Employment Agencies	
AssistU http://AssistU.com	**Electric Quill** http://Electric-Quill.com
CyberSecretaries http://YouDictate.com	**HireAbility** http://HireAbility.com
DeskTopStaff http://DeskTopStaff.com	

Virtual Staffing Services	
Global Staffing http://GlobalStaffing.com	**Staffing Services** http://StaffingServices.net

Professional Support Services http://Professionalsupportservice. com	**V Staff** http://VStaff.com
BV Staffing http://bvstaffing.com/	**Virtual Office Temps** http://VirtualAssistantJobs.com
Virtual Corp http://www.Virtual-Corp.net	**VirtualStaffing** http://VirtualStaffing.biz

To add to these lists of sites, use Google or another search engine to search on these three terms: "outsourcing services," "employment services," and "virtual staffing services," as well as other related terms.

2. Search Employment Consolidator Sites

In addition to Google and other search engines, you can also pursue searching from within some of the more active job sites, such as:

Monster.com www.monster.com	**Career Builder** www.CareerBuilder.com
Home Job Stop www.HomeJobStop.com	**Homeworkers** www.Homeworkers.org
Jobs.com www.jobs.com	**2 Work at Home** www.2Work-at-Home.com
Work at Home www.WorkAtHome.com	**Outsource 2000** www.Outsource2000.com
T Jobs www.TJobs.com	**Workaholics 4 Hire** www.Workaholics4Hire.com

If you are doing your search from within an employment site, enter terms like "telecommute" or "work from home" or "remote" into the search box on the site, or try a search without specifying a location.

Even though some employers prefer to hire a local candidate even for their online telecommuting positions, these employers know that some telecommuting jobs can be performed from any location. If you have the skills they need, prospective employers might be willing to hire you regardless of where you reside.

3. Look Through the Online Classifieds

Another place to seek online work is within the *online classified ads*. The meta-site, *Craigslist* (*Craigslist.com*), is a good place to start. *Craigslist* is the original source of many of the work-at-home leads listed on other work-at-home sites. Locate the Craigslist for your city and go to the *JOBS* section. Next select the checkbox labeled "*Is Telecommuting*" and click on the *SEARCH* button below the check boxes.

On the San Antonio Craigslist, for example, there recently were more than 300+ postings for telecommuting work. In the Charlotte area there were 139 jobs on the "*Is Telecommuting*" list, including jobs for:

- Educational sales;
- Online tutors;
- Freelance writer;
- Web developer/Web programmer;
- Staff accountant;
- Software sales;
- Inbound customer service/sales specialist;
- Dispatcher/call taker
- Administrative assistant; and
- B2B (business to business) phone sales.

Also look for recent help wanted ads on sites such as:

Fresh Jobs Classified Ads: *http://www.ClassifiedAds.com/*

Job categories that may include online jobs: Accounting & Bookkeeping, Creative, Educational, IT, Legal, Management, Marketing, Office, Sales.

Jobs Oodle: *http://jobs.oodle.com*

Site shows job listings within a radius of the area of your choice, or broader. Use the "Telecommute" category under "Job Title." Also check individual listings within your chosen area for work that can be done from home.

Help Wanted Site: *www.HelpWanted.com*

Jobs are listed by state and by category. Some can be done from home.

Jobvertise: *http://www.jobvertise.com/*

Site lists over one million jobs, with 50,000+ added each week. Search for jobs and post your résumé. Offers a free "Job Match Test" to identify careers, including some you may never have considered.

You will need to monitor these sites regularly, as their job listings change daily. Remember to bookmark relevant sites as you search. Keep notes on your results, and stay current by returning several times weekly.

4. Trawl the Online Job Boards

For many individuals who work online, especially in the initial stages of their job search, "trawling" the job boards is one of the most common methods for seeking work. This strategy also works if your goal is to find contract work, to offer services, or to start your own business. More about these online options follows in Chapters 5–10.

Searching the online job boards works well until you are able to establish a stable group of clients who use you regularly. As you gain more repeat customers, you will become less dependent on this method. But even after you've become successful, it is always advisable to return to these locations to discover new clients.

Some job board sites are operated as auctions, where the potential employer posts a job on a public online board and potential employees (such as yourself) bid against each other to get hired. One caveat, though, about this method. Although this process sounds great in theory, an unfortunate side effect of this type of solicitation is that the bidding process tends to reduce pay rates. While job auctions may work well for the employer, and may even benefit the low bidder, a talented person, who deserves to be paid well for his quality services, often loses.

The websites below are examples of popular job board sites:

Genuine Jobs: *http://www.genuinejobs.com/*

Sign up as a free member to gain access to work from home and freelance job listings. You will receive an email whenever new jobs are added to the members-only database.

Yahoo Hotjobs: *http://hotjobs.yahoo.com/*

Search for telecommuting jobs in your area. Refine the search by job category for better results.

Quintessential Careers: *http://www.quintcareers.com/*

Use the search feature. This site also offers free expert career and job-hunting advice (through articles, tools, tips, and tutorials), as well as links to many of the best job sites.

Guru.com: *http://www.guru.com/*

Find jobs and more jobs to bid on, including jobs in:

- Technology (websites, ECommerce, programming, databases),
- Creative arts (graphic design, writing, illustration, photography, fashion & interior design),
- Business (administrative support, marketing & communications, sales, legal, finance & accounting).

Employment 911: http://www.employment911.com

Use the on-site *Job Search* to search three million+ jobs posted on hundreds of job-listing and employment sites. The site also offers expert résumé writing services and many other features.

JuJu Job Search Engine: http://www.job-search-engine.com/

Use this search engine for jobs by job title, company, location or keyword. Search for job titles that can be done online, such as *virtual assistant* or Web writer. The site allows you to sign up for email alerts.

Job Line: http://jobline.net/

Use the search feature to check many nationwide and international job boards. Also check out the *Information and Advice* pages for job seekers.

5. Join Freelance Networks

Working as a freelancer means that you are self-employed and charge by the hour, day, or project. Typically, on a freelance network site, an employer posts a project to be completed. Freelancers from within the network express interest in completing the project, usually through a bidding process, with the lowest bid often emerging the winner.

Freelancer networks allow freelancers to look for work within their own fields, or to break into a new career market. These networks provide access to hundreds, or even thousands, of potential legitimate income opportunities.

If you are interested in working as a freelancer, perhaps in combination with a more predictable online job, or if you seek to expand your work experience into new areas, check out some of the freelancer networks to determine which ones might be a good fit for your particular skills.

For example, _http://www.freelancers.net/_ has been helping freelancers find work and clients find freelancers since 1999. _Freelancers.net_ is focused on the United Kingdom, but lists many job opportunities from across the globe that regularly use freelancers from outside Great Britain.

Listing yourself on _freelancers.net_ is free, both for freelancers looking for work as well as for employers seeking freelancers.

Other freelancer networks include:

Freelancer	_VWorker_
http://www.freelancer.com/	_http://www.vworker.com/_
Elance	_All Freelance Directory_
http://www.Elance.com/	_http://www.allfreelance.com/_

How many freelance jobs are posted on these sites? At the time of printing, _Elance_ had 36,000+ new jobs that had been posted within the past 30 days. Total earnings for freelance services delivered that month were $322 million.

Among the new jobs posted on _Elance_ were:

- _Web Design—Resolution Upgrade._ Budget: Between $500 and $1000;
- _Facebook & Mobile Application & Website._ Budget: Between $500 and $1000;
- _Online Tutor._ Budget: Between $1000 and $5000;

- *Build a Wedding Website.* Budget: Between $500 and $1000.

Recent sample projects posted for bid on *www.freelancer.com* include:

- 1256 Website design projects;
- 902 graphic design projects;
- 644 article writing projects;
- 348 link building projects;
- 230 blog projects;
- 102 research projects; and
- 94 *virtual assistant* projects.

The downside of freelancer networks—as more freelancers register, the competition increases, resulting in more people who are willing to work for less money. Also, be aware that some freelancer sites charge monthly fees.

6. Search Using a Search Engine

As with anything else you are looking for online, a good place to start is by conducting a search using Google and other search engines. To confine your results to the types of work that you can do online from home, use search terms like these in various combinations with the type of work you are seeking:

Telecommute	Home office	Virtual jobs
Home-based office	Work from home	Work at home jobs
Outsourced jobs	Remote jobs	Online jobs

For example, a search combining the term "telecommute" with "bookkeeping," yielded results that included these:

Bookkeeping Telecommuting and Part-Time Jobs
www.flexjobs.com/jobs/bookkeeping ▾ FlexJobs ▾
Find **Bookkeeping** jobs that offer **telecommuting**, part-time schedules, or freelance
contracts. Every **Bookkeeping** job listing is hand-screened. Find a

Flexible & Telecommuting Bookkeeping Jobs
www.flexjobs.com/jobs/telecommuting-bookkeeping-jobs ▾ FlexJobs ▾
Find **telecommuting bookkeeping** jobs and professional part-time bookkeeping jobs
that are hand-screened and legitimate, ranging from freelance to employee.

Telecommute Bookkeeper Jobs - Simply Hired
www.simplyhired.com/k-telecommute-bookkeeper-jobs.html ▾
135 **telecommute bookkeeper** jobs available. Find your next **telecommute
bookkeeper** job and jump-start your career with Simply Hired's job search engine.

Telecommuting Accounting Jobs - Virtual Vocations
www.virtualvocations.com › Browse Jobs ▾
Find **Telecommuting Accounting** Jobs that allow telecommuting, part-time, full-time, or
freelance contracts. Every **Telecommuting Accounting** Jobs is screened

7. Search the "Careers" Area of Company Sites

Most companies have their own *Careers* link on their websites. Visit sites of companies relevant to your job hunt: Verizon? Amazon? USAir? Holland America? Then scroll to the bottom of the homepage, or look for a small link towards the top of the page. Here's a sample from the Holland America site:

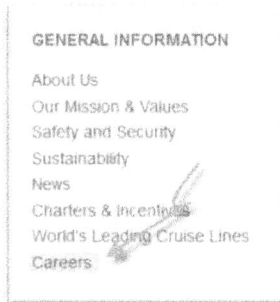

GENERAL INFORMATION

About Us
Our Mission & Values
Safety and Security
Sustainability
News
Charters & Incentives
World's Leading Cruise Lines
Careers

You'll be surprised to learn how user-friendly and job specific these corporate links are. Many include detailed job descriptions, contact information and a link enabling prospective applicants to upload a résumé. Don't automatically assume that you lack the qualifications to be employed by a major company. These organizations are so large that the skills they require are broad and varied. Although you may not be in a position to work directly within the realm of a given company's specific product, you may be well qualified to fill one of the many other related support positions within the company.

For example, you may not be qualified to work in the research and development department of a large technology company, but your experience as a tech writer may well position you to develop instructional manuals for their end products.

You may have no knowledge of computer code, but your graphic design background may be just what a company needs to create the visuals to promote their products. Even if you don't have the slightest idea how those new 3-D printers are designed, your innate mechanical ability may position you to be an efficient installer and troubleshooter of the company's equipment at their client sites, or through their online or phone-based help desk.

These same realities apply to organizations that provide a service, rather than a product. As an online worker, you may not want to be a driver within a large city's major limousine service business, but your organizational skills and your ability to multi-task, together with your experience working with difficult clients as a customer service rep, might make you a prime candidate for their opening as a dispatcher.

8. Subscribe to Newsletters, Email Alerts & Newsgroups

Many helpful jobs-at-home websites will send you recent job advertisements in a newsletter or ezine format. You can join their mailing lists or subscribe to their newsletters free at their websites.

Examples are:

- *Bassador.com*
- *HomeJobStop.com*
- *Telework-Connection.com*

Email alerts are available from many job and career websites including:

- *CareerBuilder.com,*
- *HelpWantedSite.com*
- *IHireAccounting.com*.

Internet Newsgroups comprise another resource for job search and help wanted advertisements. At *http://Google.com*, for example, newsgroups that post *help wanted* advertisements include:

- alt.jobs.offered
- misc.jobs.offered
- biz.jobs.offered
- us.jobs.offered
- misc.jobs.offered.entry

Many more jobs-at-home opportunities are listed in Yahoo Groups and MSN Groups.

Be Wary of Extreme Offers and Claims

To reiterate the warnings in Chapter 3, be aware that there are abuses out there on the Web. If a job "opportunity" sounds "too good to be true," it probably is.

If you are hoping to earn money through online work, be careful not to fall for any "earn $500 a day without working" types of scams. These scams come and go with different faces, but, unfortunately, they cost many future and current webworkers valuable time and money.

Work-at-home scams typically follow one of several recognizable themes. Beware of any "opportunity" that touts high earnings for no skills and very little actual work. There is no such thing as something for nothing, online or anywhere else.

Some work-at-home scams are pure cons, while others are simply poor money-making opportunities promoted to sound suspiciously instant and easy. Sometimes these "opportunities" come complete with false testimonials.

To protect yourself from scams, answer this question for yourself when you are considering an option: "Is this company seeking to hire and pay someone to work for them, or is it attempting to sell something to job seekers?"

Also ask yourself: "Which way does the money flow in this situation?" Do they pay you, or do you pay them? If they are in business to make money from you, instead of the other way around, then move on.

Apply these two simple, obvious clues to protect yourself completely from sales sites that are pretending to be employers:

1) Businesses that will pay you certainly *do* expect that you will work in exchange for that pay. No work, no pay.
2) Any company that claims you will not need to work to earn money is not planning to pay you money. They are planning to make money from you.

Seven Tips for Finding Real Jobs Online

To summarize, it is essential that as you translate yourself into an online worker, you put yourself in charge. Know what you are looking for. Look in the right places. And Litmus Test the results. Determine what it is that you plan to offer an employer or client. Specifically highlight the benefits and value of your product or service. And steer clear of something-for-nothing offers.

Then follow these seven tips:

1) Know and focus on what you do well and what engages you fully.
2) Identify any gaps in what you can already do and know, and move quickly and decisively to fill these voids.
3) Learn to speak the language of your new work environment—the language of the Internet.
4) Translate yourself and what you can do now into Internet language, and be ready to present yourself in these terms.
5) Redefine yourself beyond your local area. You may live in a small town, or even a large city that has lost its job base, but as an online worker, you can work anywhere.
6) Think of the search process for online work as an important form of matchmaking—finding the right match between yourself and what you have to offer, and work that needs to be done.
7) Be ready to *show* potential employers what you can do that would be of value to them.

And So...

Now that you've explored the depth and breadth of online job opportunities, you may be experiencing the confusion, or even the intermittent frustration, of "too much possibility." But simultaneously, you may be starting to feel increased excitement and an eagerness to make a choice and start working online "now or sooner." But wait. First, it's time to step back, take a deep breathe, and focus, focus, *focus*—from a floodlight to a laser beam.

The remaining chapters deal with what career you will choose to pursue, what work you will decide to do, what product or service you will offer to your clients. Will it be as a writer, an artist, a *graphic designer*, a business support person, an entrepreneur, a teacher, an arts and crafts creator? Explore and consider all the options and possibilities that may apply to you. Whatever your choice, you are about to discover a treasure chest of hints and helpers, all online, all designed to make your new venture a successful reality!

Chapter 5:
The Web is Word Hungry—Be an Online Writer

"People on the outside think there's something magical about writing, that you go up in the attic at midnight and cast the bones and come down in the morning with a story, but it isn't like that. You sit [at your computer] and you work, and that's all there is to it."

—Harlan Ellison

Are you really a writer at heart? Have you always felt the urge to capture on paper that book within you? Perhaps you have entertained the possibility of actually earning money as a writer. In fact, because of the Internet, more people than ever before are realizing this ambition.

While pundits have decried the death of the printed word and the demise of reading and traditional books, the opposite has become the reality. Why? Because the Web is word-hungry—a vast blank sheet of paper, beckoning to be filled with words. The need for effective, persuasive writing on the Internet continues to grow exponentially. If you have been harboring an inner writer, your time has come.

If you were born during the information revolution, then you are young enough to anticipate making a living as a Web writer for a very long time. If you are somewhat older, thinking that you might rekindle the latent embers of a life as a writer, new literary avenues are open to you too. Yes, you can finally make your wistful wishes a reality, and write for a living, from the comfort of your home—or from just about anywhere.

New markets for online writers are constantly emerging. Many of these markets, and the terms to describe them, did not exist 20 or 10 or even 5 years ago. Today businesses and organizations, site owners and marketers, information providers and online media are hungry for well-written material.

What types of writing are in demand online? In this chapter we will consider the major writing opportunities available for aspiring Web writers. They include:

Web Content Writer	*Direct Response Advertising Copywriter*
Search Engine Optimization (SEO) Writer	*E-Book Author*
Freelance Writer/Editor	*E-Book Ghostwriter*
Blog Ghostwriter	*Grant Writer*
White Paper Writer	*Technical Writer*

While all of these types of writing have common characteristics and criteria, each has its own set of skills, requirements and strengths. Let's first explore the commonalities and then the differences of each.

All web writing requires the following nine competencies:

1. Thorough knowledge of standard writing practice;
2. Ability to focus on a specific topic, incorporating accurate, current, and factual information;

3. Capacity to write content that entices and engages users so that they continue to browse the site and return again as regular patrons, clients or customers;

4. Capability at presenting written information in a style that is immediately accessible, providing the user with a maximum amount of relevant data within a minimum of browse time;

5. Ability to write for readability, presenting information in headlined clusters or listed as bullet points;

6. Skill at writing for maximum "searchability," incorporating as many relevant key words as possible, in as many formats and combinations as the Web recognizes;

7. Capacity to meet strict, sometimes short deadlines, and to manage time efficiently;

8. High comfort level in communicating effectively with clients, both in person and online;

9. Access to essential and current software and hardware in a high-speed online digital work environment.

Some of these general competencies for online writing are ones that you may consider to be among your current strengths. Others may be on the list of competencies you will be adding in order to be more viable as a member of the online workforce.

Want to be a *Web Content Writer*?

Every website has a specific target audience and requires a different type and level of content. You read the work of a *web content writer* every time you visit a website.

Guided by the needs of the site owner, the *web content writer* creates the content of the pages for the site, populating the pages with relevant words. It is essential that website content contains words that match those search terms that targeted visitors for the site may be expected to use when seeking the types of information, products or services that the website has to offer. These terms are called "key words." Depending upon a given site's purpose, these words might be informational, data or research driven, promotional, creative, or inspirational.

What Does a Web Content Writer Do?

A *web content writer* really is a well-rounded writer who is able to write on many topics and for multiple purposes, all on short notice, and within a set timeframe. *Web content writer*s produce a wide variety of content for the Web, from articles and reviews to game scripts. To be successful at *web content writing* you will need to adapt your writing style and content to the site's purpose, while writing in a dynamic, engaging, thought-provoking way.

If a website is information-based, you will need to ensure that your information is accurate and current, and be skilled at breaking down complex ideas into understandable explanations. If the site's goal is product sales, your approach may require use of direct advertising language.

A client's expectations might include that the *web content writer:*

- Start from scratch on a new site, using information provided by the client;
- Write short, informative content for site pages;
- Develop additional content to make a site more substantive;
- Edit and proof a site that has already been created;
- Rewrite an existing site to increase and improve its effectiveness and engagement;
- Optimize the pages of an existing site to improve its Google page rank; and
- Provide subject-relevant content on a regular basis.

Most *web content writer*s are self-employed and work as freelancers. They can often set their own schedules, but they may also need to work odd hours to meet the demands of multiple clients. A reality check—until they have established a solid reputation, *web content writer*s also may have the added pressure of constantly searching for additional writing assignments.

What Are the Qualifications for *Web Content Writer*?

A thorough knowledge of standard writing practices is necessary for *web content writer*s. Bachelor's degree programs in journalism, English and other mass communication disciplines are ideal college majors, but many other majors will suffice so long as writing skills are strong.

Specialized training programs are available that focus on grammar, editorial writing, magazine writing and ethics, electronic writing and digital media production. Certificate programs for these and other specialties often are offered at community and junior colleges, and serve to enhance a *web content writer*'s qualifications and to provide that competitive edge.

How Much Does Web Content Writing Pay?

Quality *web content writer*s are in high demand. According to the U.S. *Bureau of Labor Statistics* (BLS), writing positions in general were expected to increase 6% between 2010 and 2020. (*www.bls.gov*). Web writers who can adapt quickly to new technologies will have an advantage in the job market.

The BLS reported that the mean yearly salary for writers of all types was $68,420 as of May 2012. Some writers at the top of their form earned as much as $100,000 a year.

How much you earn as a *web content writer* depends on:

- how well you can produce quality content on a variety of topics in vastly different categories,
- how quickly you can produce quality work, and
- how effective your writing is at accomplishing its intended purposes.

Payment may be by the project, by the word, or by the hour. Projects can be one-time, or parlayed into an ongoing demand for regular content.

Working *web content writer*s report that they have no problem finding work and projects when charging $20-$30 a page (about 400-500 words). Rates per word range from $0.05 to $1.50.

Brian Scott, a freelance writer for *http://www.FreelanceWriting.com*, says that articles for web content pay from $10-$50 per article, based on word count and other aspects of the job such as keyword usage. If you are a new writer building a reputation and clientele, you may initially need to quote prices conservatively in order to win work.

Many content writing projects listed on the freelance job boards are open to a bidding process. This practice accounts for a wide variation in rates charged and paid for written content. If you have a particular specialty area, you can expect to be able to charge a premium rate for a writing job.

As a *web content writer*, it's important that you factor in the cost of the amount of research needed on a given topic. When quoting and negotiating a price for a writing opportunity, factor in any specialized expertise you bring to the topic, as well as how much research time you will need to invest.

When you are what I refer to as "speaking from your abundance"—writing about a topic that you have lived and breathed over a period of time—your research needs might be minimal, but your writing should be compensated at a high level. As an example, if you have a financial background and are writing a piece on money markets, you should expect to be paid a premium for your combination of knowledge and writing. If your background is education, you may be able to quickly pull together a segment about online learning based on your expertise, but may need some serious research time before writing on a technical topic.

A professional colleague, who has established his reputation as an experienced, well-travelled fly fisherman, has also become an authority on the topic. As such, he has written extensively on this topic, so that his writing repertoire has become a rich resource in itself. Accordingly, he can and does command a more than average fee for his expertise.

Where to Find Work as a *Web Content Writer*

Begin with exploring the freelancing or outsourcing sites listed in Chapter 4. Additionally, consider developing and using your own website to showcase your writing skills—more about this in Chapter 11. Remember, the Web contains millions of websites, all of them needing words. Finding work should not be too difficult!

You can find potential customers by accessing the eight categories of job hunting resources discussed in Chapter 4. A significant proportion of work-for-hire on these sites is for writers.

You also may consider work-search strategies that include:

- advertising online,
- blogging about your talents and availability, and
- writing articles for article directories such as *www.ezine.com*.

When an article directory like *ezine* publishes your article, you are able to add a "resource box" following your article that highlights your name, expertise and website information. The exposure you gain by writing and publishing articles that showcase your writing abilities, and that point to your website, can result in your making professional contacts that lead to paid work.

Another good way to ensure a continued, secure income as a *web content writer* is to team up with a talented Web developer. Through such a collaboration, you and the developer combined will be able to provide a full range of services for clients, delivering both the content and the functionality for their websites. And each of you will be able to focus on those aspects of the website design and development process that you do best, thus offering potential clients a high-performance one-stop shopping venue.

Could You Be an *SEO Content Writer*?

Of all the career opportunities available to you as an online writer, one of the most pressing is that of a *search engine optimization (SEO) content writer*, which is a web writing specialty in itself. You may have created the most content rich, aesthetically pleasing, relevant website on the Internet. But unless users can readily find and access it, your site might just as well be non-existent.

What is the top strategy for assuring that your site is gaining maximum exposure to the right visitors? SEO is the answer! Since most searchers read only the first page of search results, your website needs to be "ranked" high enough by the search engines for it to appear on the first page in order for it to attract visitors and, ultimately, to make money.

Just as SEO is the key to gaining site visitors, "keywords" are the key to SEO. An *SEO content writer* is an expert in the identification and use of *keywords* to "optimize" the site to be recognized and listed by Google. For a webpage to "rank" high on Google (and other search engines), it needs to be "relevant" to the words or phrases the user has entered as her search. The most "relevant" sites rise to the top of the results list.

How does Google figure out what search results will be most relevant? And then how does Google put all these search results in a specific order so quickly? One method search engines use is to create indexes that prioritize in advance the billions of pages on the Web (*4.6 billion pages* in March, 2015), based on the keywords listed in the "metatags" of the html code for the page, as compared to the actual words ("content") in the headings and text. This comparison is used to create a score that forms the basis for prioritizing each webpage in terms of its "relevancy" for any given search term. The higher the relevancy, the higher the page will appear in the results list.

This means that the metatags and text of each webpage must actually contain the relevant keywords and phrases that users are most likely to enter in their Web searches when they are seeking information, products or services associated with the topics addressed by the site.

The key to effective SEO is to think:

- If I wanted access to what this site has to offer, what words or phrases would I be likely to type into the Google search box? "Travel guide to London and Edinburgh?" "Extra wide shoes?" "Toner cartridges for Magicolor 5650EN?" "Tickets to Alcatraz?" "Algebra II tutor in Charlotte?"
- When presented with a list of website results based on my search, which link or links would I select to visit from reading the "description" shown as part of the result?

What Does an SEO Content Writer Do?

The specialty of an SEO content writer is to maximize the use of relevant key words to achieve the highest possible search engine rankings in order that a site's pages will appear on the first page of search results.

To accomplish this, your job as a writer of SEO content will be to ensure that the keywords your client's potential customers are likely to use when searching are actually present in the text and in the metatags on the web page where your client wants these site visitors to "land."

For most effective search engine optimization, a keyword should appear in these four locations:

1) Metatags,

2) Headings,

3) First and last paragraphs, and

4) Several times throughout the body of the article or web page.

Most web pages will need to be "optimized" for more than one keyword. Additionally, the necessary keywords must not only be properly inserted within the content of the page, the page text also must:

- Make sense,
- Be well-written,
- Be free from technical grammar/usage errors, and
- Be engaging to the reader.

Above all, these pages must provide the reader with useful information on the topic at hand.

In a word, for someone who has an analytical mind and is adept in the use of language, work as an *SEO writer* can be an appealing challenge. If you understand the purpose and power of SEO content, and if you can write to specifications and incorporate a particular set of relevant words into your writing, you have the ability to write SEO content.

Beyond the well-chosen words on each webpage of the website itself, lots of additional SEO content is needed in the form of substantive articles. These articles are to be submitted and published to article directories that then will point back to the website. And so the articles too will need to be "optimized" for SEO, each highlighting one or more specific words or phrases the site owner expects his potential clients will be using in their searches.

SEO is all about the words. If you're good with words, you will find many opportunities to write for all those website owners out there who don't have the time, the patience, the interest, or the talent to attend to this critical website development component.

How Great is the Need for SEO Writers?

According to Adam Short of *www.NicheProfitClassroom.com,* in order to "rank" for a particular set of search terms, an initial "traffic-generating" article campaign for a website will need at least 21 days of consistent article publishing, with one new article submitted each day, each targeting one important keyword. These articles are *in addition to* the content that is being written for the pages of the website itself.

You do the math. Most websites contain at least 5-10 pages. Each page needs SEO content to be written. Additionally, to establish a prime ranking for the site, the site owner will need 21 or more articles to submit to article directories that point back to her site. Multiply this by the number of sites on the Web and you begin to have an idea of how much SEO material needs to be written.

The quantity of writing tasks needed for successful SEO can seem daunting to anyone who is not inclined to do this focused, detailed and demanding type of writing. Many site owners would rather pay someone else to do this writing for them than to do it themselves. This becomes an advantage and an opportunity that is not lost on a would-be *SEO writer,* as it increases the demand for his contribution.

In addition to webpage copy and submitted articles, a successful website business initiative needs to carry out email campaigns, and possibly offer a blog or a mini-course. These will require even *more* well-crafted words. Are you now forming an idea of the amount of potential work there is available to anyone inclined to choose a career as an *SEO writer*?

What Does Work as an SEO Writer Pay?

How do you know what your writing is worth? You will find a range of pay rates, from customers who will want to pay as little as $5 for a 400- to 500-word article, to clients who will pay $10, or as much as $20–$30, for the same number of words.

If you are new to writing for pay, you may need to begin at the lower end of the payment scale until you have compiled a respectable portfolio of your work to demonstrate to potential customers. Once you have established your reputation as an expert *SEO writer*, then you can raise your rates, selectively choosing clients who are willing to pay a fair price for your proven work.

Where to Find Work as an *SEO Content Writer*

Two of the best sources of *SEO writer* work have already been mentioned: *Elance.com* and *Guru.com*. These sites are similar to each other. Choose one, or join both for maximum coverage. Just know that some sites carry a monthly membership fee.

At time of printing, *Elance* had 309,900 jobs posted for writers. One example is *"The New York Writing Project"* that is shown below. The writing task for this project involved 60 to 70 pages of website content, that is "properly researched, keyword driven, and original."

The New York writing project

Fixed Price: Less than $500 | Posted: 3 minutes ago | Ends: 14d, 23h | 0 Proposals

We have a fully laid out website with 60-70 pages that need to be researched and written. Some are longer then others. I will provide the list of all the pages once I shortlist the candidate. Here is a sample: - General Information --- Directions --- Operating Hours & Seasons --- Fees & Reservations - Plan Your Visit --- Tours --- Places to Eat --- Lodging - History & Culture --- People --- Stories - Nature & Science --- Animals --- Plants --- Natural Features & Ecosystems - FAQ - Fun Facts All articles would need to be keyword driven, original content and needs to go through copyscape. ▲

Category: Creative Writing   Skills: Article Writing, Content Writing, Creative Writing

Preferred Location: North America

Websites where you may find SEO writing work include:

FreelanceWriting	*Freelancer*
http://freelancewriting.com/	*http://www.freelancer.com/*
FreelanceWritingGigs	*ClickNWork*
http://www.freelancewritinggigs.com/	*http://ClickNWork.com/*

A Hidden Source of SEO Writing Jobs

A hidden source of some of your best SEO writing opportunities may lie closer to home. Do you have a friend or family member who has an online business, or who is about to initiate one?

If so, you know now that, in order for her's or any online business to succeed, that endeavor will need a steady source of high-quality SEO material. And you could become that source.

To position yourself favorably, reread the last few pages about SEO content several more times until you feel confident that you will be able to present and discuss these concepts clearly. Then set up a meeting with your friend or family member to explain the critical need for SEO content, and how this will greatly enhance the success of her business. Then present your proposal to become the SEO writer who will provide all of this written content, at a fair price.

One word of firm advance advice: If you agree to do the SEO content writing for a friend or family member, *do not* perform this work gratis. Negotiate a *written* contract agreement in advance, allowing for flexibility, if necessary.

If finances on the part of a start-up are limited, as they often are, consider an arrangement where some portion of your payment is in cash and the rest is through a small percentage of the profits from the business as it grows. This strategy not only creates good will, it also assures a long-term involvement on your part. And you will know that you are making a genuine contribution to that business's ultimate success.

Work as a *Freelance Editor*

Are you meticulous about grammar? Do you know the mechanics of sentence structure as well as you know the vital stats of every member in your favorite musical group? Can you transform a colleague's lack-luster vocabulary into prose that grabs the reader? Do you catch errors when you're reading, and silently moan? Are you the "go to" person when bosses and colleagues want their correspondence tweaked to perfection?

Your online work-from-home niche might be freelance editing. Every word written, even by the best writers, needs to be edited. And the Web has produced an avalanche of words, sometimes of mediocre or inferior quality, multiplying daily. There are many needy non-writers and reluctant writers out there, online and offline, who struggle to create quality, coherent writing, and who will welcome your services. Even writers who are competent and eloquent themselves need "that second set of eyes" to catch any flaws that have managed to slip by them because they are too close to their work.

What Does a *Freelance Editor* Do?

As a *freelance editor*, you would edit materials such as web pages and articles, books and eBooks, presentations and manuals, and, in general, all things written. Yours would be the final set of eyes to review that material before it is presented to the world in its final version. You would be the last best proofreader before publication.

If your client is self-publishing a book, for example, your editing efforts may be the only ones performed before that book makes its public appearance as an eBook, or before it reaches the printing press. Your reputation as an editor is enhanced or diminished according to how precise and perceptive you are.

Even given the current lightning speed publishing process from conception to press, it is still a certainty that no one can afford to "publish" anything that falls short of being perfect! Errors in print, on websites, in emails, in articles, in blogs—all jeopardize a writer's credibility. A professional would never allow an error to escape his critical eye. Online publications are held to the same high standards of professional quality expected of traditional publishing houses.

When you are being paid to edit website content, your client will have the right to assume that you will catch and correct every single error. Once that website goes live, or that hard copy book reaches the printer, he doesn't expect to hear from readers about copy errors.

Now let's be realistic. No matter how sophisticated a grammar usage guru you might be, you would be well served to keep a few old standbys next to your computer, either in hard copy versions or within your favorite bookmarks list. Begin with the *Elements of Style* by William Strunk and E.B. White. Writers for years have regarded this gem (referred to fondly as "Strunk and White") as the first and last word in style, grammar and word usage.

Also recommended are the *McGraw-Hill Handbook of English Grammar and Usage* (Lester & Beason) or the *Handbook of English Grammar, Style, and Writing*, published by the Research & Education Association (REA). Confirm through one of these, or via a Google search, any grammar or style element about which you are not 100% certain.

Also you will definitely need to have on hand, either in hard copy or online, a standard dictionary to verify not only the spelling but the proper usage of certain words, and a thesaurus to provide adequate variations in wording.

Depending on the client, editing will likely need to be done according to either APA style or MLA style. Have copies handy of both style manuals to ensure that you are editing according to the style each client requires. Houghton & Houghton publishes two user-friendly booklets entitled, *MLA: The Easy Way!* and *APA: The Easy Way!* *(http://houghtonandhoughton.com/)*. One of my favorite online reference sites for both APA and MLA research and reference is the *Purdue Writing Lab* at *https://owl.english.purdue.edu*.

Other excellent online resources are:

- www.grammar.com
- www.grammarbook.com
- www.proofreadnow.com
- www.Englishrules.com
- www.getitwriteonline.com.

Most clients also will expect you to be highly proficient in MS Office applications, including Word, Excel and PowerPoint, in order that you can complete editing tasks electronically. Your proficiency will need to include knowing how to use "Track Changes" so that you can collaborate with your client as he sees and approves your changes.

In addition, you will need to be extremely well organized at file management and version saving—renaming files to record accurately the dates and authors of each set of changes to ensure you both are working from the most current document file.

How Much Does Freelance Editing Pay?

As a *freelance editor*, you can charge by the project or by the hour. Because editing work is detail intensive, you seriously may want to consider charging an hourly rate.

According to the *Career Research Center* on *Payscale.com* (*http://www.payscale.com/research*), a reliable resource for checking the current pay rates for various online jobs, the current hourly rate for a *web editor* is $14–$20 with 1–4 years' experience; $15–$40 with 5–9 years' experience.

Find Work as a *Blog Ghostwriter*

"Blog" is one of those words that didn't even exist just a few years ago, let alone provide a talented writer with a living. Named as a short form of the term "weblog," a "blog" is similar to a personal journal, only it is posted online.

Thus it becomes not so personal—or, at least, not so private. Blog postings are out there for the entire world to view. Blogs often provide commentary or news on a particular subject. In addition to text, blogs sometimes also include graphics, photos or video.

What Does a *Blog Ghostwriter* Do?

Many individuals—marketers, writers, and others making a name on the Web—keep blogs to communicate with customers or a fan base. Doctors often utilize the blog format to keep their patients up-to-date on the latest news on clinical trials, health issues, and prescription drugs, or just to stay in touch.

Today, it is not unusual to find that these exchanges between a *blog writer* and his readers are actually written by a *blog ghostwriter*. So, yes, as a blog ghostwriter *you* would be the one writing *his* blog. Generally you would be creating three or four 350 to 400 word blog posts each week.

Sample Job Posting for a Blog Ghostwriter

Are you into local food and staying away from the supermarket as much as possible? Do you have a blog dedicated to gardening and growing your own?

Our website is looking for a few good bloggers to cover gardening and homesteading topics with an attitude—we aren't talkin' black plastic mulch, manicured gardens here; the focus is on food empowerment and DIY living. Windowsill gardens in the city, rooftop gardens, chickens in your backyard in the burbs, seed saving and canning your own heirloom tomatoes—we love it all.

We are expanding our site and looking to share your blog with the indie gardening world. We will mirror your existing blog, so without any extra work, you will get a guaranteed audience of more than 30,000 people a month, and get paid to share your blog on our site too. Please send us a link to your blog so we can check it out. We pay per post and will link back to your blog for more shared promotion.

We want urban homesteaders, suburban gardeners, and first time gardeners. If you are focused on where your place in the food pyramid is, we want to hear from you.

How Large is the Need for *Blog Ghostwriters*?

To understand how much blog writing there is to be done, consider the demands faced by anyone who starts a blog and builds a following. The problem with the blog format is that once you initiate it, you need to maintain and update it regularly. This means you must post to it consistently, week after week, in order to retain your audience. For a busy professional or an online merchant with other priorities, this can be challenging at best, and ultimately, overwhelming.

Blog sites that are news-based can be even more demanding. It is not unusual for a *blog writer* to stay up into the night waiting for a breaking story so that her site (or her employer's) can be the first to post a comment on a currently hot, relevant topic.

How Much Does Blog Writing Pay?

Pay depends on the topic, the urgency for posting, and the demands and financial situation of the employer. In some cases, the fee is as low as $5 to $10 per blog post. Other sites pay exceedingly well. In general, you can expect to be paid around $10 per 100 words. A 350-word blog post would then pay approximately $35.

Where to Find Work as a Blog Writer

Again, you'll want to start with *Elance.com* and *Guru.com*, or one of the other freelancer sites we featured earlier. Can you think of any subject on this earth that does not appear on the Web? You will always find clients looking for professional bloggers to write on a broad variety of topics. The key is to write for a blog that is aligned with your area of expertise, or at least within your areas of interest.

Consider Becoming an Online *White Paper Writer*

What on earth, you say, is a "white paper"? White papers once were written by and read primarily within the academic community. More recently, the white paper has been growing in popularity as a content-rich, value-promoting marketing tool.

Within the marketing community, the term white paper has come to mean: *a short report on an industry or a product.*

What Does a White Paper Writer Do?

In a marketing-focused white paper, the writer convinces the reader—who is, hopefully, a potential consumer—to see the benefits of the product, book, software program, widget or service his client is selling. Your job as a white paper author is to present a compelling and persuasive argument in support of the seller's product or service.

In order to assure that white paper writing is an effective marketing tool, the writer needs to be aware of and adhere to certain important constraints on what can and cannot be said. A white paper cannot be written in the style of a blatant sales letter. As a *white paper writer*, you must be careful *not* to actually name or promote your particular product by name. Yet you *do* need to make sure that all the product characteristics that you are declaring to be good are advantages or features that your product (or service) actually does have.

In other words, while you are making written pronouncements about what is good and necessary in a certain type of product, you are not actually naming your own product. However, as it happens, your product does have everything you have defined to be good and necessary.A white paper usually contains a table of contents, as well as several short chapters. Most white papers are not longer than 10–20 pages.

How Much Does White Paper Writing Pay?

As the white paper grows in popularity as an Internet marketing tool, writers are making a respectable living by discovering the secrets of effective, compelling white paper writing. Pay for this type of work ranges widely, depending on skill level, experience and demonstrated success. If you can establish a reputable track record, this niche can be an extremely profitable one. You can expect to be paid from $300 up to a few thousand dollars per paper.

Where to Find Work as a *White Paper Writer*

This branch of the writing trade falls under the umbrella category of "direct-response advertising writing." Look online on *Guru.com* or *Elance.com*, or on any site that lists freelance writing jobs. You will be pleasantly surprised to learn how many such jobs are available once you begin to explore this specific writing niche.

An example of this type of posting, shown below from *Guru.com,* is a writing project on *International Relations* that involves a 55-page research paper on *"The Challenge of Modern Maritime Piracy for the International Community.*

Writing project -International Relations

Posted in Writing & Translation on 19-Sep - 13 days left

Description

Developing a research paper in English on the following topic: "The challenge of modern maritime piracy for the International community".

The paper should be about 55 pages (1800 characters / page).

Outline, basic bibliography and major points are available.

I expect the writer to have a MA/PhD in a related field (International relations, Security studies, Social sciences).
The completed paper has to pass PLAGIARISM test.

The project has to be finished in a month.

"

Work as a *Direct Response Advertising Copywriter*

"Direct marketing" is any attempt to sell something to you directly—bypassing the need for a retail store. A *direct response copywriter* is the individual who writes the words, slogan, headlines and other material aimed at selling directly to a particular marketing audience.

You may not be familiar with the term *direct response copywriter*, but you certainly are well acquainted with the promotional material she writes. Glance at the sales letters on the websites you visit, encouraging you to earn a degree from home, for example. Or the letters attempting to sell you health supplements, or some amazing weight loss product. These, plus all those sales brochures stuffed in your daily email and mailbox, are the work of some *direct response copywriter.*

With the race to promote all types of web-based sales and service businesses, there is a heavy demand for direct response advertising copy. Where the sales staff of a brick-and-mortar store is the communications source that sells products or services to potential customers, the sales copywriter is the source of these communications online.

If you are a natural at sales in person, you may have what it takes to be an ace at writing sales copy. This will be like "talking" to a customer, but through a keyboard, not face-to-face.

What Does a Direct Response Advertising Copywriter Do and Pay?

As a *direct response advertising copywriter*, your job is to persuade the consumer that the product your client is selling is absolutely necessary to his or her wellbeing or success. If you are interested in competing in this demanding type of writing, you might start by enrolling in a training course before you attempt to secure employment.

The competition for work as a *direct response advertising copywriter* is keen—and rightly so. One wrong sentence can lose your client hundreds, if not thousands of dollars. The Web itself is an excellent source of training for this type of writing. There are several very reputable firms that teach the fundamentals. One caveat—this training tends to be expensive, because the marketing stakes for this type of writing are high.

Pay for *direct response advertising* is based on the level of experience and responsibility, with *Marketing Representatives* earning a national average of $36,793, and *Direct Marketing Managers* and *Email Marketing Managers* averaging $60,000–$64,000 (according to *Payscale.com*).

Become an *EBook Author*

Initially, you may not think that you're smart enough or know enough to become an *eBook author*. Think again. Conventional wisdom is that to be something of an "expert" in any area, you need to read a minimum of five books on that topic. You will thereby know more about that subject than 95% of the general population. Writing your own eBook will begin with a combination of the knowledge you already have, plus everything else you need to learn by reading and doing *research*. Extensive reading will, in effect, make you enough of an "expert" to earn the right to speak knowledgeably, coherently, and credibly on the subject.

If you have excellent skills at web- and print-based research—and if you can read and compile that information, organizing it into a flow that is interesting, understandable, and useful—and if you write well—you have what it takes to write an eBook. And you probably will be able to achieve the necessary level of preparation to write an eBook on just about any topic of your choosing.

After all, it *is* the *Information Age*, and people are earning their living selling information to others. You can become one of those well-rewarded individuals, as you simultaneously explore and learn about a myriad of subjects.

One caveat. If this is what you want to do, do not attempt to skip the step of becoming at least a five-book "expert" on the subject about which you choose to write. Your book will need to be informational and useful, not just a diary of your thoughts and opinions, and certainly not just fluff. The task goes beyond crafting pretty words and catchy phrases. Those words and phrases need to *mean* something, not just "sound good."

What Does it Take to Write Your Own eBook

Once you have taken the leap and decided to write an eBook, the questions will begin. *What* will you write about? *How* will you write it? *Who* will your readers be? *Where* will you find the customers who want or need to read your book?

Taking one question at a time—*what* will you write about? If you have a subject about which you are passionate, why not write about that? It's quite possible that, yes, there is a substantial audience to share your enthusiasm for scuba diving, raising bees, or restoring vintage Corvettes. What about writing a book in your particular area of expertise, whether it be raising llamas, writing code for a digital game, or designing a domestic drone? Hoards of writers are doing just that—writing about what they know and do best.

Once you decide on your eBook topic, *how* do you go about the actual process of writing? Two recommended books that you might find helpful are:

- *How to Write and Publish your Own eBook in as Little as 7 Days*, by Jim Edwards and Joe Vitale. (Note: But don't take the "7 day" promise literally. Think more like 7 months.)
- *Instant Book Writing Kit: How to Write, Publish and Market Your Own Money-Making Book (or eBook) Online*, by Shaun Fawcett.

Next, determine *who* your readers will be and *where* they will discover your book. To answer these questions, first think about where you would find this book you are about to write if you yourself were the reader, not the writer. Where do you go to find resources and to purchase books or eBooks on your chosen topic? You probably start with an Internet search or a search on *Amazon.com*.

Your readers will be doing this, too. This takes us back again to keywords and SEO. Begin any project by carefully thinking through what "keywords" your potential readers will use to search for books and resources that are relevant to them on your subject. Then make specific plans to help these readers to find your book by incorporating these words into the title, the URL for the book website, and the focus of the book itself.

Before you start to write, ask yourself "What do people want to read?" and then write about that. This is a much more useful, and potentially more profitable, approach than asking yourself "What do I want to write?" and then hoping you will be able to find people who want to read about it.

To assure maximum success for your writing efforts, determine the market for your book *before* you expend the considerable time and effort it will require for you to write it. By deriving in advance a clear picture of the size of your potential audience, you will be in a better position to make a more intelligent decision as to whether it makes sense to enter a given market.

Before you begin writing a book, it is possible to determine the potential profitability of the topic you are considering by conducting keyword research up front. Resources are readily available that will enable you to determine in advance the potential profitability of a niche market. These tools provide estimates of the total number of people who are conducting searches for information on any given topic.

Resources to be consulted before you begin to write include:

Google Keyword Planner
https://adwords.google.com/KeywordPlanner
Wordtracker
www.wordtracker.com
Niche Profit Classroom
(*www.nicheprofitclassroom.com*)

More about eBook writing will be covered in the Chapter 10 section on *Information Marketing.*

Or Be a Ghostwriter for EBooks

If you are newly attempting to break into the eBook market, you might want to start by ghost writing an eBook for someone else. Try searching *Guru.com* and *Elance.com*, as well as sites such as *freelancewriting.com*. Each of these sites has at least one person in search of a ghostwriter for his eBook.

Sample Ghostwriter Job

Here's an example of a posting on *www.guru.com* for a ghostwriter:

> ### Police Leadership Book: (Ghostwriter)
>
> I would like to begin compiling content for a general book concerning the elements of good police leadership. I have included a general outline of the topics that what I would like to cover in the book. I completed my doctoral research on this topic, but have a hard time articulating concepts into an easy to read format. I tend to gravitate to a more theoretical perspective and focus on peer review and research. In other words, I find it hard to write in a readable manner to the general public.
>
> I would like to have someone take the below listed concepts and write them in a practical manner for the average law enforcement officer to understand. Aside from the below included outline I can provide my dissertation to the writer to help round out some of the areas.
>
> Please note that the outline below is not hard and fast and I am willing to adapt and make the necessary changes. I believe that my target audience (law enforcement officers) may have a shorter attention span and cramming too much information into a book will either make the book too long or very superficial.
>
> Since the topic of leadership is so vast I believe that one route is to strategize the content into multiple smaller books (approximately 60 to 80 pages) that can be rolled out in a modular fashion. I would also like to entertain the notion of having a complementary workbook to accompany the text.

Starting with someone else's book may propel your thinking through plans for your own publication. It also serves as a practice exercise for going through the full process, concept to publication to SEO.

Pay Expectations as an *Ebook Ghostwriter*

Payment obviously depends on the length of the eBook, the nature of the content, and on the type of customer you attract. Is the topic highly technical, requiring you to consult other experts? Does it demand considerable background research? Will you need to spend time developing and conducting interviews, and then using that data to draw conclusions? Factor in how fast you write, rewrite and edit, and propose a price for your services that is somewhere in between what would be ideal for you and what your client can manage.

Although your estimates may begin with the amount of time it will take you for the writing, do not underestimate the importance and level of effort required for revising and careful editing. And do not plan to cut corners during the rewriting and editing process. Your reputation depends upon many factors—accuracy in citing data, writing style, meeting deadlines—but attention to careful precise rewriting and editing is paramount.

All the above variations help determine what you can expect to earn. When you first begin, you will need to have realistic monetary expectations. Working by the project, you should receive at least $200 to $250 for a mini-book, from 15–20 pages long—$10–$14 per finished page. For a 75-page eBook, your payment should be $800–$900. According to *www.payscale.com*, this translates to an hourly rate ranging from $12 to $30.

Could You Become a *Grant Writer*?

If you are looking for a legitimate career that can easily pay you $50 to $70 an hour once you gain experience and establish a reputation for success, grant writing is a career worth exploring. An accomplished *grant writer* persuades those with money to part with it for a worthy cause. Today's demand for *grant writers* is driven in part by nonprofit agencies' increasing needs to discover new ways to fund long-term projects, as well as many day-to-day operations.

Wealthy individuals, foundations, and corporations with funding allowances, provide substantial amounts of money for grant projects. Yet each year, millions of dollars in available grant moneys remain unused. Why? Lack of time, limited human resources, lack of knowledge regarding grant resources and opportunities, and a critical lack of writers who have the tenacity to pursue grant writing, and the talent to adhere to grant parameters and guidelines.

Most nonprofit organizations cannot afford to employ a full-time *grant writer*, and their staff members have neither the time nor the expertise to research grant opportunities or to actually write a grant. As experienced *grant writer*s will attest, this type of writing is an art and a skill unto itself.

"Secret" Skills of a *Grant Writer*

Your role as a *grant writer* is to write and develop grant proposals that attract needed money. As you complete this process, you will find yourself wearing several different hats. Be prepared to be consultant, researcher, writer, manager and "matchmaker."

In fact, your first role will be that of matchmaking—aligning your customer's needs and goals with the guidelines and initiatives of available funding sources. Take as much time as you need to learn about your client's organization—its goals, needs, and unique mission. Think of yourself as the bridge between your customer and the donor. The grantor must be convinced that his money will be used wisely and productively, and that your client is a worthy recipient of these funds.

Next, do your research on the broad range and types of grants available. More often than not, the client will depend upon you to find potential donors and funding sources. You become the point person to discover and uncover potential and actual groups and resources who are interested in a particular project and who are willing and able to partner by providing money to promote their cause.

Learn how to access and download a *Request for Proposal* (RFP), and then study the limitations and requirements that the grant imposes on potential recipients. Pay particular attention to technical and mechanical details. Attendance to details and deadlines is critical, as well as strict adherence to page-count restrictions.

Grant writing requires quintessential writing skills. You will need to be able to communicate clearly to the potential donor exactly why your client deserves to receive a large amount of money. You also need to have an excellent understanding of the grant process itself. Your mission, in large part, will be to convert your client's ideas and concepts into a viable, concrete proposal and program that impresses the potential donor, complete with broad goals, specific measurable objectives, a sound rationale, a practical timeline, relevant tasks, a detailed budget, and a plan for evaluating and assessing results.

Grant writing, like every other type of writing, is its own animal. It requires an economy of words (don't use 100 words when 80 will do), precision (address each grant requirement directly and concisely), and factual, accurate content. Don't exaggerate or fabricate your current situation or future success.

In a word, pretend you're the grant reader who has the authority to approve or reject your proposal. Is your grant clear, credible, realistically doable? Have you built in strong, measurable assessments? Is your timeline for implementation and completion reasonable? Remember that you are competing with an unknown number of applicants for a finite pot of gold.

The sober reality is that, of necessity, because of intense competition for grant funds, the grant reader/awarder is seeking any "excuse" to deny your grant because of a technical issue. This is how he narrows the playing field. Don't provide the professional grant reader any opportunity to detect a weakness or technical mistake within the content of your proposal, thereby prompting him to relegate your work to the "no go" pile.

Once you have written a grant, your job is not over yet. The client will expect you to remain in contact with the potential funding source, and to follow up on the initial submission. You will need to be available to provide the funding agency with any additional materials and information until the request for funds morphs into a grant award.

Additionally, you may be written into the grant to provide periodic and final reports, as required by the granting agency. Accountability measures are always built into every grant to assure the proper use of funds. These follow-up reports are often detailed and time consuming. If there is no one within the recipient's organization who has the time and the expertise to prepare these reports, your client may call on you to do so, on a contract basis. After all, you were the writer who created the grant. Who else, other than the overly busy grant administrator herself, is better prepared than you are to periodically report on the grant's progress?

Throughout the entire grant process, you will need to be self-disciplined and highly organized. Your clients are relying on you to adhere to submission deadlines and to maintain a follow-up schedule on the actions required to compete for funds from these donors.

Lastly, it's important to remain current in the latest trends in grant resources and where to find them. New grant sources appear daily. An Amazon search, or a trip to your local bookstore, will provide you with books that list the latest and greatest grant resources.

How Much Does a *Grant Writer* Earn?

Grant writing can be extremely lucrative. As a member of this profession, you will find that, depending on the customer, you may receive payment in any of three ways: hourly pay, project fee or commission. Or your pay may be some combination of the above. When paid by the hour, experienced *grant writers* can earn as much as $70 an hour. Since most grants will require at least 40 hours to write, this translates to a baseline of $2800 per grant. If the agreed means of payment is by-the-project, a grant writer could earn $1,000 for a simple grant, or three or four times that for a more complex grant.

Some of the best *grant writers* realize that the real money to be made is by charging, at least in part, a performance-based commission, linking their fee to the amount of money the organization is awarded. A percentage of the final grant is agreed upon by the *grant writer* and the recipient—typically 1% to 5%. So for an grant award of $150,000, the commission could range from $1500 to $7500.

Obviously, from a financial point of view, this last alternative carries a high level of risk for the grant writer. No grant award, no pay! Also, from a regulatory standpoint, some funding agencies do not allow grant monies to be used to pay for grant writing services that occurred prior to the grant award.

An excellent solution is for the grant writer to be written into the grant as an active participant in the ongoing work of the proposed project. Most grant projects will end up requiring writing of all sorts. If the grant writer is written into a winning grant, he will receive a sustained income over the life of the grant, which can sometime span several years.

Carolee can attest to this from personal experience. The 10 major grants (and their renewals) for which she served as *grant writer,* yielded over $9.5 million in grant funding, and provided her 14 years of engaging and well-compensated work.

Finding Work as a Grant Writer

For the most part, grant-seeking clients will emerge from the non-profit sector, especially community-based organizations. Other customers may include universities and colleges, public school districts, as well as various other institutions.

You may want to start out locally. Many *grant writers* begin by making a list of potential clients in their own area. Larger organizations often employ their own full-time *grant writers*, so start with the smaller groups that you know are in need of money. Develop essential contacts within these groups and begin to network. To be a successful *grant writer*, you need to realize the vital importance of active networking.

Work as a *Technical Writer*

How many times have you purchased even the simplest of gadgets that came with instructions, illustrations, and "how to assemble" directions, only to find yourself pulling your hair out, grinding your teeth, reaching for a sledge hammer, and whispering a litany of four-letter words before turning to your spouse or best friend in desperation. Blame the *technical writer*!

What Does A *Technical Writer* Do?

A *technical writer* creates and writes various types of user documentation, including how-to guides, references, manuals, "cheat sheets," or instructions. The material a *technical writer* produces is designed to allow the end user to assemble or to operate and use a particular gadget, appliance, or piece of equipment, or to understand or learn a subject. The technical author needs enough knowledge to understand the subject thoroughly. However, when writing she must bear in mind the perspective of her users or readers, who may be encountering the subject for the first time.

This skill involves interpreting technology or applications and then designing and writing documentation. The information may be presented in the form of user guides for software applications, reference manuals, training guides or online help incorporated into software and operating guides. Technical authors also provide software demos and interactive tutorials in a range of media such as 2-D and 3-D graphics, PowerPoint presentations, and video.

As an example, Marie recently purchased a wireless keyboard that came with a wireless mouse and a set of batteries for each. Of course, the batteries came in two different sizes. Since the visual in the one-page instruction sheet was miniscule in size, and since there were no written directions indicating which set of batteries was meant for which device, she (wrongly, of course) assumed the two larger batteries belonged to the keyboard, and the two small batteries belonged to the mouse. *Wrong!*

After recovering from her mental meltdown, she shifted strategy and began to calmly apply reason to her efforts. By process of elimination, she determined which set of batteries belonged where. Such a simple task could have been a non-event if only the instructions had indicated which batteries belonged to which device. Where was the *technical writer* when Marie needed her?!

What are The Requirements for *Technical Writing*?

A *technical writer* must have a clear and concise writing style and a flair for turning technical subjects and jargon into easily understood text. She needs an analytical mind, an inquisitive nature, a curiosity about how things work, and the ability to absorb information quickly. It is essential that she has an eye for detail, and competence with integrating graphics into the text in order to enhance communication.

Professional backgrounds for *technical writers* are broad and varied. Some *technical writers* have scientific or technical backgrounds. Others move into technical writing after gaining experience in journalism.

Excellent English usage is essential, together with some kind of specialist knowledge. Some technical writers have college degrees;

others have earned a two-year Associate's Degree from a Community or Technical College.

A *technical writer* needs to be able to:

- Understand the technology and applications for which documentation is to be prepared.
- Gather and analyze the information needs of the user.
- Organize information in logical order, according to the user's needs.
- Study drawings, specifications, mockups, and product samples.
- Create user documentation for a variety of material, including how-to guides and instruction manuals.
- Write, edit and present information sequentially.
- Explain scientific and technical ideas in simple language to ensure that technical verbiage is easy to understand by the layperson.
- Write clear and concise policies and procedures.
- Prepare charts, graphs, or forms to go along with rough drafts.
- Collaborate with developers and managers to clarify technical issues.
- Write scripts for online tutorials.
- Commission, coordinate or prepare matching illustrations.
- Edit industrial publications.
- Adjust copy, as necessary; proofread for grammar and spelling.
- Field test written instructions with potential users.
- Work with translators, printers and service providers.
- Provide updates and different editions, as necessary.

Is There A Need for *Technical Writers*?

The *Occupational Outlook Handbook* (http://www.bls.gov/ooh/) estimates that the employment of technical writers is projected to grow 15% from 2012 to 2022, faster than the combined average for all occupations. Employment growth will be driven by the continuing expansion of scientific and technical products, and by the growth in online product support services.

Expansion of professional, scientific and technical service firms is expected to drive demand for those who can write instruction manuals and communicate information to users with clarity.

What Does a *Technical Writer* Earn?

The *Occupational Outlook Handbook (http://www.bls.gov/ooh/)* listed the May 2012 median annual wage for technical writers as $65,500. An experienced *technical writer* can expect a six-figure salary at the high end.

Glassdoor.com presents a salary range for *technical writers* starting at $46,800 through $177,400. The *Bureau of Labor Statistics* (BLS) indicates a salary range of $38,700–$101,700, with a mean of $67,910.

Where Does a *Technical Writer* Find Work?

Technical authors work for a range of industries including automation, avionics, chemical, defense, finance, government, manufacturing, medical and pharmaceutical supplies, nuclear energy, quality assurance, hardware, software, telecommunications, transport and utilities.

In addition to these industries, some authors work for technical publishing companies. Others are self-employed, working on a project basis. Many opportunities exist in high-tech companies. Vacancies are found in specialist publications and on the Internet. Many openings are handled by specialist recruitment agencies. For starters, go to the websites we have previously mentioned, as well as others such as *www.careerbuilder.com,* and follow the same search guidelines.

And So...

Did you ever in your wildest imagination realize there were so many ways to earn money just by knowing how to use words effectively? In fact, millions of writers, authors, editors, are doing just that—word-smithing for profit, professional pleasure, and meaningful purpose.

If you have chosen to earn an online living in any field related to writing, hopefully this chapter has provided you with enough resources and leads to last you throughout your literary lifetime.

On the other hand, your talents may be more visual than verbal. You know who you are! As a kid, your school notebooks were filled with mosaic doodles and cartoon drawings. To this day you can't pass a dusty car without drawing a smiley face. The word "icon" is your favorite four-letter word. You're admittedly a YouTube addict. Then Chapter 6 is where you'll be more likely to discover your online future—exploring, imagining, creating. Read on.

Chapter 6:
The Web is Visual: Design Graphics & Multimedia

"As the global market shrinks with the ever-growing reach of technology, the need for that eye-catching graphic becomes more and more valuable to a business."
—Santana Graphix

It's no secret that before the advent of digital media, our primary means of communication were either the printed or the oral word. Computer and video formats have completely changed the landscape for reaching an audience. No longer is the linear medium of print the only, or, some may argue, the primary, way in which the messenger can deliver his message.

Now the Web is dominated by graphics of all types—full motion and live video, virtual reality, 3-D animation, photography, clip art, and original art work. In fact, advocates of a digital society might well argue that these visual media have become far more effective ways of communicating ideas than by using words alone.

As proof of this revolution in the way we receive and share information, learn new skills, and discover phenomena of the world around us, just walk into your local school or public or university library. Count the number of users researching in hard copy books versus the number of patrons using computers. In fact, even the staunchest of traditional librarians now admit, many reluctantly and with chagrin, that they would gladly relinquish their book budgets for more computers.

Moreover, for the first time in the history of mankind, visual learners are now able to assume their place front and center in the world of communication. At last all you visual learners, who best absorb information through digital, video, film, animation, pictures, and every other type of graphic media, now have heretofore unforeseen opportunities to learn, to create, and to work.

This is not to suggest that graphics can mask or substitute for weak content; but visual images not only help to make content more appealing, they provide an alternative and powerful way to communicate the message.

Well-designed graphics enhance a website, encourage visitors to stay and read, and render it unique and consistently recognizable. Graphics, professionally done, also add significantly to a publication's or website's readability. Furthermore, compelling, appropriate graphics create the opportunity for branding, which is critical to all businesses, including Web businesses. A brand is what sets a business apart from its competitors.

Think about the universal recognition factors of the CBS eye logo, MGM's roaring lion, McDonald's golden arches, or the logos of the major auto manufacturers. Each is a powerful visual communicator representing a distinct, successful, and immediately recognizable and widely understood symbol of a product. Or consider the Apple Computer logo—the age-old education image of an apple, but infused with renewed vibrancy and uniqueness by its rainbow of stripes.

Online Visual Design: The Broad Spectrum

Visual design is the art or skill of communicating, attracting an audience, marketing a product or service, or problem solving by creatively combining various types of media, both print and non-print. Visual designers combine words, symbols, and images to create a visual representation of ideas and messages to produce a final result. Visual design often refers to both the process (designing) by which the communication is created, and the products (designs) that are generated.

Where the old paradigm required that a visual designer possess the unique innate artistic gifts and talents of a Michelangelo or a Leonardo DaVinci, today's current and emerging technologies have opened up new avenues for artistic creativity. Now those who have conceptual ideas also have access to computer-generated images and graphics tools that enable them to translate those ideas into tangible, marketable entities of remarkable beauty, entertaining media and heretofore unimagined usefulness.

Who Needs a Visual Designer?

The need for visual designers has escalated in the current visual era. Whereas books, marketing materials, journals, and even the Web once were primarily text-based, these and most other mediums now have "gone graphic." Since the beginning of the millennium, the impetus for more and more graphics has come from multiple directions. But the most significant changes fueling the graphics phenomenon have emerged from the Web.

The visual design process has become a problem solving process that requires substantial creativity, innovation and technical expertise, yet one that offers many opportunities for online work. For example, just reflect on the number of workers who now make their living creating computer games, phone apps, and digitally animated films. In fact, this digital age has generated an explosion of new and exciting career opportunities for the artistic creator—so many specialized niches and potential online careers.

Six Types of Visual Professionals

Since the Web has become highly graphic and richly visual, with other communication mediums following suit, job opportunities are abundant for those skilled in photography, graphic design, layout, animation, illustration, drafting—all things visual. Let's consider six types of visual professions that can be engaged in as online careers.

Photographer	Illustrator	Desktop Publisher
Graphic Designer	Animator	Draftsman

You may already know in general what each of these types of visual design work involve. But if you were to enter one or more of these areas as an online worker, what would be required? Let's delve specifically into the online version of each of these six areas of visual design, focusing on three aspects of each:

1) Brief overview of the work itself,
2) Approximation of potential earnings, and
3) Select list of appropriate and useful websites to:
   - Promote your own work.
   - Select software.
   - Learn and upgrade associated critical skills.

We emphasize that the websites we've included are not meant in any way to be all-inclusive or evaluative. Rather, we hope you'll use them as launching pads to provide you with a flexible overview and starting point of exploration. Consider each group an introductory sampler that you most certainly will want to expand upon by doing your own Google search, where you will undoubtedly uncover lots of valuable sites to add to your repertoire.

Some sites are free to the end user, while others require purchasing software or a subscription. The sites' contents cover various degrees and levels of sophistication, from novice to professional. You will also find that some sites "overlap," in that they can apply to and be helpful in more than one career category.

So be adventurous enough to browse through these web resources. Our inclusions are meant to help you determine the competition, learn what free and paid services are available, view the entire range of both free and non-free software, access the premier learning venues, and gain a broad perspective on the depth, width, and extent of career options and challenges available in your chosen career path.

Home-based Photographer

A home-based photography career can be exciting, versatile, and lucrative. Professional and freelance photographers are needed for fine art and commercial purposes. They may be hired by publications such as newspapers and fashion magazines; organizations such as museums and advertising agencies; and event planners for weddings and all sorts of social engagements.

Although the work of taking photographs would, of course, be performed in the field, each of these major areas of demand for photography work—fine arts, commercial, publications, organizations, events—offer online possibilities for contracts, promotion and sales. Photography is an instance of "glocal" work, the combination of "global" and "local" as discussed in Chapter 3—combining a *global* market demand with *local* customization and follow through.

Taking Photos of What?

The *Minneapolis College of Art & Design* (*http://mcad.edu/*) provides an excellent break down of various types of photography careers that you might pursue, depending on your interests, experience, and training.

Fine art photographers sell work to individuals, galleries, interior designers, architects, libraries, community centers, churches, banks, hotels, and government organizations on a freelance basis or by commission. These photographers enjoy creative freedom not generally allowed to freelance or staff photographers, but they must also be extremely self-motivated.

Staff photographers produce images for magazines, advertisements, brochures, catalogs, corporate reports, publishers, architects or other individuals and businesses that want an event documented or an image that conveys a specific thought or story. The ability to meet deadlines is critical for success as a staff photographer.

Freelance photographers are hired out on a job-by-job basis, a nice perk for those who prefer to make their own schedule or to work on a variety of projects. Freelancers do many of the same jobs as staff photographers, but without the benefit of a consistent paycheck. Some freelancers specialize in areas such as portraits, aerial photography, weddings or fashion.

Medical or forensic photographers document medical symptoms and patient progress as well as evidence for the law enforcement community. Crime scenes, as well as autopsy results, are often prime subjects. An education or experience in criminal justice and/or medical science is an advantageous prerequisite.

Photojournalists document history with a camera by photographing newsworthy people, places, or events. They typically work for a newspaper, journal, magazine or television network, and produce powerful photographs that capture for posterity events in the world around them. Often photojournalists can expect to travel locally, nationally, and internationally.

How Much Does Photography Work Pay?

- Commercial photography averages $45,705 per year (according to www.payscale.com.
- Photo editing earns an equivalent annual wage of around $45K.
- General photography averages $14.56 per hour, ranging in hourly rate from $9 to $50.
- Commercial Photography ($16.58) and Product Photography ($15.24) command the highest hourly earnings.

Websites for Promotions, Software and Learning

The sites below will shed light on Web resources available should you choose photography as your online career.

Sites to Promote Your Photography Work	
Flickr http://www.flickr.com	**RedFrame** http://redframe.com
SquareSpace http://www.squarespace.com	**IntoTheDarkRoom** http://intothedarkroom.com/
SmugMug http://www.smugmug.com/	**PhotoShelter** http://www.photoshelter.com/
ZenFolio http://www.zenfolio.com/	**Thumbtack** http://www.thumbtack.com

Sites to Select Your Photography Software

AdobePhotoshopLightRoom *http://www.adobe.com/*	**DXOImageScience** *http://www.dxo.com/intl*
ACDSystems *http://www.acdsee.com*	**Gimp (free software)** *http://www.gimp.com/*
CorelPaintShopPro *https://store.paintshoppro.com*	**Paint.Net (free software)** *http://www.getpaint.net/*
TimeExposure *https://www.timeexposure.com/*	**PhaseOneCaptureOnePro7** *http://www.phaseone.com*
TenTopTenReviews *http://photo-editing-softwarereview.toptenreviews.com/*	
PortraitPro *http://www.portraitprofessional.com/*	
Aperture *http://www.apple.com/aperture/*	

Sites to Learn & Upgrade Your Skills

CreativeLive *http://www.creativelive.com*	**SmashingMagazine** *http://www.smashingmagazine.com*
SmashingMagazine *http://www.smashingmagazine.com*	

Home-based Illustrator

Just look around you. Open any Web site, book, magazine, newspaper, circular, brochure, flyer, catalog and what do you see? Sketches, icons, symbols, drawings, pictures, cartoons, images—all examples of illustrations created by someone. Depending upon your age, you probably have very different ideas of what an illustrator was, is and has become in this *Internet Age*.

Illustrating for Whom? Illustrating What?

As an *online home-based illustrator*, your market for contracts and assignments expands from your immediate geographical area to the world. You might be creating illustrations for the traditional media formats mentioned above; but you also may find yourself illustrating a host of material to which you never really gave much thought. How about illustrating textiles? Or wrapping paper? Or wall paper? Or what about creating illustrations for greeting cards, calendars and stationery. . .or the cover of an e-Book? Think about the need for illustrators in the video game industry or in advertising.

Whether it be a hand-drawn illustration or a digital one, at the heart of every illustration, there is a story to be told, a problem to be solved or a point of view to be expressed. The illustrator visually communicates his message in his own personal style and artistic voice, using acquired technical skills in a variety of media.

Some illustrators specialize as *medical illustrators*. These illustrators must have a full understanding of surgical and medical procedures, as well as the mechanics of living organisms and anatomy. They typically work with doctors and researchers to create illustrations for medical journals, scientific exhibits, medical advertising or textbooks.

Another area of specialization is technical illustration. Again this requires additional background and preparation. *Technical illustrators*, also known as scientific illustrators, prepare detailed drawings to help people understand often complex scientific or technical information. Their illustrations are used in textbooks, reference books, instruction manuals and technical sales brochures. They may also produce images for multimedia software, film and television, websites and architectural visualizations. *Technical illustrators* need to be familiar with a variety of software programs, including AutoCAD, Photoshop, and Adobe Flash Builder.

How Much Does Online Illustration Work Pay?

Illustrators earn an average of $53,400 per year (according to the *Bureau of Labor and Statistics*—BLS). PayScale (*www.payscale.com*) cites an average hourly wages of $20.45.

Medical illustrators earn more, averaging $61,000, but require a higher level of education and skill (*www.ami.org*). *Technical illustrators* earn an average of $62,757 (*www.salary.com*).

Sample Job Listing for a *Home-based Illustrator*

Consider these sample job listings posted on *www.oDesk.com* to get an idea of the types of work you may have open to you.

Looking for 2D/3D Artists Excited to Create Simple Mobile Game Assets. Less than 1 month. 10-30 hours/week

Notes: Looking to hire a few part-time and full-time artists. If you are interested in creating various unique assets for games and freely expressing your creativity at the same time, consider buzzing us. We are exploring a lot of themes for the games from arcade, retro games, fighting, shooting, racing etc.

Creative Mobile App (IOS and Android) Designer. 3-6 months, 30+ hours per week.

Notes: This is an epic opportunity to work with a world-wide mobile campaigns organization. You will need to be passionate about designing for mobile and eager to launch your career and learn from an extremely talented bunch of people. The role requires a team player who has a proven track record of effective collaboration, both within digital teams and in a multi-disciplinary agency environment. You will thrive on delivering big ideas by bringing the content to life, and presenting and selling your ideas with passion.

Websites for Promotions, Software and Learning

These sites will be useful Web resources if you are interested in online illustration as a career.

Sites to Locate Illustration Work	
oDesk http://www.oDesk.com	**Illustration** http://www.illustrationWeb.us/
MyBookIllustrator http://www.tmcreations.com	**BigBlackBag.com** http://www.bigblackbag.com
Awwwards http://www.awwwards.com/	**SiteSlinger** http://thesiteslinger.com
IllustrationMundo http://www.illustrationmundo.com/	

Sites to Aid Selection of Illustration Software	
OXP http://www.onextrapixel.com	**CreativeBloq** http://www.creativebloq.com

SpoonGraphics *http://blog.spoongraphics.co.uk*
TopTenReviews for PCs *http://illustratorsoftwarereview.toptenreviews.com/*
TopTenReviews for Macs *http://mac-illustrator-software-review.toptenreviews.com/*
Adobe *http://www.adobe.com/products/illustrator.html*

Sites to Learn & Upgrade Your Skills	
Noupe *http://www.noupe.com*	**DzineBlog** *http://dzineblog.com*

Desktop Publisher

Can you think of any company or organization, large or small, that does not need desktop publishing services to produce newsletters, presentations and other graphic materials? A desktop publisher fills this need by creating printable material from data, photographs or text. She combines knowledge of graphic design and aesthetic science to create functional and eye-catching materials.

Using appropriate computer software that formats and combines text, numerical data, photographs, illustrations, charts and other visual graphic elements, the *desktop publisher* produces publication-ready material including brochures, financial reports, business proposals, menus, books, newspapers, magazines, newsletters, packaging, tickets and business cards.

The following "punch list" indicates that, in addition to being creative and having an eye for graphic design, a *desktop publisher* must be detail-oriented. Some of the routine, mundane duties include:

- Operate desktop publishing software and equipment to design, lay out, and produce camera-ready copy;
- Position text and art elements from a variety of databases in a visually appealing way in order to design print or webpages. Use knowledge of type styles and size and layout patterns to position text;
- Check preliminary and final proofs for errors; make needed corrections;
- Store copies of publications in hard copy as well as digitally.

What education is needed to become a *desktop publisher*? A college degree is not necessarily a requirement to work as a desktop publisher—many skills are learned on-the-job. But those with either an associate's degree or earned certificate seize the best job opportunities.

First and foremost, you will need strong computer skills, specifically proficiency with desktop publishing software packages such as InDesign, PageMaker, Illustrator and Photoshop. It is also essential that you have excellent file management skills to organize the assets for each project so that they are readily accessible, and to control the versions of each master file as you receive input and feedback from clients, contributors, and reviewers.

How Much Does Online Desktop Publishing Work Pay?

How much do desktop publishers typically earn? This career pays an average of $37K ($17.81/hour) to $40K per year. Pay-scales vary depending on education and experience. The highest wages are earned in the electronic and legal services industries, at $27+ per hour, or $57K annually.

Sample Job Listing for Online Desktop Publishing

Consider these four sample job listings posted on _www.oDesk.com_ to get an idea of the types of work you may have open to you.

Email Newsletter Manager. More than 6 months. Less than 10 hours/week. We are using _mailchimp_, integrated with _magento_. If you know these two platforms, it will be a plus. We require you to:

1. Have graphic design skills—we would like to view your work first;
2. Be creative with our newsletter advertising/marketing;
3. Demonstrate to us your past experience providing similar services.

InDesign Expert Needed. 1–3 months. 30+ hours/week.

Help me with 3 books needed to complete within a month.

Desktop Publishing. Less than 1 month. 10–30 hours/week.

We will have lots of files that may need to be formatted. They will be translated and then the layout will need to be adjusted to make sure it is correct and it matches English. There will be some Word documents and also some _InDesign_ files, so candidates will need to have _InDesign_ skills. There will be 13 languages in total, with about 7 files in each language.

MS Word Expert. More than 6 months. 10–30 hours/week

Formatting of CVs/résumés using MS Word. Gathering of all info provided via email and placement of all data into MS Word template provided. Must have excellent written English, writing and editing skills. Résumés compiled and formatted to a high standard. Work must be emailed back within 24 hours so our writers can then word and prepare the finished CV's for our clients.

Websites for Promotions, Software and Learning

The following sites will assist you in seeking out career opportunities in this field, and improving your desktop publishing skills.

Sites to Promote Your Desktop Publishing Work	
Elecks'Localization *http://eleks.com/*	**Thumbtack** *http://www.thumbtack.com*
FlexJobs *http://www.flexjobs.com/jobs/telecommuting-publishing-jobs*	
oDesk *https://www.oDesk.com/o/jobs/browse/skill/desktop-publishing/*	

Sites to Select Your Desktop Publishing Software	
PageSuite *http://www.pagesuite.com*	**AdobeInDesign** *http://www.adobe.com/*
Scribus *http://www.scribus.net*	**StockLayouts** *http://www.stocklayouts.com*
Serif *http://www.serif.com*	**Gizmo'sFreeware** *http://www.techsupportalert.com/*

Sites to Learn & Upgrade Your Skills	
Inkling *http://discover.inkling.com*	**AboutTechnology** *http://desktoppub.about.com*
Virtual Training Company *http://www.vtc.com/showall.htm*	**SkillPath** *http://www.skillpath.com*

Graphic designer

A *graphic designer* uses visual elements to communicate messages through print and electronic media. He may design magazines and newspapers, websites, packaging, video games, promotional displays and marketing materials. *Graphic designers* work with images as well as text in order to design and create visually appealing elements, including brochures, logos, advertisements, and websites.

In order to create these items, *graphic designers* will often work with a variety of different types of images, including photographs, paintings, and digital media. Photo and image editing software is often used to manipulate images and create the designs.

Most clients hire *graphic designers* to create something that communicates an obvious or subliminal message. This means that not only do these artists need to make their creations look great, they also usually need to assure that their creations deliver a message that grabs and holds the audience.

In today's world of flashy visual elements and subliminal messages, graphic design is a growing industry, and talented *graphic designers* are in high demand.

Some *graphic designers* work as logo designers, advertisement designers, Web designers, photograph editors, book layout artists, magazine or newspaper layout artists, illustrators, or art directors. Other designers work for advertising, publishing and design firms.

One of the most common—and obvious—places to find an online graphic design job is with a graphic design firm that hires several *graphic designers* to work on a variety of different projects for multiple clients. Some companies also hire their own *graphic designers*. For example, advertising agencies often have several *graphic designer*s on staff.

You can also work as a self-employed freelance designer. Although you then would have the option of picking and choosing which types of projects you work on, as a freelance *graphic designer* you also would be responsible for procuring your own clients. As a freelancer in any occupation, one trades the security of a regular paycheck for freedom and mobility in managing one's time and life.

How Much Is An *Online Graphic Designer* Paid?

A *graphic designer* earns an average annual salary of $40,073, but wages vary based on experience. Experienced designers earn 17% above the national average. Late-career designers earn 23% above. Self-employed *graphic designer*s show higher annual earning averages—around $59K, ranging from $39K to $104K.

Sample Job Listing for Online Graphic Design

Consider this sample job listing posted on *www.oDesk.com* to get an idea of the kind of work you may want to pursue:

Freelance *Graphic designer*s for Boutique Graphic Design Agency Wanted: More than 6 months; Less than 10 hours/week.

Notes: *Art Affairs* is a well-established, worldwide collaborative design agency in India. We are currently setting roots in Australia and are in need of 4 freelance designers who are willing to work remotely with us. Our team is comprised of people from all over the globe—India, Australia & Venezuela—we work remotely from our own offices and homes, we are excellent professionals and team players who enjoy what we do, and we look forward to new members to make our business grow. Targeted Countries: Asia, Northern Europe, Latin America and the Caribbean.

Websites for Promotions, Software and Learning

Below are some relevant graphic-design websites that you as a future *graphic designer* might want to explore.

Sites to Promote Your Graphic Design Work	
DesignIsKinky *http://designiskinky.com*	**AAWWWARDS** *http://www.awwwards.com/*
JustCreative *http://justcreative.com/*	**SimplyHired** *http://www.simplyhired.com*

Sites to Select Your Graphic Design Software	
JustCreative *http://justcreative.com/*	**CorelDraw** *http://www.corel.com/*
WebGraphics *http://wegraphics.net/*	**TheTopTens** *http://www.thetoptens.com/*
TopTenReviews *http://graphic-design-softwarereview.toptenreviews.com/*	

Sites to Learn & Upgrade Your Skills	
MediaMilitia *http://mediamilitia.com/*	**HOW** *http://www.howdesign.com/*
CreativeBloq *www.creativebloq.com/*	**Lynda.com** *http://www.lynda.com/*

DesignInspirationMagazine

http://designinspirationmagazine.com

Animator

Animators create 2D and 3D images in motion for animated films, video games, commercials, and music videos. They provide special effects and visual images using video, film, or computer software. An animator produces multiple images called frames that, when sequenced together rapidly, create an illusion of movement known as animation. The images can be made up of digital or hand-drawn pictures, models or puppets.

Computer-generated animation features strongly in motion pictures to create special effects or an animated film in its own right, as well as in television work, the Internet and the computer games industry.

Since the advent of computers, digital animation has taken on a life of its own. Just witness the success of *Pixar, Industrial Light and Magic*, and *Dreamworks* over the past 15 or so years, and how these corporations have raised the bar in terms of the richness and capabilities rendered through digital animation.

While the basic skill of animation still relies heavily on the animator's artistic ability, in this era of technological sophistication and capability, it is absolutely essential that aspiring animators be experts in using the latest computer animation packages.

Some of the most common technology programs used by animators includes: *Adobe, AutoDesk 3DS Max, VectorDesigner, Ability Photopaint, After Effects*, and *Cinema 4D*.

How Much Does Online Animation Work Pay?

About three out of five of animators have less than five years of experience. Relatively new workers average around $51K in annual earnings, ranging from $35K to $80K. Experience is the biggest factor affecting pay for this group.

Sample Animator Job Listing

DIGITAL ARTIST / ANIMATOR

Primary Responsibilities: Design and develop interactive interfaces, instructional media and 2D animations, graphics and web pages for use in educational products. Provide input into product design requirements and branding, monitor resource allocations and applications to project and guide design process throughout product development.

Other responsibilities will include creating, testing and maintaining web based and other learning products. Ideal candidate will work in an integrated team environment with other *graphic designers*, instructional designers, application developers, videographers and subject matter experts to develop other previously noted products but must be able to work independently as well.

Basic Qualifications:

- Qualified candidate must have minimum of BA in Graphic Design, Interaction Design, Multimedia or a related discipline, and 1-3 years of experience in the field.
- Knowledge of graphic design theory, electronic design layout, use of color, design theory, 2D animation and typography required.
- Knowledge of *Adobe Photoshop*, *Adobe Illustrator*, and *Flash* required.
- Knowledge of instructional design concepts is a bonus.
- Portfolio required at time of interview.

Websites for Self-Promotion, Software and Learning

As a future animator, you might find some of these sites helpful.

Sites to Promote Your Animation Work	
DeviantArt	**Aniboom**
http://www/deviantart/com/	http://www.aniboom.com/
Moovly	**Wideo**
http://www.moovly.com/	http://wideo.co/
GoAnimate	
http://goanimate.com/	

Sites to Select Your Animation Software	
AnimeStudio	**FlipBook**
http://anime.smithmicro.com/	http://www.digicelinc.com/
OXP	**CorelDraw**
http://www.onextrapixel.com	http://www.corel.com/
GoAnimate	**Bloop**
http://goanimate.com/	http://www.bloopanimation.com
Maya&Softimage	**FreeMake**
http://www.autodesk.com/	http://www.freemake.com/
KeyShot	**ToonBoom**
http://www.keyshot.com	http://www.toonboom.com
TopTenReviews	
http://2d-animation-software-review.toptenreviews.com/	

Sites to Learn & Upgrade Your Skills	
FullSailUniversity *https://learn.fullsail.edu/*	**ComputerGraphicsWorld** *http://www.cgw.com/*
Lynda.com *http://www.lynda.com*	**AnimSchool** *http://www.animschool.com*
AnimationMentor *http://www.animationmentor.com*	

Draftsman/Draftswoman

A *draftsman/draftswoman* is essentially an artist with the ability to prepare schematics based on given specifications and calculations. Drafters use software to convert the designs of engineers and architects into detailed mechanical technical drawings and plans. They specialize in architectural, civil, electrical, electronic, aeronautical or mechanical drafting, using their technical expertise to help design everything from microchips to skyscrapers.

Besides creating drawings and plans that are used in manufacturing and construction, draftsmen are expected to calculate structural strength, assess building capacity limits and estimate material needs and construction costs.

Depending on the project, draftsmen may use traditional drafting methods, such as drafting pencils and T-squares, to create their drawings. However, most draftsmen today use CAD (Computer Assisted Drafting) software to create, save, view and distribute their drawings and plans. This software enables drafters to create detailed schematics to guide product manufacturing or building construction, incorporating the input of engineers, architects, and surveyors, and specifying dimensions, codes, materials, and production methods.

The three major areas of drafting specialization are:

- *Architectural/Civil Drafter*—creates drawings of buildings or engineering projects such as highways, bridges, and airports;
- *Mechanical Drafter*—focuses on technical drawings of machines and mechanical devices;
- *Electrical/Electronic Drafter*—prepares diagrams for wiring, circuit boards and electrical equipment.

How Much Does Online Drafting Work Pay?

The *Bureau of Labor Statistics (http://www.bls.gov/)* states that, as of 2012, the median salary for *drafters* was $49,630, or $23.86 per hour. *Drafters* typically need specialized training that can be accomplished through a certificate or associate's degree drafting program.

While not required for employment, acquiring a professional credential can increase chances of advancement. The *American Design Drafting Association (ADDA)* offers certification programs for architectural, civil, and mechanical drafting (*www.adda.org*). The *ADDA* requires that individuals have three years of professional experience to be eligible to take the certification examination. Certification is valid for five years.

Sample Job Listing for Online Drafting

Check out this sample job listing, posted on *www.careerbuilder.com*.

Hartman Windows & Doors, LLC is currently seeking an experienced *CAD Draftsman* to join their team.

About Us: Hartman Windows & Doors is a highly-respected custom, wood window and door manufacturer, specializing in design and fabrication of custom wood windows and doors for high-end residential and commercial projects.
Job Summary:

The *draftsman* is responsible for making and revising detailed technical drawings of our windows and doors according to project specifications. In addition to being technically proficient, the candidate should demonstrate a capacity for innovation in making the shop drawing process more standardized and efficient.

Job Responsibilities:

- Use CAD to create technical window and door drawings based on project specifications to be sent to architects and to manufacturing floor for production.
- Incorporate needed changes and modifications to shop drawings.
- Focus on standardization and continuous improvement in drawing process to increase efficiency and decrease error rate.
- Create standardized library of products to simplify creation of shop drawings going forward.
- Performs additional duties as assigned.

Experience:

- Minimum of 2 years of relevant work experience.
- Demonstrated experience as a draftsman, preferably in wood windows and doors.

Skills and Abilities:

- Excellent verbal and written communication skills.
- Excellent presentation and demonstrated organizational skills.
- Proficiency in AutoCAD. Fluency in Microsoft Word, Excel, and Outlook.
- Must have strong work ethic, be detail-oriented and technically proficient.
- Ability to juggle many projects simultaneously, to work independently and to show initiative.
- Ability to work with others in the organization to complete drawings to the correct specifications.

Websites for Promotion, Software, and Learning

The following sites are meant to help you promote your work and locate available online resources to hone your drafting skills.

Sites to Promote Your Drafting Work	
HomeAdvisor	**Elance**
http://www.homeadvisor.com/	*http://www.Elance.com/*

iFreelance	Alibaba.com
http://www.ifreelance.com/	http://www.alibaba.com/

Sites to Select Your Drafting Software	
PTCCre0	**SmartDraw**
http://3hti.com/	http://www.smartdraw.com/
Download.com	**AutoDesk**
http://download.cnet.com/	http://www.autodesk.com/
Softonic	
http://draftsman.en.softonic.com/	
Soft112	
http://autorun-draftsman-deluxe.soft112.com/	

Sites to Learn & Upgrade Your Drafting Skills	
Ant3DStudio	**DegreeDirectory**
http://ant3dstudio.com/	http://degreedirectory.org/
TechnicalInstituteOfAmerica	**LEDET**
http://www.tiaedu.com/	https://www.ledet.com/
ISeekEducation	**Murray'sTechnicalEducation**
http://www.iseek.org/	http://www.homeschoolingus.com/

StratfordCareerInstitute	EducationalPortal
http://www.scitraining.com/	*http://education-portal.com/*

MechanicalDrafting101
http://mechanicaldrawing.8m.com/

For More Information...

Do you want to know more about what these and other types of visual careers involve and the potential opportunities available in each? The quintessential reliable, current source to learn more about these professions is the *Bureau of Labor Statistics Occupational Outlook Handbook (http://www.bls.gov/ooh/)*, where each career is described in detail, together with:

- Summary Job Description
- Work Environment
- Necessary Qualifications
- Salary Expectations
- Employment Outlook
- Related Occupations

Another great site for additional information about these careers is *http://degreedirectory.org.* Touted as the "world's largest education and career help desk," this site answers education requirement questions for a wide variety of careers and occupations. Led by a team of educators and researchers, this group makes an authentic attempt to publish only accurate, unbiased, peer-reviewed data.

We also highly recommend the *Art Career Project* website at *http://www.theartcareerproject.com* that covers not only the entire traditional range of graphic design and multimedia career options, but also features some unusual career directions to consider, such as a floral designer, shoe designer, and video game designer. The site provides an excellent job description snapshot, educational requirements, and job venues for every specific career.

You owe it to yourself to devote serious time and effort to researching all three sites, where you'll find reliable, informative, current and accurate data on any and all occupations. After all, before you embark on any journey, you need to arm yourself with the following realistic expectations:

- What is my final destination?
- Is this really where I want to go?
- What are the steps I need to take to arrive there?
- What obstacles and challenges might I encounter along the way?
- What external tools and internal assets will I need to meet these challenges?

And So...

This chapter's essential challenge has been to consider how you might maximize your skills and talents to be successful at doing online graphics work that you love while earning money in the process. But if you are among those individuals who have neither the desire nor the talent for wielding an artist's brush, operating a digital camera, designing a shack, or even drawing a hangman stick figure, take heart.

If you have not yet found any career that actually suits you, look ahead to Chapter 7. Perhaps your expertise rests not so much in creating words or visuals as it gravitates towards areas that involve business support, administration and other types of business-related work. This next chapter deals with providing support for both online and offline businesses, large and small.

If you have a business head, Chapter 7 aligns with your aspirations and talents. After all, we all know that someone has to do the daily detailed work of record-keeping, organizing, planning, and otherwise serving as the person behind the curtain.

Are you skilled at these types of work? Do you derive great satisfaction in dealing with data, keeping things organized, and servicing frustrated customers? Have you come to appreciate, through your own personal experience, how 21st century technology often confounds and puzzles the average user? Is your forté hand-holding, diffusing potential client confrontations, and trouble-shooting customers' daily frustrations?

Then read on. A world of online business-related careers awaits you in Chapter 7. Learn how the new cyber-economy breeds opportunities for all types of business support services—from *virtual assistants* to *at-home call-center managers* to *data entry specialists*.

You might find that your greatest challenge will be to choose which of the many available job opportunities you should pursue.

Chapter 7:
The Web is Global & "Glocal": Provide Support for Businesses

"The ability to deal with people is as purchasable a commodity as sugar or coffee. And I pay more for that ability than for any other under the sun."
—*John D. Rockefeller*

Are you highly organized and attentive to details? These are personality traits that may earn you a respectable living providing online support for online, or even offline, businesses. If you are business-minded and professional, and if working with people is your forté, then the Internet is your potential income engine!

Your talents at organizing, selling, solving customer problems, or performing other business-supportive services, may make all the difference to a myriad of businesses, small and large. If you are able to provide organizational assistance, clerical or recordkeeping help, or any number of other services as an independent contractor, you are potentially exactly what a small business person needs. Large businesses are looking for help, too, for all the reasons we talked about in Chapter 3, including globalization, glocalization, increases in outsourcing, and the expanded expectations of consumers.

Because of increasing salary demands, and the cost of health care and other benefits, many small businesses can no longer afford to hire even part-time employees to work on-site. Even large businesses are increasingly seeking reliable, capable offsite help to avoid the costs associated with hiring and housing permanent staff.

This chapter is intended to explore some challenging online career options you might not have considered. Let's start with these six.

Virtual Assistant	Virtual Concierge	At-Home Call Center
Manufacturer's Representative	Online Executive Recruiter	Data Entry Specialist

Could You Be a *Virtual Assistant*?

The position of *virtual assistant* is a relatively new category in the administrative profession. A *virtual assistant* is a professional who aids small business owners and managers by providing them with long distance personal and administrative support.

If long distance personal support sounds counterintuitive to you, let's take an in-depth look into what such a job entails. Individuals who have these organizational and people skills are making the life of the small business owner easier in so many ways, while simultaneously earning an income.

A *virtual assistant* (VA) can support his client without ever meeting her in person or visiting her place of business. In other words, as a VA, you may live in Ohio, but work for a client who is based in New York City. Or you might live in Colorado and perform VA services for a firm in India or Finland or Brazil.

The fact is, we have all experienced such arrangements in our own lives. How often do we find ourselves speaking with a VA in a foreign country when we place a service call or seek information via phone or Internet?

For the most part, *virtual assistant* relationships are long term. In order to provide impeccable, focused administrative support to each client, most VAs work with only a handful of different clients at a time. The standard tools of the *virtual assistant*? Internet access, email, phone, scanner and fax, Microsoft Office—and any other method or tools to perform online office functions and communications.

Who Needs a Virtual Assistant?

Why would a small business owner need a VA? Perhaps because the workload is beginning to increase, yet hiring new permanent staff is not financially feasible. Perhaps because organizational and administrative tasks simply are not the business owner's particular strength or interest, and she prefers to spend her time on other business priorities, such as building her customer base or researching her competition.

With a *virtual assistant* instead of an on-site assistant, the business owner will not need to rent additional office space or purchase more equipment. And she will compensate the VA only for actual work accomplished, not for unproductive "face time" when the work load slacks off and there's nothing productive to be done.

Here are just a few professional categories of employers who currently hire *virtual assistant*s and use them successfully:

- Certified Public Accountants
- Professional speakers
- Attorneys
- Writers/Authors/Novelists
- Celebrities
- Therapists
- Financial planners
- Stock brokers
- Executive recruiters

- Entrepreneurs
- Politicians

Why Would You Want to Be a *Virtual Assistant*?

Here are some reasons to determine whether a career as a *virtual assistant* would be a good fit for you:

- To become involved in, and to learn firsthand, a variety of interesting businesses or projects;
- To develop critical professional relationships;
- To operate your own business while working on someone else's payroll;
- To gain independence, flexibility and control over your career as well as your personal life; and
- To become a success on your own terms.

How Much Do *Virtual Assistant*s Earn?

If you decide to become a *virtual assistant*, what can you expect to be paid? If you already have developed an administrative and organizational skills reputation in the brick-and-mortar world, and are transferring your skills to cyber space, you can expect your starting wage to be about $20–$30 an hour. Those individuals with more experience working as an assistant in the "virtual world" can earn upwards of $40–$50 an hour.

The Importance of Quality

One outsourcing agency, *ClickNWork*, frequently hires *virtual assistants* to serve the needs of their business clients. Their quality requirements for work performance are typical:

"We are unforgiving about our quality standards. Our clients are exacting professionals, and we have to impose the same standards they do. Performance is tracked on every task. For some assignments our task management software gives automatic feedback; for others

it will be an email from a reviewer. If you meet our high standards, you have nothing to worry about. But those who fail to meet our standards are quickly replaced. Every task is graded by people within ClickNWork and by the ultimate arbiter—the client.

We judge quality with measures suitable for the work, but in all cases we look for accuracy, excellent and clear English, timeliness, and correct formatting (we often work with client templates)."

How About a Career as a *Virtual Concierge*?

You know what a concierge is. You've seen the Concierge Desk at the Hilton and the Marriott, where the persons sitting at those desks appear to be perpetually engaged assisting guests. Exactly what are they doing? And would you be able to perform these services from the comfort of your home?

Let's start with the question about what exactly the concierge is doing. Think back on your past stays at resorts, hotels or ocean liners. You probably relied on the concierge to:

- Provide expertise on his environs;
- Map out ways to walk or taxi to your various destinations, including critical information such as walking distances or estimated taxi costs;
- Recommend and make reservations for restaurants to meet your dining preferences;
- Guide you in planning your days, including the best types of activities available, and where to shop;
- Meet your needs as they arise, such as the location of the nearest drug store, deli, wine shop or post office; and
- Purchase play or concert tickets.

To work as a concierge, you will need to know all this and more. The list goes on. What are the schedules for nearby churches or synagogues? Where is the nearest laundromat, post office, subway station or bus stop? And what's the best way to get there from here?

Also you will need to help solve problems. My camera battery just died, where can I buy another one? I need a great place to meet up with my important customer, my long-lost aunt, my pre-teen niece, my about-to-be fiancé (I hope!). I forgot to bring my phone charger... my bathing suit... my comfortable walking shoes. I'd like to pick up a couple nice bottles of wine for an impromptu gathering in my room.

Now for the second question. Can these types of services be performed online? In a word, yes they can. Again, you will need to be thoroughly familiar with the types of services a concierge actually performs, and expert on the local area, with a thorough knowledge of everything within the immediate surroundings, including its unique qualities, as well as its cultural and recreational amenities and offerings. You will still be dealing with the same types of needs and questions, and the same varieties of problems to be solved. The difference will be that you will provide concierge services online instead of face-to-face.

How to Find *Virtual Concierge* Jobs

It is a fact that concierge services are growing in popularity. Businesses of all types and sizes are using them. To find a job as a *virtual concierge*, start with a Google search using the search term *"virtual concierge."* Also visit online employment posting sites like:

Monster.com http://www.monster.com/	SimplyHired.com http://www.simplyhired.com/
TipTopJob.com http://www.tiptopjob.com/	JobFox.com http://jobfox.com/
FoundValue.com http://www.foundvalue.com/	VIPDesk.com http://www.vipdesk.com/info/

Sample Job Posting for a *Virtual Concierge*

This position with Expedia as a *virtual concierge* in Las Vegas is an example of a *virtual concierge*'s duties and qualifications.

Virtual Concierge—Las Vegas

Company: Expedia Local Expert
Location: USA—NV—Las Vegas
Employment Type: Full-Time Regular
Education Required: High School Diploma
Experience Required: 1-2 Years

Position Overview:

The *virtual concierge* is responsible for contacting *Expedia.com* guests via phone, assessing guest needs and selling attractions and activity tickets that ensure a memorable vacation experience. Qualified candidates bring previous outbound phone sales experience and high-touch customer service phone skills to the team.

The *virtual concierge* is expert on the local area, attractions and tours and activities. As a member of the team, they will be expected to uphold the *Expedia Local Expert* oath: "I promise to delight every guest by sharing my passion and local knowledge to arrange memorable experiences."

Responsibilities:

- Provide each guest with a professional and courteous phone greeting and outstanding guest service.
- Demonstrate the ability to balance guest service with sales results.

- Build rapport with the guest and assist guest in selecting the product that matches their needs. Needs are assessed via the discovery process (i.e. asking questions).
- Meet or exceed established sales targets in a commissioned environment.
- Demonstrate the ability to generate sales and upsell product by "painting the picture" and planning out the guest's stay to maximize their experience.
- Take responsibility for solving guest issues in a timely fashion, with satisfaction and a sense of urgency. Follow up on issues to ensure that they are resolved.
- Use sales tools to invoke a sense of urgency to commit.
- Close and book the sale and get guest to make payment.
- Provide a thorough, detailed recap of the purchase, along with properly thanking the guest for their business.

Qualifications:

- Exceptional phone demeanor and guest service skills.
- Ability to adapt to and support change within the business.
- Ability to overcome objections and offer alternate solutions.
- Knowledge of the local area and attractions.
- Excellent written and verbal communication skills a must (fluent English required, bilingual a plus).
- Strong listening skills to be able to identify customer needs.
- Self-motivated, with the ability to work independently in a sales driven environment.
- Proven ability to juggle multiple duties and prioritize.
- Able to work flexible hours (available for any shifts

> assigned, including late afternoon and evening).
> - Computer literate. Should have basic Excel skills.
> - Knowledge of travel industry; concierge experience a plus.

Establish Your Own *Virtual Concierge* Service Career

After working for an online service in this field for a period of time to obtain a clear idea of what types of tasks you'd be required to perform, and for what types of clients, you may even want to consider establishing your own concierge service. One place to start would be by testing the waters and contacting various businesses in your area to see if they might have a need for such a service, for themselves or for their clients.

Do not limit yourself to travel, leisure, or recreational types of establishments. Broaden your horizons to include:

- Busy working parents,
- Retired older couples,
- Professionals whose work demands extensive travel,
- Local businesses.

Each of these groups has its own needs and priorities. For example, a professional couple with children may need help with researching and checking out quality daycare programs, planning a party event, or locating reliable pet care for when they are called away on a business trip. An older couple may require assistance booking travel and possibly travel support services—transportation to and from the airport; wheel-chair assist, if needed; drivers at the other end. A business may need someone to take charge of making the arrangements for a conference or an important luncheon meeting—food catering, technology set up in the conference rooms, hotel arrangements and chauffeurs for business colleagues, translation services for international visitors.

There is such a diversity of demographic groups needing so many different goods and service, that if you are ready, willing, able, and resourceful, you will soon find yourself adding more and more items to your concierge services business card.

Establish an *At-Home Call Center*

Currently, more than 100,000 home-based operators are employed as at-home call-center workers. Within several years, this number is expected to nearly triple. If you are really interested in testing the online work waters, you may want to consider establishing an "at-home" call center. The *at-home call center* idea has come into its own as a viable work-from-home option. All you need is your telephone, your computer, a headset, and most important of all, *yourself,* as a reliable, flexible employee.

Are there really such job opportunities? Yes, many companies currently pay individuals to take phone calls from their homes. One set of examples are the airlines that utilize *at-home call center*s during inclement weather to handle the large overflow of calls about flight delays and cancellations. Some additional examples of companies that hire individuals as "at-home" call centers include:

- *1-800-FLOWERS* (only in specific geographic regions)
- *Freedom Telework*
- *VIPDesk*
- *Working Solutions*

The Requirements for an *At-Home Call Center*

Organizations and corporations specify their requirements for your *at-home call center,* generally to include:

- High-speed, broadband Internet access;
- One or more phone landlines;
- A relatively new, powerful computer;
- Current software;
- Printer/fax/scanner capabilities; and
- A quiet, reliable, consistent, professional environment, devoid of interruptions, loud noises, and personal distractions.

Most often, each company will install its own software on your computer, with a tech support system in place to assist you with installation, training, and technical troubleshooting.

That's the easy part. Now let's talk about the most important asset required of an *at-home call center* employee—*people skills and work ethic*. Your ability and skill in dealing with all types of personalities is by far your most important asset. Are you patient, tactful, empathetic, competent, and able to diffuse potentially explosive situations? Are you a problem solver? Do you have the skills to resolve client conflict? Do you have the temperament to deal with clients who are difficult, frustrated, untrusting, impatient, angry, rude, and technically illiterate— and all within the same day?

Not to be underestimated is a highly self-disciplined work ethic. Ask yourself these questions:

- Does my lifestyle support a flexible yet tightly defined work schedule?
- Can I establish a physical work environment that is devoid of distractions and interruptions?
- Am I sufficiently self-motivated to realize the importance of time-on-task?

If you're confident that you can provide and embody the above three elements (lifestyle, work environment, self-motivation), then read on.

The Application Process

The first step in the hiring process for call center work is simply the completion of an online application and skills assessment. Since most of the application screening process is automated, you will need to be as thorough and descriptive as possible when filling out these forms.

If you have experience in a variety of work settings, be sure to make this clear on your application. Many call center outsourcing firms hire home agents for more than one type of industry. Broad experience renders you more marketable, since you can be called on to handle several product or service areas.

The application usually contains a checklist to inform the company of what equipment and technology you have in your home office compared to what they require. You will need to make sure that your computer, phone and other systems meet their requirements.

Following a successful online application, you might be surprised to learn that the next step may be an "audition." This process is fairly straight forward, if a bit intimidating. Usually, you will be asked to call in and leave a message, after which the employer will provide you with several scripts to prepare for your audition.

The purpose of this screening is to determine your phone personality. They also want to hear the tone of your voice, and how you project yourself—your "phone presence"—the degree to which you sound sincere, friendly, helpful, knowledgeable, and professional.

Practice Makes Perfect

If the idea of an audition unnerves you, or if you're unsure of how well you will perform during a phone interview, try relying on a friend to help you rehearse your script. When you finally do call in for your audition, make sure that there is absolutely no noise in the background, and that there will be no interruptions during your call.

Designate a quiet area of your home. The best place would be your home office. We cannot stress enough the importance of providing a quiet, professional interview environment. Disable call waiting in advance of the interview, again to ensure that there will be no interruptions from other incoming calls.

At interview time, speak slowly and clearly. And *do* put a smile on your face as you speak. Customers can always "hear" a sincere smile right through those phone lines—and so can potential employers. Take a deep breathe, and strive to be calm, cool, and confident. Most important of all, let your dynamic, capable personality shine through.

Some interviewers may want to involve you in a video interview using *Skype*, where you will be able to see, as well as hear, each other. Your technical capability and willingness to accommodate this type of request for a virtual "face-to-face" encounter will only enhance your marketability.

The questions you are asked during your audition will vary depending on the type of business for which you are interviewing. For example, if a pharmacy is a possible assignment for your call center employment, then part of the interview process may be to ask you to engage in a technical dialogue.

If possible, review the company's online profile in advance of your interview. This will give you an idea of what types of questions you might be asked. A Google search will provide you with valuable corporate background information to which you can refer during the interview.

After your interview, callbacks may not be prompt. Some companies compile waiting lists to ensure they always will have the coverage they require. Others purposely delay contacting a potential employee until the project they will be assigned is about ready to launch. Another reason for a delayed response may be that the employer wishes to be sure that you are a serious candidate and have not had a change of heart during the ensuing weeks.

Choose a Career as a *Manufacturer's Rep*

Manufacturer's reps—sometimes called or *sales reps*—are the backbone of just about any manufacturing or wholesale business. Regardless of the type of product he sells, the primary mandate of a manufacturer's rep remains relatively the same—entice the customer's interest in the product, address any concerns or issues, then close the sale. After the initial sale, the rep follows up with support, and hopefully cultivates a productive long-term customer relationship.

A career as a *manufacturer's rep* differs from a sales position in which products are sold directly to consumers. Instead, products generally are sold to other businesses, government agencies and organizations.

The actual process of promoting and then selling a product can be an extensive one. It may take up to several months just to close one sale. But a single sale can lead to an ongoing account that will yield sales for years to come. A seasoned sales rep knows that the general success ratio for any sales transaction is 10:1—ten calls to yield one sale.

Sales services can be performed over the phone, in person or online. The rep's primary tasks are to describe the products and explain their benefits, conduct demonstrations of the products, and field any and all questions that arise.

For the most part, *manufacturer's reps* work for manufacturers, wholesalers or technology companies. Some representatives are employed by a single corporation, while others may represent several companies.

Manufacturer's reps who represent several companies and sell a range of products will need to have a broader scope of company and product knowledge in order to successfully represent each of their products and organizations.

Some *manufacturer's representatives* elect to specialize in a particular product area—the technical arena, scientific products, agriculturally-based items, pharmaceutical goods. Still others deal with broader categories of products such as food, office supplies, home furnishings or apparel.

One important part of your duties as a *manufacturer's rep* will be to stay attuned to the advances and additions in your product line, as well as the changing needs of your customers. You will need to attend trade shows, conferences and conventions that showcase new products and new technological breakthroughs. In the process, you also will meet and get to know other representatives, thereby expanding your list of business-to-business clients and making valuable networking connections.

The Challenge of Technical Expertise

if you choose to attempt to secure online work as a *manufacturing representative*, don't let any deficiencies in technical expertise deter you. What you do not know yet, you certainly will be able to learn if you make the effort. The company generally will provide extensive product training.

Some companies team a *manufacturer's representative* with a technical expert—possibly an engineer—who is tasked with attending all sales presentations in order to provide technical specifications and explanations, and to field all necessary questions about product performance. The *manufacturer's rep*, who made the initial contact with the customer, formed the relationship, and introduced the potential client to the product, then closes the sale, following the technical expert's presentation and explanation.

If you think the role of *manufacturer's rep* is solely to sell products, then think again. You may actually welcome the broader range of tasks the position involves. *Manufacturer's representatives* really do much more than just sell. They also analyze sales statistics as well as prepare any number of reports, and even handle some administrative duties. In addition, they are constantly keeping track of discounts, prices and any new products their competitors may offer.

For the most part, the position of *manufacturer's representative* requires some training beyond a high school diploma, but not necessarily a college degree. Even more important than formal education, though, are the specific skills that enable you to recruit business, communicate effectively, and close the sale.

Personal traits that can carry you far in this position include the ability to set and follow through with goals, a talent for persuasion, self-confidence, the drive to work without supervision and the capacity to be an effective team member.

The Bottom Line: What Does It Pay?

The median annual wage of a *manufacturer's representative* varies by industry. If you choose to do this on a full-time basis, you can expect to earn a minimum of $40,000, up to around $70,000, per year. Some positions also provide bonuses and/or include profit sharing. These perks can add from $1,000 to $12,000 per year to a base salary.

Become an *Online Executive Recruiter*

An *executive recruiter* works in conjunction with companies, organizations and other businesses, searching for the perfect applicant to match an open career position. This potentially lucrative career also can be performed from the comfort of your own home.

What It Takes to be an *Executive Recruiter*

Online recruiting requires specific character and personality traits. An *executive recruiter* must be organized and detail-oriented. Above all, she must possess an uncanny ability to read people, to discern critical character and personality traits, and to match people with positions. Previous experience in a job placement service or human resources position is a competitive asset for an *executive recruiter*.

For an initial exposure to this particular job market, visit the larger job boards such as:

HotJobs.com	CareerBuilder.com
(*http://hotjobs.yahoo.com/*)	(*http://www.careerbuilder.com/*)
Monster.com	
(*http://www.monster.com/*)	

Where to Look for a Job as an *Executive Recruiter*

Search for this type of job by using keywords such as "virtual recruiter," or "home-based recruiter." Or enter the term "remote" in the "work location" box of a list of executive recruiter positions, then scan through the filtered results.

You may also want to go directly to Google or Yahoo and look for "contingency search firms" or "placement agencies"—or both. Carefully scour these sites, again using terms like "virtual recruiter" and "home-based recruiter."

Your next step from here will be to contact or "cold call" these organizations and ask them outright if they use home-based recruiters. This phone discussion will provide you the perfect opportunity to impress them with your phone skills. Many of these companies may not actually advertise for "recruiters" because they secure leads through word-of-mouth. But if you can demonstrate that you already have a record of success behind you, you might be invited to join a team.

Data Entry for Fun & Profit

Undoubtedly, *data entry specialist* is one of those "work-at-home" jobs you have seen advertised frequently. The question arises, "Are these offers legitimate?" Unfortunately, some of the ads you see may not be; but fortunately, the activity itself certainly is.

What is data entry? The words themselves define the job. A *data entry specialist* takes various forms of information—or data—and enters it into whatever program or format or database a particular company requires. The actual type and amount of data depends on the needs of the employer and the nature of her business.

If you are a fast typist and accurate typist, and you enjoy computer work, you may find data entry to be an ideal method of earning money from home. Most *data entry* work can be performed on your own time schedule, although within a set timeframe. This can mean that you would be able to work an occasional evening in order to free yourself for a busy personal day ahead.

For the thousands of data entry jobs that are legitimate, *data entry* work is a win-win situation for both employer and employee. The employer assigns work, knowing that important deadlines will be met, and home-based employees benefit by being able to earn a reliable income, month after month, from home.

The immediate drawback to this type of work is the necessity of sitting at a computer for extended time periods in order to record what often constitutes volumes of information. If you decide to work as a *data entry specialist*, you will need to design regular breaks into your work day and invest in an ultra-comfortable chair.

How to Find Data Entry Specialist Jobs

You can find *data entry specialist* employment on the Internet through job providers who specialize in this area. You may also find data entry work through the other approaches discussed at length in Chapter 4, such as:

- conducting a Web search,
- using outsourcing sites, like *ClickNWork.com*, and
- searching through online classifieds.

If you have experience in the accounting field or in transcription, your expertise will be worth even more to a potential employer. As you go through the hiring process, be sure to inform the interviewer about any additional skills you have, especially any advanced computer skills or data analysis background. This additional expertise will provide you with a competitive edge over other candidates.

Before You Start Your Search

Before you seriously apply for any position, it's important that you determine whether you can or want to work full-time or part-time. The tasks of a *data entry specialist* are not difficult, but they can become tedious, especially when you are approaching that 40-hour a week mark. For this reason, many individuals opt to engage in data entry work only part-time, possibly combining this with another type of online work, or even with an online business of their own.

Sometimes your employer will want to assign and pay you by the project. This arrangement sometimes actually can work to your advantage. When you work by the project, and complete a given assignment quickly and accurately, your per hour rate increases accordingly.

Even if the position requires a full-time person and you wish to work only part-time, you may be able to establish a job sharing arrangement, teaming up with a family member, a friend, or a professional colleague, to accomplish a project that is too extensive for you to assume on your own. However, if you do partner with someone, make sure in advance that both of you share the same skill level and work ethic in terms of reliability, accuracy and efficiency.

How Much Does *Data Entry* Pay?

For the most part, current promises of $500 per week full-time coincide with national guidelines. For a *data entry clerk*, this equals $10–$13.50 per hour, and up to $20 per hour for overtime work. Higher level *data entry specialist* jobs generally pay more, between $11 and $15 per hour, and up to $22 per hour for overtime.

And So...

One thing you've learned in and through this chapter—every major successful enterprise requires a back-up workforce to take care of the business of doing business. Therein lies the reason why the Web abounds with all the support service opportunities we are exploring. Hopefully, you've found more than one career avenue that you can and plan to pursue—all from the comfort and convenience of your own home office, with a work schedule that suits your current lifestyle and that meets your personal financial needs.

In our next chapter, we turn our attention to those whose gift in life is to impart knowledge to others. If you are a current or former teacher, tutor, instructor, or researcher, you'll soon learn that the Web is a gold mine for anyone with a marketable knowledge bank or skill.

Do you know how to cane a chair? Make cheesecake? Solve quadratic equations? Scale fish? Design a Web site? Speak Mongolian? Trust us, there is a ready audience for your talent—someone who is eager to pay you to teach them what you know and what you know how to do.

Chapter 8 helps connect teachers and learners. But even more than that, you'll learn how anyone adept at the art and skill of teaching can parlay this talent into related career opportunities, such as researching and language training.

Chapter 8:
The Web is a Font of Information: Research & Teach

"If you want to build a ship, don't drum up people together to collect wood and don't assign them tasks and work, but rather teach them to long for the endless immensity of the sea."

—Antoine de Saint-Exupery

Whether you are old enough to remember the first TRON movie or have seen the 2010 version, the image that never leaves your mind is that of the main character transported from the outside world into the cyber world, possibly never to return.

This is an apt metaphor for thinking about many of today's businesses. Although there are still many businesses that have one foot in and one foot out of the Web, an increasing number of businesses are strictly online.

These online businesses have no physical presence out in the world. The whole business, including its workforce and its clients, is "virtual." All work is announced online, assigned online, accomplished online, submitted online, reviewed and managed online, and compensated online. These businesses live and act entirely within the Web.

Many of these businesses were conceived with the Web in mind, and thus take full advantage of the global, distributed interconnectedness of the Web. In a word, these businesses were started on the Web and have grown up there. They have never left the Web, and in all probability, never will. Many of them could neither exist nor function without the Web.

So what are the implications of this Web business phenomenon? And what are the new career opportunities this movement has generated?

First and foremost, these online businesses require an online workforce. In this chapter we will explore six Internet-only ventures so you can better determine if one (or more) of them might be your perfect match, including:

Online Search & Data Analyst	Social Media Analyst	Market Researcher
Criminal Records Researcher	Language Trainer	Online Tutor

The first three of these Internet-based careers are related, and to some degree, overlap each other. *Online search & data analyst* work involves the broad scope of web search and data analysis. *Social media analysts* and *market researchers* focus in on social media and market research, respectively, within the vast range of web search in general.

Become an *Online Search & Data Analyst*

In this era of fast-paced decision-making, everyone wants the right information right now. And they want it in an understandable, readable, measurable, compressed format for fast and easy access, as a basis for making effective business and marketing decisions. Given how rich the data collection potential is on the Web, businesses know that they need to access and understand that data in order to guide their own product and marketing decisions, and thereby to remain competitive and profitable.

A highly valuable player in determining direction and addressing questions that are essential to the success of businesses is the *online search & data analyst.* This is an individual who can quickly locate answers to business questions using information on the Web, then collate those findings into summary documents that form a basis for decision-making.

Requirements for *Online Search and Data Analyst* Jobs

In addition to being able to find information that precisely answers complex business questions, *online search and data analysts* must have impeccable English speaking and writing skills.

When recruiting *online search and data analysts* as potential online employees for their client employers, online outsourcing agencies like *ClickNWork* prefer to work with analysts who also are able to perform the full range of related services. These services include data entry and analysis, chart preparation, and writing—the skill base necessary to fully complete a client's search and analysis project, then to report the results accurately by combining well-designed spreadsheets and charts with clearly-written text that describes and summarizes the results and what they indicate.

Pay for *Online Search and Data Analyst* Jobs

Pay for the work of *online search and data analysts* averages $54K per year, ranging from $35K to $71K. There can be an additional the potential for up to $5200 in bonus pay.

Sample *Online Search and Data Analyst* Job Listing

> **JOB TITLE:** *Internet Researcher*
>
> **COMPANY NAME:** *Advertising Checking Bureau, Inc.*
>
> **DESCRIPTION:** The *Internet Researcher* is responsible for providing outstanding customer service to clients (internal and

external). Primary responsibility will be timely and accurate research of Internet sites to capture information for all accounts and record & input information gathered from various sites.

This position will ensure compliance with client's program specifications and ACB policies and procedures. Specific duties may be dependent on the client(s) they support. This person must effectively manage their time and workload to ensure all service levels are maintained.

ESSENTIAL RESPIBILITIES

- Research Internet sites to capture information.
- Compose professional and thorough communications regarding research for internal and external customers.
- Proactively communicate with the Account Specialist and Supervisor if unable to meet contractual turnaround time.
- Maintain all client program information and resources (i.e. specification sheets, account binders, ad slicks).
- Participate in creating and maintaining a high quality work environment so team members are motivated to perform at their highest level and to continue working for the company.

QUALIFICATIONS:

- Very Strong PC knowledge, including Microsoft Office products: *Outlook*, *Word*, and *Excel*.
- Extensive research experience using search engines and specialty sites.
- General mathematical, spelling and grammar skills as demonstrated by successful completion of pre-employment tests.

> **WORK EXPERIENCE:**
>
> - A minimum of one year work experience is desired.
> - Previous experience in a customer service or clerical production environment is preferred.
> - Strong organizational and time management skills are needed to manage multiple tasks/priorities.
> - Ability to communicate effectively orally and in writing.

Work as a *Social Media Analyst*

Companies today recognize that it is essential for them to craft and maintain their online brand presence. Enter the role of the *social media analytics researcher*, the provider of answers to such questions as:

- Should I concentrate on marketing my service/product on a social network, and if so, which one would provide me with the best return on my investment?
- Once I have committed to advertising my service/product on a particular site, how can I measure:
  - Total number of visitors within a specific time period?
  - How many are return visitors versus new ones?
  - What percentage of visitors take action in the form of making a purchase or posting an inquiry?
  - Where else on the Web are my visitors spending time?

According to *PRNewswire* (*http://www.prnewswire.co.uk/news*), the network analytics market is estimated to grow from $487.9 million in 2013 to $1672.5 million in 2018, at a *Compound Annual Growth Rate* (CAGR) of 27.9% from 2013 to 2018. This report says North America is expected to be the biggest market in terms of revenue contribution to the field of network analytics.

Social media analytics is highly critical and valuable to the world of online marketing. For this reason, each of the major search engines and social networks—*Google, Yahoo, Twitter, Facebook, Pinterest, LinkedIn, Instagram, Flickr, Digg*—have launched their own sophisticated analytics tools to provide marketers with real-time insights into activities on their sites, and to develop and maintain their own competitive edge in terms of attracting users to their sites.

What Does A Social Media Analyst Do?

Social media analysts collect data from social media platforms, search engine sites, and blogs, and analyze this data to extract relevant conclusions that make sense of usage patterns and provide insight into the psyche of the social consumer. This critical information is then used to make informed decisions pertaining to a given business.

Using their creativity and marketing skills, *social media analysts:*

- gather data to formulate and execute methods of brand maintenance;
- engage the target audience using social media platforms;
- stimulate brand visibility and awareness;
- maintain a consistent, positive image across the spectrum of current and emerging social media platforms; and
- devise ways to increase sales and promote customer service through the social media networks.

An analyst will study trends in social media, research popular social media platforms, study emerging social media tools and observe how often those platforms and tools are used.

For new businesses, a *social media analyst* will study the audience that the business is attempting to reach, and offer plans on how social media will work best for them and their business model. Analysts may write up reports for clients and team members to show them the strategies available to them. They also may alert clients about any potential problems or concerns that arise.

What Are the Qualifications?

Social media analysts typically have a bachelor's degree in public relations, marketing, social media management or business communications. In fact, undergraduate and graduate degrees are now offered in *social media management.*

A marketing background is a tremendous asset for an aspiring *social media analyst*, whose job it is to improve and build a company's online presence and brand awareness through use of social media networks, blogs and online search engine optimization (SEO). This growing field of business marketing requires individuals with strong online communication and business analysis skills.

What Are Social Media Analysts Paid?

According to *www.pay scale.com*, a *social media analyst* earns an average salary of $44K, ranging from $30K–$68K. Skill in social media optimization is associated with high pay for this job.

Be a *Market Researcher*

Market research specialists study market conditions to examine potential sales of a product or service, and to provide companies with critical information about what people want, who will buy, and at what price (http://www.bls.gov/ooh/).

The Internet has dramatically impacted the role of the *market researcher* in three major ways. First, since a major portion of commerce is conducted on the Internet, massive and illuminating amounts of online data are readily available through which companies can hone their products and services in order to optimize profitability and success.

Second, through the globalization of shopping, and the possibility of finding exactly the right item, part, supply or service, at the absolutely optimum price, consumers expectations have expanded (as we discussed in Chapter 3). Consumers now expect more because they are no longer limited to what is available to them locally. This increases the necessity for companies to be in the know about what their intended clients want and need, as well as what other competing options are available to them online.

Third, given the *"Reviews"* feature that proliferates on the web, both within vendor sites and through open posting boards such as www.tripadvisor.com (for travel) or www.consumersearch.com (for products) or www.ratemd.com (for doctors) or www.urbanspoon.com (for restaurants), most products and services are quickly revealed according to their strengths and weaknesses. Through strategic use of these reviews, weak products can be improved or eliminated, and strong products promoted more actively.

Job Outlook for Market Researchers

Employment of *market research analysts* is projected to grow dramatically over the next decade, in part due to the Internet and the trio of impacts discussed above:

- Availability of critical marketing data;
- Increased consumer expectations, and
- Potential for customer reviews.

This has led to widespread shifts in corporate marketing strategies. Companies now make significantly increased use of data and market research across all industries in order to understand the needs and wants of customers, and to measure the effectiveness of marketing and business strategies.

The resulting growth in job projections for this career, as cited on the in *Business and Labor Statistics* (BLS) site's *Occupational Outlook Handbook* (*BLS.gov/ooh*), shows a predicted ten-year job growth rate of 32% from 2012 to 2022, equating to projected employment of 547,200 by 2022. This growth rate is dramatically higher than the 11% average for all occupations.

What Does A *Market Researcher* Do?

A market research analyst typically performs services like these:

- Devise and evaluate methods for collecting data (interviews, surveys, questionnaires, opinion polls, data harvesting);
- Gather data about consumers, competitors, and market conditions;
- Monitor and forecast marketing and sales trends;
- Determine a company's position in the marketplace;
- Measure the effectiveness of marketing strategies and programs;
- Use market segmentation strategies to guide targeted plans for product promotion;
- Analyze data using statistical software;
- Present complex data and findings visually, using clearly understandable tables and graphs; and
- Prepare written and narrated reports to present results to clients and management.

Qualifications of a *Market Researcher*

To qualify as a *market researcher*, you will need:

- Minimum of a bachelor's degree;
- Strong math and analytical skills;
- Training in statistics, research methods, and marketing;
- Strength in oral, written, and graphic communication;

- Ability to gather information, interpret data, and present results to clients;
- Critical and strategic thinking skills; and
- Accuracy and attention to details.

What Are Market Researchers Paid?

Market research analysts show a median annual wage of $48K, ranging from a low of $35K to a peak of $70K (www.payscale.com). Additional compensation may be earned through profit-sharing. Proven skills that positively affect *marketing research analyst* salaries include data analysis (7% higher pay), market research (3% higher pay), and SPSS (1% higher pay). Note: SPSS is a widely-used statistical analysis software package.

Work as a *Virtual Criminal Records Researcher*

Do you have a legal or paralegal background? If so, an online job as a *virtual criminal records researcher,* also called *background investigator*, might be a career direction to pursue.

What Does a Virtual Criminal Records Researcher Do?

Criminal records researchers complete background screenings, interacting with courthouses to process county and state criminal background checks for pre-employment background screening.

Duties can include:

- Enter, code, and retrieve a variety of information from various computer systems related to an applicant's criminal history.
- Search and retrieve information from files, microfiche, computer records, and other documents.
- Release information and documents in accordance with the *Public Information Act*, the *Fair Credit Reporting Act*, and other applicable laws and procedures.

For this type of work, you will need to be reliable, detail-oriented and able to successfully pass a strict background check and drug test. Ideally a *Criminal Justice* degree is preferred and previous experience is an advantage, but some agencies will train promising candidates.

Who Hires Virtual Criminal Records Researchers?

An agency such as *www.pre-employ.com* recruits full and part-time *virtual criminal records researchers.* Researchers work under the direct supervision of a corporate supervisor, with whom they meet daily via video, phone and email.

Another company that actively recruits criminal records researchers is Accurate Background http://accuratebackground.com/about/jobs/, an online enterprise that offers criminal research, background screening, international searches, and other compliance services to companies, ranging from small businesses to the Fortune 100, in a wide range of industries worldwide. A sample job description for a criminal researcher involves the following job summary, responsibilities, qualifications, and pay range:

Job Summary:

The Criminal Researcher is primarily responsible for processing Public Records products related to pre-employment background screening applications. This position is accountable for working within Accurate Background's client guidelines as well as the Federal Credit Reporting Act's (FCRA) regulations to provide minimal turnaround time and high quality results on background research requests.

Responsibilities:

- Retrieves and enters a variety of information from various computer and web based systems related to applicant's history.
- Searches and retrieves information from files, computer records, and other documents.

- Locates information and documents quickly and accurately in accordance with applicable laws and procedures.
- Supplies timely updates and notifications of delays.
- Understands the court system and terminology.
- Communicates effectively with courts to retrieve additional information as needed.
- Performs duties and responsibilities as assigned.

Qualifications:

- High School Diploma or GED required.
- Bachelor's degree preferred – specializing in Criminal Justice a plus.
- 1 to 3 years related work experience.
- Familiarity with FCRA a plus.
- Intermediate knowledge of word processing software, including MS Word, Outlook, and Excel.
- Strong familiarity with the internet, including internet research experience.
- Excellent analytical, written and verbal communication skills.
- Type 60 words per minute.
- Independent and detail oriented.
- Ability to work under constant deadlines.
- Teamwork oriented attitude.

Pay Range:

$12 - $14/ hour.

What Are Virtual Criminal Records Researchers Paid?

Average annual pay for a virtual criminal records researcher is $46K, ranging from $34K to $71K. Experience is a major determinant of pay level, with entry-level researchers receiving 10% below the average and experienced researchers receiving 37% above.

Become an *Online Language Trainer*

Are you a native English speaker? Are you interested in other cultures? Would you like to learn and practice 21st century skills in cross-cultural communication, teaching and ELT (English Language Training)?

Agencies like *ISpeakUSpeak* or *ISUS* (www.jobs.ispeakuspeak.com) employ instructors to deliver language training to adults who range in age from 25 to 55. Most of these language students are employed in multinational firms and are receiving language training as a benefit from their employer.

When training has been completed, these students will be expected to apply their learning to accomplish professional tasks such as negotiations, meetings, presentations, and email communication. Their linguistics levels prior to training range from pre-intermediate to advanced.

This instruction is accomplished through a series of exercises to help students improve their spoken English and listening skills in order to boost their confidence, unlock their ability to speak, and dramatically improve their listening comprehension.

Positions as English language trainers exist for independent contractors who work from home. There is no application or training fee for potential trainers. This is another type of purely online service business that would not have been possible before the Internet.

What Does an Online Language Trainer Do?

What would you be expected to do as an *online language trainer*? You would use your native English language skills to help students from around the world improve their English. In other words, you would be making money online just for having conversations with eager, interesting people from other cultures.

When a student is assigned to you, your task would include interacting with him by discussing an assigned topic, and then providing him with feedback about the interaction. As part of your feedback, you would correct his grammar, vocabulary, pronunciation and fluency, and offer any other constructive help you could provide.

If you worked for a company like *ISUS*, you would first be trained and certified on the use of the *ISUS* proprietary language learning platform. Your responsibilities would include teaching classes through discussions and role-plays, and sometimes by monitoring student performance on the *GlobalEnglish* platform.

As a trainer, you would work up to 25 to 30 hours per week, Monday to Friday, year-round. You would be free to determine how much or how little you work. Most *ISUS* teachers prefer to work in blocks of 2 to 4 hours. Class sessions consist of half hour sessions (25 minutes of class and five minutes of feedback/correction).

You would be supplied with all lesson materials (grammar, vocabulary development, role-plays, discussions, follow-up, and "listenings"). This material has been designed to cover a full academic year (10 months).

Since students are scattered across time zones, the ISUS coordination department (responsible for assigning students to tutors) has a wide range of timetables from which you would be able to choose. So a wide variety of teaching time schedules are possible.

Language Trainer Requirements

ISUS is representative of the requirements for *language trainers,* expecting candidates to be native English speakers. *ISUS* also prefers that candidates have ESL or other teaching experience, although exceptions are made, and thorough training is provided before formal *ISUS* certification. In terms of trainer personality, *ISUS* is interested in individuals who are enthusiastic, motivated, and passionate about helping people learn.

Requirements include that a *language trainer* be:

- A native English speaker;
- IT literate and equipped (telephone, computer, broadband Internet connection); and
- Experienced in ESL or another educational field.

The hiring process for this company is generally conducted over the space of five days, requiring approximately 5 to 10 hours. To earn *ISUS* certification, you as a candidate will need to become familiar on a self-study basis with the *ISUS* and *GlobalEnglish* platforms, as well as the English language learning materials.

Trainers are hired on a freelance basis, and paid monthly, according to the number of hours they work. Rates of pay are quoted according to country of fiscal residence and local currency, and become part of a formal contract.

Additional companies that hire online language trainers to teach English include the following:

Verbal Planet
www.verbalplanet.com/tutorhome.asp
Human English
www.humanenglish.com/about/trainer-vacancies.html

What Does Virtual Language Training Pay?

Pay begins at $13 to $15 per hour in US dollars for US workers, but varies from contract to contract. If you take on this type of work, make sure you know what your rate will be if you are hired.

Work as an *Online Tutor*

If you think back to when you attended school, tutoring was always done face to face. And in many places, for many people, face-to-face tutoring is still the norm. But a growing number of individuals are finding that online tutoring is being used in conjunction with many of the Internet-based educational tools provided by both public and private schools, and businesses.

And since tutor and student location does not matter when tutoring is online, a tutor from Oregon can just as easily work with a student from Georgia as with one who lives next door. Regardless of physical location, now students can access the services of the best tutor for their specific needs.

Not only are parents searching for online tutors for their children, either to supplement traditional schooling or to help with homeschooling, but businesses nationwide are searching for online tutors. Adults also seek tutors to improve and upgrade their job skills, and to qualify for certifications of all types.

The reality is that, no matter what your skill or profession, if you are an effective communicator, you can parlay this knowledge into teaching others "how to do it." Consequently, many workers from all walks of life, who have made their primary living by producing a product or providing a service, also have earned extra income by teaching and sharing their expertise.

Requirements for Online Tutoring

It's important that you research each company first before applying. Companies have different requirements for their tutors, including levels of experience, references and even background checks. Some require that you hold a teaching certificate. Others will consider you so long as you have subject matter experience.

Experience as an educator is one of your greatest assets. If you have experience and are clearly dedicated to student learning success, opportunities for Web tutoring are plentiful.

In addition to experience, an online tutor should have:

- A high degree of computer and Internet skills;
- A minimum of a college degree;
- Possibly a teaching certificate (beneficial).

Lastly, don't be surprised if the company asks for a fee to connect you with students. Even the most reputable of firms may do this. If the organization is legitimate, your investment may be justified.

The Hiring Process for *Online Tutors*

The hiring process itself usually starts with your responding to and posting some type of online query or submission. In addition to submitting all the usual information, you also may be expected to take a test based on the academic subjects and grade levels you wish to tutor.

Eventually, you will be required to undergo some type of telephone interview. Once you are hired, you will be told everything you need to know about the company's policies, from working with materials and tutoring mediums, to communicating with students.

Because of the potential dangers to children that currently lurk on the Internet, your hiring agency may require fingerprinting and/or a background check. Nowadays, online tutoring companies not only search for a high level of professionalism from their tutors, they are diligent in making sure that all potential tutors are legitimate, with no criminal records. After all, the parents who are your potential clients will be placing their children's' academic futures in your hands. They will want assurance that you are competent, reliable, and safe.

Due diligence goes both ways. You will need to do your own "background check" to determine that the firm you are about to work for is reputable. Don't hesitate to ask for references or to call the *Better Business Bureau* to ascertain whether any complaints have been filed against a prospective tutoring employer.

Where to Find Online Tutoring Jobs

Below is a sampling of online tutoring sites for you to explore. These firms will supply you with just about everything you will need to perform your job well, including software, a tutoring medium, and lesson plan materials. But more, these organizations will connect you with students who can benefit from your expertise.

Tutor.Com	InstaEdu
http://www.tutor.com/apply	*http://instaedu.com/*
TutorVista	**Growing Stars**
http://www.tutorvista.com/	*http://www.growingstars.com/*
EduNiche	**Smart Thinking**
http://www.eduniche.com/	*http://www.smartthinking.com/*
Sylvan Learning	
http://www.sylvanlearning.com/careers	
Webwise Tutors	
https://www.Webwisetutors.com/	
Study Pool	
https://www.studypool.com/answer	

And So...

It is our hope that you are probably far enough into this book to be surprised, excited and optimistic about the online work possibilities open to you, depending upon your talents, interests, and past experiences—all factors that you can parlay into a lucrative cyber career from the comfort of your own home. In fact, our guess is that by now you are toying with exploring several different options, and are a bit uncertain about which one to pursue.

All the better! The bottom line—the purpose of these chapters is to lay before you the multiple online roads to Oz that are open to you. If and when you're ready, we encourage you to zero in on a few, devote the time to research them carefully, and then take the specific preliminary exploratory steps to test the waters.

The inherent message is that, even if you have found your dream career within a different chapter in this book, nothing prevents you from sharing your talent and skill as an instructor. In a sense, this chapter is for everyone who has a passion for their chosen work and who has the gift of communication. Why not spread the wealth of what you know to others, for a price, of course!

On the other hand, you may be numbered within that group of individuals who hasn't yet found a perfect match. Perhaps you are most fulfilled when you are working with your hands. You love to create things. Yet possibly, as a craftsperson, your creative nature has yet to find its "place in the sun."

Not to worry—there's more ahead. Our next chapter deals precisely with those of you who are the artists, the craftsmen, the creators among us. You who have the talent to create exquisite works of art in various forms—works that enhance and enrich our lives—are about to discover how the Internet has become the 21st century showcase and depository for your work. As Keats wrote, "A thing of beauty is a joy forever." Now, for the first time in history, the Web gives you the tools and capacity to promote and present your creative work to the entire world! Read on to see how!

Chapter 9:
The Web Creates Demand: Produce & Build for It

"With crafting, you can never make a mistake because it's your own unique creation."
—Heidi Rew

St. Francis of Assisi said, "He who works with his hands is a laborer. He who works with his hands and his head is a craftsman. He who works with his hands and his head and his heart is an artist."

Just as the very nature of arts or crafts work is intrinsically original, so too are the personality types who aspire to make their living as artisans and crafters. So much of this type of work is a variation on a theme, and therein lies the magic of creating and appreciating handmade works of artisans and crafters. The artisan crafter can view a colleague's work, and then embark on a totally different production, based on an off-shoot idea he conceives in his mind's eye.

Most of us secretly envy or are in awe of artisans and crafters. Where do they derive their ideas? How do they manage to bring to life such unique patterns, media, and uses—to wed functionality with creativity and aesthetic beauty?

And they do so with such a detached sense of equanimity and ease. Have you ever encountered an uptight, irascible, stressed out artisan? Probably not. They all seem to possess a built-in serenity meter that perhaps derives from the fact that they are creating a work of beauty with their hands.

Throughout our country, there has been an emergence and resurgence of artists and crafters who are creating unique and magnificent works of beauty and utility. On any given weekend, fans of estate sales, flea markets, and antique shops comb their favorite neighborhoods seeking "your trash that will become my treasure."

Simultaneously you'll find road signs, TV and radio ads, and local newspapers announcing and publicizing juried arts and crafts fairs, where you'll discover that perfect gift or that ideal object for just the right space in your home.

In order to compete with commercial outlets, such as chain stores and high end department stores, the talented folk who create arts and crafts have sought out and discovered multiple ways to vend their wares. Craft fairs, gift shops, art studios, craft co-ops and consignment shops have traditionally provided artisans and crafters outlets for their creations.

Entire American communities and towns have developed and continue to flourish as meccas for highly talented artisans and crafters. In the West, the *Taos Art Colony* in New Mexico. In the South, Gatlinburg's *Great Smoky Arts & Crafts Community.* In the Northeast, New York's *Sugarloaf Arts and Craft Village.*

Such communities have become tourist destinations where visitors are able to watch these talented workers ply their trade as well as to purchase their work. By becoming members of an arts and crafts community, these creators have the benefit of being able to sell their work from where they live.

The Web has added a powerful and global additional sales venue that has dramatically opened up new markets for creative work. Sometimes this has had the effect of increasing the demand beyond what a single artist or crafter can create on his own.

Are You Creative? Do You Love All Things Creative?

There are artists and crafters, but also there are those who are able to build to a specified design, and those who appreciate and wish to promote the creations of these other two groups. This chapter is designed to address the opportunities of the first two of these three groups (the third group will be addressed in Chapter 10):

- Those who create;
- Those who may not have the level of creative talent to create their own original designs, but do have the refined levels of skill to assemble or produce craft objects that have been designed by someone else; and
- Those who appreciate these unique, sometimes priceless, products, and are skilled at marketing and selling them.

After all, as much as we acknowledge the intrinsic beauty and value of a unique artifact, it would be nice if the artisan or craftsman could actually earn a living doing what he loves! Enter the assembler, the marketer, the advertiser, the seller!

What Does an Arts & Crafts Creator Do?

Craft artists create, either by hand or with digital software, decorative objects using various methods and talents. They employ a variety of techniques and media, such as weaving, needlepoint, pottery, embroidery, painting, welding, ceramics, glass, paper, textiles, wood and metal, to create handmade objects for sale or exhibition. They are experts in manipulating materials, using hand tools, power tools, machinery and, yes, computer software.

The craft artist tends to work outside the traditional fields of fine art (illustration, painting, and sculpture). She must be knowledgeable about materials, trained to use them effectively, and able to create works that appeal to others.

Most artists need proficiency in drawing, composition and spatial relations, but other skills required by craft artists vary widely, depending upon their specialties. Successful craft artists develop a particular artistic vision and are able to express this vision in their work. They often gain valuable expertise by being apprenticed to a master craftsman. And since most craft artists are self-employed, they often benefit from business and marketing training to help them promote and sell their work.

Where Do Arts and Crafts Creators Sell Their Work?

Where, traditionally, have craft artists gone to promote and sell their hand-crafted creations? For starters, they often exhibit in local, regional and national crafts fairs. Many such fairs are juried, requiring that only high quality materials created by uniquely talented individuals be invited to exhibit. Usually these events are theme-based or seasonal. Often crafters exhibit within a sequence of several fairs per season. Exhibit space at reputable crafts fairs is limited and costly, but artisans know that exposure at high-end fairs is invaluable and sales can be lucrative.

Artisans and crafters often place their work on consignment at local and regional gift shops and boutiques. Under this arrangement, the proprietor of the shop receives a portion of the sales price, which is mutually agreed upon in advance between shop owner and artisan.

Lastly, and totally in keeping with the theme and thrust of this book, 21st century artisans and craftsmen are increasingly broadening their customer base by establishing their presence on the Web. Because the Web is so visual, it lends itself quite naturally to becoming the ideal place for artisans to display and to sell their creations. In fact, most clients today expect an artisan/crafter to have an up-to-date, professional-looking, aesthetically-pleasing Web site.

Three excellent examples of beautiful and unique hand-created arts and crafts offered through the web, spanning from France to Sweden to the US, are:

Magna Art (France)
http://www.artmagnacreations.com/
Bendt Elde (Sweden)
http://www.nordicdesigns.se/
Crystal Underground (US)
http://crystalunderground.com

Once an artisan or crafter begins to establish a reputation and her work becomes known, individuals may commission the artist to develop a custom-made design for an agreed upon price and time line.

As illustration of this point, this past holiday season, Marie received from her friend, colleague, and co-author, a lovely wall hanging, hand crafted to reflect the theme of the first book they had published together. Marie was so taken by its beauty and uniqueness, she located on the Web the artisan who had created it, contacted him, and asked him to build her a companion wall hanging. Since a photo of a piece similar to hers was displayed on the artisan's website, he was easily able to recall the details of her first piece, comprehend her vision for a companion piece, and begin work making her concept a reality. Now her two complementary works of art hang in her living room as a constant testimony that "a thing of beauty is a joy forever."

Where to Market Arts & Crafts Work? Start with *Etsy*

Etsy (*https://www.etsy.com/*) is a peer-to-peer e-commerce website that focuses on handmade or "vintage" items and supplies, as well as unique factory-manufactured items. Vintage items must be articles that are at least 20 years old.

Items showcased on *Etsy* cover a wide range, including:

- Art,
- Photography,
- Clothing,
- Jewelry,
- Food,
- Bath and beauty products,
- Quilts,
- Knickknacks,
- Toys
- Craft supplies such as beads, wire and jewelry-making tools.

As a sales engine for creative work, *Etsy* has been compared to a cross between eBay and "your grandma's basement." Over 30 million users were registered on the website as of 2013, with projections of over $1 billion in total annual transactions.

Following in the tradition of open craft fairs, the *Etsy* website provides sellers with personal "virtual storefronts" where they are able to display and sell their goods. Chad Dickerson, CEO of *Etsy*, describes the website as "a platform that provides meaning to people, and an opportunity to validate their art, their craft."

Etsy sellers range from hobbyists to professional artists. Shoppers are drawn to the website because it enables them to purchase directly items that are highly unique, offered by artists and artisans from around the world. Reviews are made available for each item.

The *Etsy* site includes a shopping cart. Creating a shop on *Etsy* is free; but there is a charge of 20 cents per item listed in the shop. The shop owner determines the sales price for each product, with a commission of 3.5% from each sale claimed by *Etsy*. Purchasers make secure payments through Paypal. A listing remains on the shop's sales page for four months, or until the product sells out.

One sample shop on *Etsy* is *AFY Collection*, offering handmade clothing from Italy. The "unique-design, hand-created wool cape" shown below is one item offered for sale through the shop.

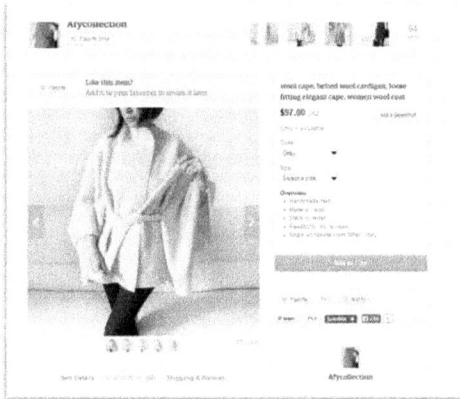

Shoppers are able to use functionality within *Etsy* that includes:

- *Search* or *Browse* for items or shops by category: art, home and living, mobile accessories, jewelry, women, men, or kids.
- *Order and Purchase* selections.
- *View trending items*: a place to explore shoppers' top finds from around the marketplace.
- *Community Taste Makers*: an area to gain inspiration from members' top picks.

Products sold on *Etsy* are created and shipped from all over the world. However, even when transatlantic shipping is required, it is possible to upgrade shipping to *DHL Express*, and thereby to shorten delivery times between Europe and the US to as little as 2–3 business days.

The following additional sites may be of value to those who plan to work as crafts artists.

Sites to Promote Your Arts & Crafts Work	
Artsy Shark http://www.artsyshark.com/	**Craftbizblog** http://www.craftbizblog.com/
Artonomy http://www.artonomy.co/	**Onlinecraftsites** http://www.onlinecraftsites.com
Pinterest http://www.pinterest.com/	**LifeScoop** http://mylifescoop.com/
OnePrettyThing http://www.oneprettything.com	**Craftster** http://www.craftster.org/
A Beautiful Mess http://www.abeautifulmess.com	**100 Craft Links** http://www.100craftlinks.com/
Crafts Sites Report http://www.artcraftmarketing.com/topsites/	
Esty https://www.etsy.com/	

Sites to Select Your Arts & Crafts Software	
CraftArtist2 http://www.serif.com/	**Craft Artist Compact** http://www.serif.com/
Craftsitedirectory http://www.craftsitedirectory.com/	

Would You Want to Build & Produce Crafts?

Even if you are not an artist yourself but are good with your hands, or if you are an artist but want to supplement your income from your own art, there opportunities for creative work in support of other artists and crafters whose businesses have grown past the point where they can produce enough work themselves to meet demands. Are you an expert at sewing, crafting or woodworking? Can you produce work that would be considered "professional" quality? If so, you may be able to make money from home doing home assembly.

Are You Good with Your Hands? Try Home-Assembly

You might be wondering what kinds of companies, making what kinds of products, pay for home assembly? And why would a company want home crafted products instead of those that are mass-produced?

Companies that hire home assemblers are those that offer "hand-made" and "hand crafted" products such as: pottery, CD cases, circuit boards, ornaments, children's clothing, holiday gifts, kimonos, stationary, scarves, moccasins, stained glass, wind chimes, wooden toys, window boxes, book ends, and on and on. The key here is the term "hand-crafted." All of these items are products that require a personal touch.

Could You Assemble Miniatures?

One possibly enjoyable type of home-assembly work is to produce hand-crafted miniatures—the collector quality, highly realistic accessories that are sought out by miniature collectors. There are over 2,000 shops in the U.S. that sell dollhouses and the miniature decorations that adorn them.

Although most miniature displays are dollhouses, some collectors make displays of stores, restaurants, and even little towns. These collections are often made to reflect a specific era such as Victorian, Turn-of-the-Century, the 50's, or Contemporary.

Tiny Details (<u>http://www.tinydetails.com</u>), a company that pays home-based artisans in the United States to produce dollhouse miniatures, is a leader in the "collector-quality" miniatures industry. Their miniatures are sold wholesale and carried by many of the 2,200 miniature shops in the USA, world-wide, and on the Internet. In operation since 1999, *Tiny Details* has employed over 71,000 people to work from home, assembling miniatures.

At press time, the specific craftsman needs *Tiny Details* was listing on their website included artisans to create:

- Miniature calandars
- Spiral notebooks
- Encyclopedia sets
- Tiny books
- Miniature bows
- Quart milk cartons
- Silver chests

As a potential assembler, you would be expected to pay a deposit for a "kit" of materials that includes most of what you will need for the assembly. You are encouraged to send in a sample of your initial work for feedback to ensure that the items you produce will be at the required quality level to be purchased. Checks are paid to you on receipt of your completed set of miniatures.

As an example of the pay scale for producing miniatures, *Tiny Details* will pay $125 for 100 assembled miniature books; $75 for a set of 100 milk cartons; $60 for 10 completed silverware chests.

Products are assigned difficulty ratings; the assembler is paid more depending upon the complexity of the project. The time required to complete a single set of miniatures varies, but many can be assembled in several hours to a day.

Though most assemblers work part-time and make under $200/week, there is the potential to make $400–$500 in a 40-hour week, or possibly more, depending upon the time you invest, as well as your skill level.

Do You Sew? How About Sewing Assembly?

Home-based sewing-assembly jobs are another option. These jobs range from basic hand stitching to advanced sewing by machine. Embroidery jobs are available for the more skilled seamstress. If you have a passion for sewing, then work-at-home-assembly jobs sewing craft products can earn you an income, assuming you have the skill level to assemble the products with professional-level workmanship.

Some examples of home-based sewing-assembly jobs include:

- *Baby bonnets*. Requires basic sewing skills and a straight-stitch sewing machine. Pay is $95.40 per unit (30 bonnets), plus $4 shipping. Limited to 5 units per week, for a possible total of $477 per week.
- *Little "Buddy Bear."* Requires basic sewing skills and a sewing machine. Pay is $80 per unit completed to quality standards. One unit consists of 10 Buddy Bears.
- *Baby Bibs*. Requires a basic sewing machine with zig-zag or satin stitch. Pay is $115 per unit (36 bibs), plus $4 towards shipping. Your output will be limited to four units per week, for possible earnings of $460 weekly.
- *Angels*. Angels are constructed of muslin and flannel, and require easy, straight stitch sewing, trimmed with simple embroidery, using floss and silk ribbon. Pay is $100 for each unit made according to specifications (24 angels), plus $5 postage.

Although the basic pattern is the same, trim varies to create an angel for each of the four seasons. You must purchase your raw materials, costing about $40, leaving a profit of $60 per unit.

If you are considering work of this type, test out various employers until you find the ones that suit you. Beware of "deals" that sound unrealistic or that require sizable investments up front.

Are You a *Wood Crafter*? Consider Home-based Wood Craft Assembly

If you are a *wood crafter*, there are wage-earning home-assembly jobs for you, too. Again, you must be highly skilled, and own basic tools, such as hammer, screwdriver, band saw, coping saw, paint brushes, nuts and bolts, and other industrial grade materials.

Sample woodworking assembly jobs include:

- *Wood American Bald Eagle Plaques.* You should have some painting skills. Pay is $3.50 for each eagle completed to quality standards, with a maximum of 72 eagles a week. Possible weekly income totals $252.
- *Small (7"–8") Wooden Pull Toys.* Workers may select from three toys: *Barnyard Chicken, Circus Zebra*, and *Pink Bunny*. Pay is $96 per unit (24 toys), with a maximum of two units per week. Potential total weekly income is $192.
- *Wooden Note Holders.* You will need a band saw or coping saw, and the ability to operate a saw and do free-hand painting. Each unit (38 holders) pays $133, plus $30 to cover the cost of supplies, plus reimbursed shipping.

Do You Concentrate Well? Then You Could Try Cut & Glue Assembly

Some home product assembly jobs require only cutting and gluing, although even these necessitate a fair level of crafting skill, as well as concentration and excellent hand/eye coordination, in order to produce products that meet professional quality specifications. Employers will not tolerate any kind of defect or shortcoming in the quality of workmanship. Since the product is to be sold commercially, it must be perfect.

New England Crafters (*http://magicalgiftdollhouses.com*) lists assembly products that require cutting and gluing such as:

Project	Difficulty Level	Income
CD Case	Easy. Glue, paint & cut.	$1 each
Cupcake Magnet	Easy. Clay, paint & glue.	$1 per set
Donut Earrings	Easy. Clay, paint & bead.	$1 each
Lollipop Necklace	Moderate. Clay, paint & bead.	$1 each

Be Wary of Home Assembly Job Scams

By taking several precautions, you will protect yourself from scams in the "work from home" market. To ensure that you're not being scammed:

- Make sure that the assembly business you are considering has a real physical address, along with a phone number listed, and preferably a customer care representative available to address all your questions to your satisfaction.
- Personally contact a company representative and chat with her directly about the product and the potential contract offered.
- Ask for references of current employees who would be willing to provide opinions and information concerning the legitimacy of the product and process.

- Be aware that even some legitimate home-assembly employers require a security deposit for materials sent out to you. This deposit should be refundable when your completed work has been accepted. Other employers charge for materials. Some will reimburse you for supplies you have purchased yourself.

Understand in advance that all home-assembly arrangements are based on a requirement of professional level work. If you are able to produce crafts with perfection and accuracy, you will make money. If not, your work will be rejected.

And So...

This chapter was designed to provide and promote authentic and helpful online venues for those talented folk who plan to showcase their own unique creations and talents on the Web. Others, who construct arts and crafts based on the designs of other artisans and crafters, are talented too. In order to produce products that can be sold, these individuals also must be capable of working accurately and skillfully with their hands, crafting flawless work.

If you fit in either group, designer or producer, your search for your optimum online career may now be complete. If not, read on to explore the online careers open to those who have an entrepreneurial bent.

Actually, read on even if you have already found your fit in this or an earlier chapter. If you are creating treasures as an artisan or builder... Or if you are offering services as a writer or graphic artist... Or if you are drawn to supporting businesses, or to research, or to teaching... In each of these cases, you have goods or services to offer. And whatever other sales venues are open to you, the entrepreneurial potential on the web could rapidly become your primary marketplace and source of income. Read on to expand the scope of your ideas about how.

Chapter 10:
The Web Connects You to the World Marketplace: Go Entrepreneurial

"You don't learn to walk by following rules. You learn by doing and falling over."

—Richard Branson, Virgin Group Founder

When we think of entrepreneurship we think of grand titans such as the likes of Jobs, Winfrey, Gates, Buffett, Singer, Ellison, Zuckerberg, Bezos. What could you or I possibly have in common with these brilliantly successful personalities? The answer to this question resides in the very nature and definition of the term "entrepreneur."

Webster defines "entrepreneurship" as: "the act of starting and running your own business or a tendency to be creative and wish to work for yourself in your own ventures." The *"Your Dictionary"* site (*http://www.yourdictionary.com/*) defines an entrepreneur as: "a person who takes an idea, product or service and does whatever is necessary to introduce it to the marketplace where it can produce revenue."

The idea could be a new procedure or a new way to provide a service. If the idea is a product, it could be something simple such as a new type of hair comb, or it could be a multi-part product such as a new electronic gadget. It could be an artisan's original creation, or a replication or derivative of it.

Another example of an entrepreneur is an experienced business manager who decides to use the skills she has learned working for others to start her own consulting firm. Entrepreneurs range from an international business tycoon who establishes a multibillion dollar organization to a stay-at-home mom who has great ideas for creative or instructional children's toys.

Enough said. Based on these definitions, is there any doubt that *you can*, if you have the will and the skill, and the right temperament, be and become an entrepreneur?

Is It Possible to Earn a Living as An Entrepreneur?

To support the premise that entrepreneurism is alive and well in America, and to confirm that, should you decide to pursue this career direction, you will number among a large cohort of colleagues, let's take a look at some interesting statistics from *http://www.forbes.com.*

Growth in Small Businesses

There are almost *28 million small businesses* in the US, about 52% of which (over 14 million) are home-based. More than 75% (22.5 million) of all small businesses in the US are "nonemployer businesses." A "nonemployer businesses" is defined as a business that consists of a self-employed individual, with no additional payroll or employees, and with annual business receipts of $1,000 or more that are subject to federal income taxes.

The ranks of nonemployer businesses has grown steadily and substantially over the past decade, from 17.6 million in 2002 to 22.5 million 2011. This represents an increase of almost 5 million businesses.

Growth in Nonemployer Businesses 2002 - 2011 (in millions)

17.6 18.6 19.5 20.4 20.8 21.7 21.3 21.7 22.1 22.5

2002 2003 2004 2005 2006 2007 2008 2009 2010 2011

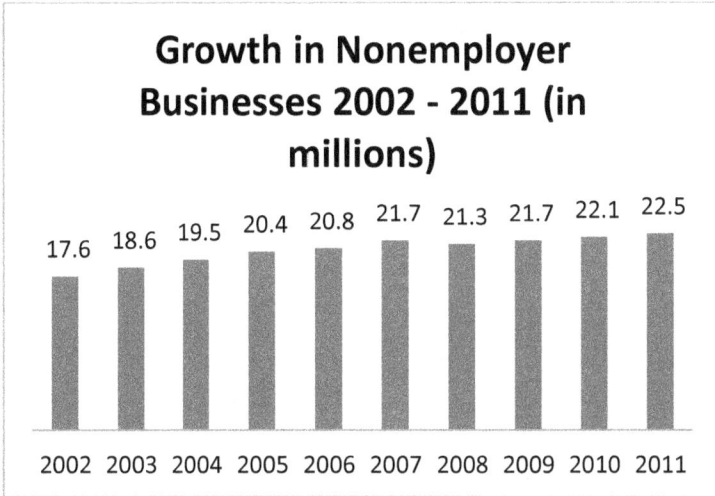

How Much Do "Nonemployer" Businesses Earn?

Revenues from "nonemployers" reached $989.6 billion in 2011 (up 4.1% from 2010). Individual *nonemployers* earned average annual revenues of $44,000, ranging from:

- less than $50,000 in receipts for 80%, equating to 18 million businesses;
- over $50,000 in receipts for 4.5 million *nonemployer* firms;
- over $100,000 a year for 2.33 million enterprises;
- over $250,000 in annual earnings for around 725,000 *nonemployer* companies; and
- over $1 million per year taken in by 29,000 *nonemployers*.

The table below illustrates the breakdown of these earning statistics.

Revenue Breakdown of Nonemployer Businesses 2011

Revenue / year	Percentage	Establishments
$989.6 Billion	100%	22,491,080

Less than $5K	24.4%	5,492,587
$5K- 10K	16.9%	3,795,785
$10K – $25K	25.3%	5,689,588
$25K – $50K	13.5%	3,029,809
$50K – 100K	9.6%	2,151,075
$100K – $250K	7.2%	1,609,507
$250K – 500K	2.2%	484,479
$500K – $1M	0.9%	209,415
$1M – 2.5M	0.1%	26,744
$2.5M – $5M	0.0%	1,723
$5M or more	0.0%	368

What Are the Options for Online Entrepreneurs?

There are many options for entrepreneurialism online. For starters there is the independent version of each of the areas we have discussed so far in the chapters of this book.

If you elect to enter a word-based career as discussed in Chapter 5, clearly you could do this either by working for someone else or by going entrepreneurial and working for yourself. Or you could combine the two. The same holds true for each type of graphics and multimedia work we covered in Chapter 6, as well as for the business support work in Chapter 7, the research and teaching work in Chapter 8, and the creating and building work in Chapter 9.

In addition to these, we will highlight three broad types of entrepreneurial work here:

Direct Sales	Information Marketing
Online Marketing	

Have You Always Wanted to Open Your Own Shop?

There are unlimited opportunities to make money through online direct sales. Direct selling is the sale of a consumer product or service, person-to-person, away from a fixed retail location, marketed through independent sales representatives, who are sometimes also referred to as associates, consultants or distributors. Direct selling can be done in one of three ways:

- Business-to-business (face-to-face or online)
- Person-to-person (face-to-face or online)
- Home parties (or online parties)

What Products? What Services?

Just about any product or service can be purchased through direct selling somewhere in the world. Many people think of cosmetics, wellness products and home décor as products that are often sold through direct sales.

But add to those areas countless other product categories including jewelry, clothing, gardening supplies, heavy equipment, technology tools, sports and athletic equipment, and so many other items. The evidence is in the numbers. Currently over 14 million people work as independent direct sales contractors.

Shifting Gears to Your Career Working Online

If you are considering a business in sales, start by choosing a company (as you research, there'll be plenty from which to select) that reflects your own personal tastes and expertise. It's easier to sell a product or service that excites you, and that you know and believe in.

Do you have taste buds for wine? Become a representative for *TravelingVineyard.com* and "start a business in a bottle." Or enlist with *Wine Shop at Home* (*http://www.wineshopathome.com/*) as a "wine consultant" and "come for the taste and stay for the lifestyle." If you're a clothes horse, and have a good eye for style and value, check into selling for the *Carlisle Collection (www.CarlisleCollection.com)*.

Perhaps you are a relatively new parent. That would make you an expert on many things—baby showers, baby gifts, baby furniture, baby clothes, baby toys, baby quilts. How about hosting an online or in-home shopping party for *Discovery Toys (www.DiscoveryToys.net)*?

If, on the other hand, you have no idea where to start, go to one of the major sources for products, such as:

Direct Selling Association	Alibaba
http://www.dsa.org	*www.alibaba.com*
Direct Selling 411	
http://www.directselling411.com/	

These organizations provide links to a variety of businesses that provide products, as well as advice on how to succeed in direct sales.

Here's a list of the product/service categories available on the *Direct Selling Association* (DSA) site. Circle any that are of potential interest to you as you read through the list.

• Air Filters/Air Filtration	• Homecare
• Animal/Pet Care	• Homeopathics

- Aromatherapy
- Art/Framing
- Audio/CDs/Cassettes
- Auto Care
- Baby/Childcare
- Baskets
- Bed and Bath
- Benefits Packages
- Books
- Business/Commercial
- Candles
- Clothing/Shoes
- Coffee/Tea/Beverages
- Cookware
- Cosmetics
- Crafts/Craft Supplies
- Crystal/China
- Cutlery
- Educational Materials
- Encyclopedias
- Fashion Accessories
- Financial Services
- Food/Gourmet Items
- Fragrances
- Garden Accessories
- Giftware
- Green/Organic
- Group Buying Service
- Hair Care/Accessories
- Health/Fitness/Wellness

- House & Kitchenware
- Insurance
- Internet Services
- Jewelry
- Legal Services
- Lingerie/Sleepwear
- Nutritional Supplements
- Oral Hygiene
- Party Supplies
- Personal Care
- Photography
- Plants/Foliage
- Religious Books/Gifts
- Rubber Stamps
- Scrapbooking/Albums
- Security Systems
- Skincare
- Software/Computers
- Spa Products
- Sporting Goods
- Stationery/Paper Products
- Tableware
- Telecommunications
- Tools
- Toys/Games
- Travel
- Utilities
- Vacuum Cleaners
- Videos

• Holiday Decorations	• Water Treatment
• Home Décor	Systems
• Home Appliances	• Weight Management
• Home Technology	• Wine/Wine Accessories

Where to Find Inventory to Sell

If you set up an online shop, you could start by selling for one of the direct sales companies who list with *Direct Selling 411*. Or you could make your own arrangements with a "drop shipper." Drop shippers handle products from thousands of suppliers and manufacturers. These drop shipping services are the route to direct access to products at deeply discounted wholesale prices.

Some drop shippers will sell you small "lots" of products at wholesale costs that you then can "resell" from your online shop at retail. Other drop shippers will fill your customer orders for you and ship directly to each customer after you make the sale.

One example of a dropship service is on the *Wholesale Central* website (*http://www.wholesalecentral.com/Dropshippers.html*). This site lists hundreds of drop shippers, sorted into categories, all of whom sell only to businesses, not to consumers.

Searching for "leather" on the *Wholesalecentral.com site*, for example, yielded a list of seven distributors, including *S & S Vegas Distributors* (*http://www.ssvegasdistributors.com/*). *S & S Vegas Distributors* represents many of today's leading brands,. from sporting goods and electronics to home furnishings and travel items. They offer an online tour of their warehouse, giving potential clients (like you?) the chance to see these products and their pricing up close.

S & S Vegas Distributors is a supplier for many eBay "powersellers," as well as flea market dealers, individual retailers and even individual wholesalers. This distributor has no minimum order requirement, but offers further reductions for orders over $2000.

All items must be prepaid prior to shipping. As the seller, however, one option is for you to collect the funds from your customer, and only then purchase the product. The distributor will ship the product directly to your customer, with no labeling on the shipment to identify the contents as having come from a source other than your company.

Using this just-in-time product purchase strategy, you would not need to store inventory or risk purchasing inventory that may not sell. And you would not need to spend the time and money required to package and ship items that have been sold. All merchandise is guaranteed for 90 days from the original date of purchase, although the distributor charges a 15% restocking fee on returns of non-defective goods.

As a sample of an item available through *S & S Vegas Distributors*, the wholesale price for this *Embassy Italian Stone Design Genuine Buffalo Leather 19" Tote Bag* (with two zippered side pockets, four front zippered pockets and a detachable shoulder strap) is $16.53 per item, with an additional discount to $14.88 each for orders of 10 or more. The retail value of this item would be upwards of $40.

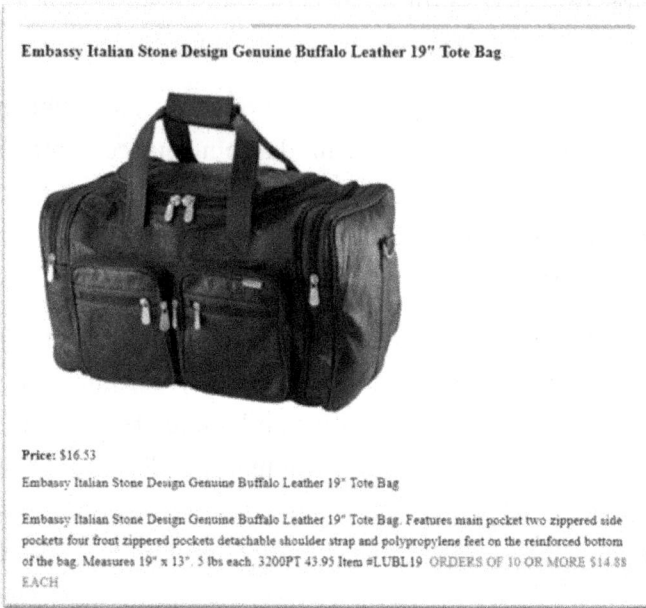

Embassy Italian Stone Design Genuine Buffalo Leather 19" Tote Bag

Price: $16.53

Embassy Italian Stone Design Genuine Buffalo Leather 19" Tote Bag

Embassy Italian Stone Design Genuine Buffalo Leather 19" Tote Bag. Features main pocket two zippered side pockets four front zippered pockets detachable shoulder strap and polypropylene feet on the reinforced bottom of the bag. Measures 19" x 13". 5 lbs each. 3200PT 43.95 Item #LUBL19 ORDERS OF 10 OR MORE $14.88 EACH

Another resource where you can locate products to sell, including electronics, arts, gifts, apparel, sports, jewelry, and automotive parts, is *Drop Ship Direct* (*http://dropshipdirect.com/warehouse*). Once you establish a free account on *DropshipDirect.com* as a "reseller," you will be able to purchase inventory wholesale.

As well as obtaining products to sell online, you will need to:

- Set up your shopping site;
- Promote and advertise;
- Write articles to increase the relevancy rank of your site;
- Plan campaigns to attract a customer base; and
- Stimulate return business and possible referrals.

Work as an *Information Marketer*

"Information marketing." Even if you've never heard the term, if you have ever purchased an eBook, downloaded a song or an app,

participated in an online Webinar, or taken an online course, you have already experienced in the process of *information marketing*. By purchasing one of these products or services, you saved time, energy, and dollars. In this current age, where information is voluminous and ubiquitous, and even potentially overwhelming, the task of packaging information and selling it in useful forms has become its own product.

And that's exactly why, in the last decade, the *information marketing* industry—incentivized by the popularity of the Internet—has grown by leaps and bounds. There is an overwhelming quantity of information available online. People want products that synthesize and summarize from this virtual deluge the essential intelligence on topics they need to learn about or goods they plan to purchase.

These "information products" may be in the form of books, eBooks, audio books, training courses, or "webinars" (web-based seminars). They may be a series of online videos or a CD set or a mini-course or a blog. Or they may be some combination of these formats.

The Growing Market for Packaged Information

Who are the individuals who create the information products other people need? This industry is composed almost entirely of small businesses. Considering only eBooks—just one part of *information marketing*—annual revenues (as reported by the *Association of American Publishers)* have risen precipitously, as these estimates illustrate:

- under $6 million in 2002
- $20 million by 2006
- $54 million by 2008
- $166 million by 2009
- $220 million by 2011
- $282 million by 2012

We would be hard pressed to find any other business that equally offers the fascinating and lucrative opportunities found in and through *information marketing*. The reason is simple. In this business, you actually are able to research and pursue topics that are of personal interest to you, then write about them, and thereby generate income.

Robert Skrob, president of the *Information Marketing Association*, explains the creation of wealth through *information marketing* (yes, many individuals have become wealthy selling information) as "working once and receiving payment over and over again." He cites his own experience doing this. Several years back, over the course of three weekends, Skrob spent 31 hours creating an information product. Not only was he able to sell that product once, but to this day it is continuing to bring in revenue.

Do You Have a Career as an *Online Marketer*?

As an *information marketer*, you will need not only access to a rich collection of resource materials on a chosen topic, but, just as vitally important, an adequate potential audience with interests in the information niche you are promoting.

How do you know your potential market is out there? And, if it is, how do you connect with them? The Web, combined with Google (and other search engines), makes all this possible, enabling the information provider to connect with the information seeker, and vice versa.

And as well as satisfying the quest for information, the Web has become the engine that fuels the demand for information products, as information consumers' expectations have dramatically increased. Readers now fully expect to be able to have readily available to them the means to pursue learning about anything that sparks their interest.

In addition, the evolution of "keyword research" has enabled writers to learn in advance what information readers are seeking, since they now are able to determine the total number of searches per month for every possible search term or phrase. How many people are searching for information on "vacations in France" or "Algebra II tutors" or "working in retirement"? Are more people interested in Italy than France? Algebra I than Algebra II? Traveling in retirement instead of, or combined with, working?

The combined effect is that readers want and expect more. And writers are more able to meet these wants and expectations, with each factor further fueling the other.

By reviewing these search numbers in advance of writing a book or eBook, you will be better able to provide potential readers with the information products they want and need, and to be well compensated for your efforts.

Discover the Security of Multiple Streams of Income

Many of the entrepreneurs who do become wealthy in this area of *information marketing*, do so because they work to develop more than just one source of income. In fact, most successful *information marketers* have discovered that the key to success is to have several products working simultaneously at any given time. This strategy is known as *generating multiple streams of income.*

As an example, imagine that you have created a CD on fitness, and have your sales website active and operating, with everything in place to bring traffic to your site. As an offshoot, you may move on to design a new style of workout clothing. You then could decide to tackle a new project—for example, an eBook on a breed of dog known as the *Australian Shepherd,* and from there opt to develop a new line of health foods for dogs. After you have completed and launched this second project, you could move on to your next project, or a spin-off of your first, and so forth. Meanwhile, your initial projects will continue to generate income. Over time, these various sources of ongoing income begin to accumulate.

Although earlier projects may continue to earn income, it's important to note that you will need to monitor the websites for these products regularly. Each site will peak in sales and then possibly wane. But if you provide even a moderate stream of new articles on the Web that point back to the sales page for each site, and occasionally use Google Adwords and other forms of advertising, you will find that a continuing stream of customers will be interested in your product, possibly for years to come.

Remember, too, that you have the option of regularly creating and marketing updated versions and formats of all your products and projects. You can easily see how your income would grow as you continue to add new products, versions and formats. After all, the entire Web is your resource, and the entire world of information seekers is your potential client base. You are limited only by your creative imagination, your investment of time, and your work ethic.

For example, when my colleague and I co-authored and published our first book, *Shifting Gears to Your Life & Work After Retirement* (*www.ShiftingGearstoYourLifeandWorkAfterRetirement.com*), we not only made it available through Amazon, Barnes & Noble and other online booksellers, both in paperback and eBook formats, but we also transformed the entire work and marketed it to community colleges as a continuing education "Course-in-a-Box" (complete with PowerPoint slides, activities and handouts), and to HR directors as an outplacement workshop.

The medium you select for your information product depends on your particular interests and your main communication strengths. Are you a writer? Then you can write eBooks. Are you an ace at video creation or multi-talented enough to work with several mediums, including both video and audio? Then create informational videos, or team up with a writer and take charge of the video and audio versions of his books and e-books. Or produce informational audio products by using your own content or by seeking out a colleague with whom to collaborate in producing a dynamic finished product.

Information Marketing as an Affiliate

If time is at a premium... If you are too eager to get started to take the time now to create your own information product... If no particular product idea comes to mind right now... Consider making your start by marketing and selling information products designed by others.

Go to *Clickbank.com* (*http://www.clickbank.com/index.html*), where you'll find information products that might interest you. Select one that you find exciting and sign on as an affiliate. Then start by selling someone else's product while you research and create your own.

To initiate your own *information marketing* business selling other people's products, it is essential to select a product "niche" that excites you. "Niche" is the marketing terminology for a specified and highly specialized segment of a chosen market.

Thanks to the power of the Internet, marketers can profit by targeting even very small niches. Those who love the *Australian Shepherd*, for example. Or people interested in genealogy. Or *Celtic music*. Or *batik*. Targeting a small niche, and providing that niche with information products, was not even a possibility before the advent of the Web. Having the full world as the marketplace has enabled the small niche marketplace to flourish.

Do You Have a Career in Online Marketing

Effective marketing is critical to selling of anything at any level of enterprise—large corporation, small company, for-profit or non-profit organization. In a world of varied media that ranges from television to the Internet, the demand for outstanding marketing professionals has never been stronger.

Marketing professionals are involved in developing marketing campaigns to promote a product, service or idea. Their job includes planning, advertising, public relations, event organization, product development, distribution, sponsorship and research. The work is often challenging and fast-paced.

Because marketing is such a diverse field, today's marketing professionals may have one specialty area, while others handle multiple areas. Data-driven marketing increasingly focuses on the consumer, data and accountability—and how these attributes interact. Marketing departments and agencies are looking for well-rounded individuals who possess communication skills and who are comfortable in measuring, analyzing and manipulating numbers and data. In other words, marketers help companies figure out which campaigns work best and how to use advertising and marketing to enhance their bottom line.

There is a wide array of paths to choose from in this field including:

- Account coordinator,
- *Search Engine Optimization* (SEO) specialist,
- Community manager,
- Database marketing coordinator,
- Email and Internet marketing specialist,
- Marketing analyst,
- Social media coordinator, and
- Web content writer.

The responsibilities of an *online marketing manager* vary depending on the size of the organization and sector, and whether the focus is on selling a product or service or on raising awareness of an issue that affects the public. Their goals are to grow brand awareness, increase sales and improve customer acquisition and retention by using various online marketing tools and analytics. Ideal online marketing managers are both creatively and analytically minded.

How Much Does Online Marketing Work Pay?

An online marketing manager earns an average salary of $61K per year, ranging from $40K to $89K. Highest pay goes to those skilled at e-commerce and marketing management. Hourly rates range from $10–$36 per hour, plus profit-sharing bonuses of $500 to $10,000.

Websites for Promotions, Software and Learning

Below is a list of marketing and advertising websites meant to shed light on this career.

Sites to Promote Your Advertising/Marketing Work	
JustPromoteMarketingCompany *http://www.justpromote.biz*	**ClickZ** *http://www.clickz.com/*
RedFusion *http://www.redfusionmedia.com*	**Yodle** *http://www.yodle.com/*
AdvertisingAge *http://adage.com/*	**Marketing Eye** *http://www.marketingeye.com*
AmericanMarketingAssociation *http://www.jointheama.com*	**Dunnhumby** *http://www.dunnhumby.com/*
Teradata *http://marketing.teradata.com/*	

Sites to Select Your Advertising/Marketing Software	
IntuitQuickBas *http://try.quickbase.intuit.com/*	**CampaignMonitor** *http://www.campaignmonitor.com*
APRIXSolutions *http://aprixsolutions.com/*	**StatSoft** *http://www.statsoft.com/*
PICA9 *http://pica9.com/*	**WorkZone** *http://www.workzone.com/*
WordStream *http://www.wordstream.com/*	**MarinSoftware** *http://www.marinsoftware.com/*
AD-IN-ONE.COM *http://www.ad-in-one.com*	**ChaseSoftware** *https://www.chasesoftware.com/*
TopTen EmailMarketingServices *http://www.top10emailmarketingservices.com*	
Revolver *http://www.revolversoftware.com/*	

Sites to Learn & Upgrade Your Skills	
BureauofConsumerProtection *http://www.business.ftc.gov/*	**BrianSolis** *http://www.briansolis.com/*

eMarketer
http://www.emarketer.com/

How & Where to Sell Your Products: Universal Online Marketplaces

Whether you're an entrepreneur, eager to introduce the world to your latest brainchild, or an artisan craftsman seeking a buying audience, or a natural in the art and skill of connecting buyers with sellers, or a professional ready to vend your particular knowledge or product, it behooves you to be aware of and to befriend the online marketplaces where you will be able to publicize and sell your product or service. Start with these five:

eBay	Products
http://www.ebay.com/	
Alibaba	**Products**
http://www.alibaba.com/	
Craigslist	**Products &**
https://www.craigslist.org/about/sites	**Services**
Kickstarter	**Project funding**
https://www.kickstarter.com/	

eBay

It is highly likely that you are already familiar with *eBay*, the technology company that provides everyone and anyone with the opportunity to buy and to sell anything and everything from buttons, bows, belt buckles, and bread boxes, to items too large to fit in your neighbor's pickup.

Think about the sometimes exotic, often absurd, dust collecting "stuff" you have accumulated in your garage, attic, and basement over the years. Remember that *Thigh Master* you were going to use to whip those legs into shape? Someone on eBay awaits it. Or what about that *Cabbage Patch* doll you bought after standing in line for four hours at a local department store, starting at 4 a.m. one Christmas, because, after all, your granddaughter could not weather disappointment at the tender age of four?

Yes, there's someone trawling the eBay site right now waiting to pounce on your treasure. Or that collection of intact puzzles, reminders of those puzzle contests you won (or lost!) during those memorable annual extended family summer vacations at the lake? Boxes and boxes of puzzles that a nursing home activities director might just be waiting to scoop up for her residents.

On eBay you can offer your fashions, your auto parts, your home and garden materials, your electronics... all for sale to everybody everywhere, worldwide. At press time, *eBay* had over 155 million active registered users, both buyers and sellers, offering more than 16 million items for sale.

Clearly *eBay* has been highly successful at connecting buyers with sellers in a virtual marketplace made up of billions of computers and mobile devices. According to Forbes (*www.forbes.com*), a total of 8.7 billion devices were internet-connected in 2012.

EBay lists items by category, indicating their conditions of wear, and even providing a *Buyer Protection Plan* that covers items that are not received, or that are not as they were described in the eBay listing.

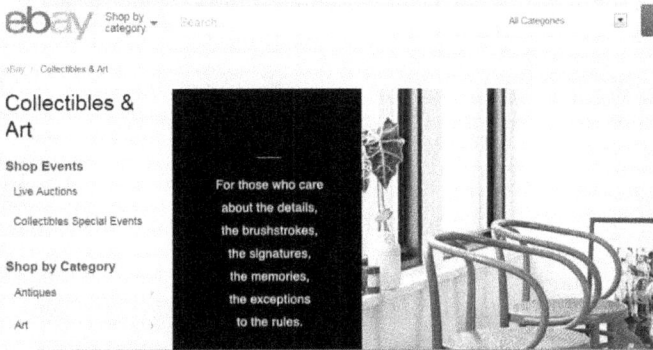

The *Daily Deals* feature on *eBay* offers various products, in multiple categories, at discounted prices, with free shipping. *Stub Hub* is the eBay venue where fans can buy and sell tickets to sports, concert, theatre and other live entertainment events.

How is money transferred? Payments are processed through eBay's payment brand, PayPal, enabling buyers and sellers to send and receive payments confidently and securely.

In his online descriptive article, *"What Is eBay? An Introduction to the World's Online Marketplace,"* Aron Hsiao aptly describes eBay as "a meeting place, not a store... eBay doesn't actually sell any goods itself. All of the goods on *eBay* are sold and delivered by third party sellers who are neither employed by, nor have any other relationship with, eBay itself. Instead, *eBay's* business is to give entrepreneurs and sellers a place to reach buyers, and to give buyers access to the world's largest collection of things for sale."

Alibaba

Another heavily used shopping search engine, serving 240 countries and regions, and bringing together millions of buyers and suppliers, is *Alibaba* (*http://www.alibaba.com/*). Similar to *eBay.com*, and featuring nearly a billion products, Alibaba is one of the 20 most-visited websites globally. By providing a fundamental infrastructure for commerce and data technology, *Alibaba* supports the building of small businesses. Joining Alibaba is free, but for full services and utilities there is a charge.

The *Alibaba* Group was founded in 1999 by 18 people, led by Jack Ma, a former English teacher from Hangzhou, China. Their intent was to "champion small businesses, in the belief that the Internet would level the playing field by enabling small enterprises to leverage innovation and technology to grow and compete more effectively in the domestic and global economies." *Alibaba's* vision and mission, as stated on their website, is "to build the future infrastructure of commerce."

As a seller on *Alibaba*, you will have the use of a tool that allows you to research buyer demand, the better to understand your buyers' search behaviors and to identify market opportunities. This is an excellent way to get a sense of how to market and sell your product globally, or even to determine what product to offer for sale.

For example, a compiled report on buyer trends in searching for "leather motorcycle jackets" cites a strong demand for this product in December 2014, with 56% of the demand coming from Western Europe, Asia, and North America. The highest search volume came from Portugal.

In addition to being a sales engine, *Alibaba* is also used as a global source of inventory to be sold. When purchasing inventory through your own e-commerce sites, you are able to do a search for a particular item and browse the potential sources of inventory available to you. Prices vary, tending to be lower for suppliers who require larger minimum order quantities. Some suppliers require only one piece as a minimum order.

As an example, the supplier of men's leather jackets shown below will supply a single item for $10-$20 per piece. By following the "Get Latest Price" link, you are able to seek the best quotes from multiple verified suppliers based on the item and the quantity you need.

Alibaba offers an escrow service as protection from Internet scam artists. This service will hold your payment in escrow while the order is being processed, and release payment to the supplier upon your confirmation that you have received the goods and are satisfied with their quality. The charge for this escrow service is 5% of the total order, including the costs of shipping.

Craigslist

Craigslist is a website for classified advertisements, with sections devoted to:

- jobs
- housing
- personals
- for sale
- items wanted
- services
- community

- gigs
- résumés
- discussion forums

You may already be familiar with *Craigslist*. Perhaps a family member found his current job on this site. Or your best friend posted his summer home for sale. Or you yourself have listed your restored classic sailboat, together with a "selfie" of you at the helm. Or this is where your daughter found and hired the DJ who provided the lively music at her wedding.

If, on the other hand, you're new to the world of online buying, selling, negotiating services, and bartering goods, then you might start at *http://www.craigslist.org/about/*, where you'll be introduced to the entire range of how to use *Craigslist* and all about the Craigslist online environment.

More than 60 million people use *Craigslist* each month in the US alone, generating Internet traffic of more than 50 billion page views per month. Users post over 80 million classified ads each month, including reposts and renewals. Job hunters can, on a monthly basis, find more than 1 million new jobs listed.

Although Craigslist is a global enterprise, it is set up by region, with more than 700 local sites in 70 countries. *Within Craigslist you will be able to identify and use your own regional list or explore lists anywhere in the world.*

How does *Craigslist* differ from *eBay*? First, the focus of *eBay* is on the purchase and sale of products. In addition to *products* available for sale, Craigslist also deals with the whole range of *services* available for hire, as well as potential jobs and gigs.

services	
automotive	legal
beauty	lessons
computer	marine
creative	pet
cycle	real estate
event	skill'd trade
farm+garden	sm biz ads
financial	therapeutic
household	travel/vac
labor/move	write/ed/tr8

Secondly, *Craigslist* listings are free, and no monetary transactions take place through *Craigslist*. Rather, thje provider and the customer connect and deal directly with each other when negotiating an exchange or a financial arrangement.

Kickstarter

What, actually, is *Kickstarter*? In short, the *Kickstarter* website (*https://www.kickstarter.com*) is a funding community where anyone can launch a project, large or small, for the purpose of raising a pre-set amount of money within a finite time period in order to help the creator or entrepreneur successfully create and market his/her product. The creator sets his own funding goal and timeline, in the hope that financial backers will find the product or project investment-worthy.

If people like a project, they can pledge money to make it happen. The project creator or product entrepreneur is charged only if he successfully reaches his financial goal by the deadline he sets. Since its launch in 2009, 6.7 million people have pledged $1 billion, funding

66,000 creative projects on *Kickstarter*. To date, an impressive 44% of projects have reached their funding goals.

Why would anyone pledge financial backing to a *Kickstarter* project? Because the entire *Kickstarter* culture embodies and informs a grass roots effort to give ordinary folk the opportunity to invest in an entrepreneurial idea that may become a marketing success, while simultaneously providing the entrepreneur with necessary financial capital to launch his product or invention.

Backers who support a project on *Kickstarter* gain the opportunity to have an inside look at the creative process. Also, they enjoy the satisfaction of helping that potential project idea become a reality. In terms of more tangible rewards, backers also get to choose from a variety of unique rewards offered by the project creator. Rewards vary from project to project, but often include a copy of what is being produced or an experience unique to the project.

To better understand the *Kickstarter* community, spend some time on the *Kickstarter* website. Here you will be able to search and sort by various categories and criteria to see what projects are currently seeking funds. This will serve two purposes. You may find a project that interests you. But also, these posted projects can serve as models for a possible project for which you want to seek funding yourself.

Sample Kickstarter Project

Sense: Know More. Sleep Better by Hello. San Francisco, CA

Sense is a simple system that tracks your sleep behavior, monitors the environment of your bedroom and reinvents the alarm.

1,732% Funded. **$1,732,660** Pledged

16 Days To Go

Now you decide...

Which of these different, but all-productive and promising sites will best serve your purposes and goals, or your products and services? Perhaps all of them. Or would it be more realistic and productive to concentrate your energies on developing one venue to its fullest before branching out to another?

Only you can determine your best career launching pad. But in order to inform your decision, we suggest that you fully explore several, noting the pros and cons of each as they apply to your particular circumstances, limitations, and aspirations. Then, and only then, should you begin the hard work of expending maximum effort and resources to promote your own service or product.

And So...

There is an expression—"Everyone to his or her own skill." Perhaps your idea of the perfect career has never consisted of working for someone else. You function best and are happiest when you can function as "the captain of your fate, the master of your soul." The entrepreneurial spirit is alive and well in your career frame of reference.

If you find yourself very much at home in this chapter, our intent was to provide you with the motivation and some practical resources to launch you into doing your own thing, in your own way, in your own timeframe.

Whatever your decisions about the specific area of online work you hope to pursue, you will need to refine your skills at promoting yourself online. This is what the next chapter is about. So put aside your humility, for a moment, and prepare to "blow your own horn"— but tastefully.

Chapter 11:
Promote Yourself Online

"Don't put a ceiling on yourself."

—Oprah Winfrey

Now it is time to synthesize the discoveries and choices you have made so far. In Chapter 2, you established, furnished and equipped your home office. In Chapter 3, you completed a *7-Step Process*:

1) Understand the seven trends that define the current online workplace;
2) Define yourself;
3) Upskill yourself;
4) Select from the four categories of online work;
5) Translate yourself;
6) Present yourself;
7) Plan your trajectory.

Now you have defined yourself and know what you have to offer, and have added to your skill base, as needed, to make yourself highly marketable as an online contributor. And you know what category (or combination of categories) of online work you want to pursue: find an employer; find contract work; self-employ; or start your own business.

You have translated yourself into cyber terms, and prepared your résumé and portfolio, including samples of relevant work to show-and-tell your capabilities. And, starting in Chapter 4, you have considered *seven types of online work*, and selected the area of focus that will best engage you and your talents, leading you to an online career that makes full use of your abilities, and at which you can make a contribution and add value. The seven types of online work you considered, each with a range of potential careers, included:

1) Find work for hire (Chapter 4);
2) Become an online writer (Chapter 5);
3) Work in graphic design and multimedia (Chapter 6);
4) Provide support for businesses (Chapter 7);
5) Research or teach (Chapter 8);
6) Create or build (Chapter 9);
7) Go entrepreneurial (Chapter 10).

With all that accomplished, it is time to synthesize all this valuable information, plan your trajectory, then move forward... To reach out and become very active and proactive.

From this point forward, it will be your task to promote yourself and thus to enable the online world of work to *find you* in the vastness of cyberspace. In addition to having your résumé and portfolio ready to post when responding to a job opening, you have at your disposal other essential web-based ways to promote yourself.

But, first, a general word about self-promotion. We all walk a fine line between bragging or exaggerating—behaviors that no-one admires—and demonstrating our capabilities to the extent that employers and clients will be convinced that it's in their best interest to employ us. Your task here will be to "show and tell" yourself and your abilities in ways that best demonstrate how much others stand to benefit from having you work for them, but without appearing to be too full of yourself.

Eight Channels to Promote Yourself

There are many channels available to promote yourself online. What it comes down to is one single question: "Here I am! How do I make myself 'visible' to the online world?" As you shift to your career working online, you will need to deliberately and diligently create and telegraph your "presence"— transforming yourself from the "physical you" to the "virtual you."

Your main concern and challenge will be to become fully aware of how the virtual world of meeting, collaborating, engaging, and working happens. Who is looking for what? Who sees what? Why do they look? How do they find what they are looking for? And, most importantly now, how will they find *you*, and how will they know that *you* are the one they want to find?

The eight channels that follow are ones that you need to act upon immediately.

1. *Present Yourself on ZipRecruiter.*	5. *Establish Your Web Presence.*
2. *Link Up on LinkedIn.*	6. *Write & Publish Articles to Establish Your Expertise.*
3. *Post to Directories.*	7. *Join a Forum and/or Create a Blog. Post Regularly.*
4. *Notify Your Email Contacts.*	8. *Conduct a Google Adwords Campaign.*

The first four of these—*ZipRecruiter, LinkedIn, Directories* and *email contacts*—are essential to you regardless of which of the four types of online work you have selected: find an employer; find contract work; self-employ; or start your own business.

The next two channels—*establish your web presence* and *write and publish articles* to establish your expertise—are particularly important if you are moving in the direction of online contract work, selling your services, or starting your own business.

The final two channels—*forum and/or blog* and *AdWords campaign*—are optional but highly effective ways to get the word out about yourself and what you have to offer.

Present Yourself on ZipRecruiter

Let's start with a one-stop shopping website that might simplify the process of launching yourself, your product, and/or your service into the online job searching world. *ZipRecruiter* will make it easier for you to "multitask" the steps you need to take to publicize yourself.

When you register on *ZipRecruiter*, your professional profile and résumé will post to over 50 job sites simultaneously, including these six major job search sites:

Monster.com	Indeed.com
http://www.monster.com/	*http://www.indeed.com/*
SimplyHired.com	**GlassDoor.com**
http://www.simplyhired.com/	*http://www.glassdoor.com*
BackPage.com	**Craigslist**
http://www.backpage.com/	*http://www.craigslist.org*

There is no cost to register and search on *ZipRecruiter*. You will be able to post your résumé, create job alerts, save jobs that are of interest, and apply for jobs. Consider the career benefits that will accrue from registering on this mega-career-search site to promote your professional work future.

As a potential worker or employee, take advantage of *ZipRecruiter's* many features, including:

- Upload your résumé to be posted automatically to 50+ job boards simultaneously;
- Complete a job seeker profile to allow *ZipRecruiter* to make job recommendations;
- Apply for jobs, adding a cover letter that is appropriately customized to each;
- Automatically receive email updates;
- Download a mobile app to access relevant job alerts;
- Access links for job seekers, including articles, tips and other resources to help you find a job faster;
- Seek work that is hourly, full-time, part-time, or seasonal.

Some employers and recruiters who post jobs may require that you answer questions online as part of your initial application process. Some of these questions may be open-ended, while others may be in the form of multiple-choice or yes/no responses. It is imperative that you make a serious effort to address these questions, as they will constitute the first impression you make on a potential employer. Provide high-quality and complete answers to all questions asked. And check your spelling and grammar to be certain that it is flawless before you click "send."

Link Up on LinkedIn

LinkedIn (*www.LinkedIn.com*) is currently one of the most prominent social media outlets for professional networking. As such, it is one of the top priority online locations where it is essential that you establish a professional presence.

On *LinkedIn*, you will be able to post your entire work profile, connect with familiar colleagues and new associates world-wide, and view and apply for job openings. *LinkedIn* goes beyond *ZipRecruiter* and other job search sites because it allows you to "manage your professional identity."

Using *LinkedIn*, you will be able to become selectively connected to people from your past or present with whom you choose to continue to have a relationship after you have shifted gears. One feature of the *LinkedIn* networking environment is to enable these colleagues to "endorse" you for particular skills and abilities, and vice versa. So, over time, your professional strengths and capabilities will become increasingly apparent and reinforced. Your *LinkedIn* profile, once you fully complete it, serves as a version of an online résumé.

In the past, what would it have cost you to publish your credentials in every major newspaper and trade publication on a daily, weekly or monthly basis? On LinkedIn, *at no cost*, you can permanently showcase your past and current work experience, indicate your future career aspirations, list your academic accomplishments and skills levels and preparation, update your profile as often as you'd like, and search for and apply for available job openings.

For an additional fee you have the option of upgrading your *LinkedIn* account to the "premium" level, where you will have use of additional features, including:

- *Open Profile*— Increased visibility that allows you to let anyone on LinkedIn see your full profile and message you for free;
- Access to information about everyone in your network and everyone in their networks (to the first, second, and third degree); and
- *InMail*—a system that allows you to communicate directly with recruiters and other professionals anywhere on *LinkedIn* (totaling over 300 million profiles).

With a premium-level *LinkedIn* account, your job applications will be featured at the top of applicant lists. And you will be able to see how you compare to other applicants, as well as to view detailed salary information for each job. Also, you will know who has been viewing your profile. And you will have the option of building a "premium profile," including visuals that express your "professional brand."

Of particular potential value to you if you are building your own business is the *Lead Builder* feature of a premium account. *Lead Builder* will enable you to create lead lists using custom searches—up to 1500 leads with a "Professional Level" membership, or 3000 leads at the "Team Level."

The process of upgrading to a premium *LinkedIn* account, and then reverting back to a basic account, is very straightforward. So it is possible to upgrade at times when you plan to make heavy use of the premium features, then downgrade back to a basic account when you have accomplished your goals, at least for the time being.

Post to Directories

If you are planning to join one of the three self-managed, independent online career groups—contract worker, self-employed, or business owner—it is essential that you list yourself in the directories for your particular skill or profession. Take the time now to double back to the chapter about your specific choice of focus area, and add the associated list of sites and contacts to your "to do" list:

- Writing (Chapter 5);
- Designing graphics and multimedia (Chapter 6);
- Supporting businesses (Chapter 7);
- Researching or teaching (Chapter 8);
- Creating or building (Chapter 9); or
- Going entrepreneurial (Chapter 10).

Then delve into the specific directories where you need to list yourself, according to your area of focus. Use the general directories, as well as the specific ones. Here are a few examples:

For Freelance Writers *http://www.writersplace.org*
For Freelance Designers *http://www.freelancedesigners.com/*
For Freelance Translators *http://aquarius.net/*
For Freelance Technical Consultants *http://www.freelancelocaltech.com/*
Complete Directory of Freelancers *http://freelancersdirectory.org/* [Directories for: Web Design, Web Marketing, Illustration, CAD, Legal, Software/Database Development, Sales/Telemarketing, Graphic Design, Marketing, Admin/Support, Translation Editing/Writing, , Business]

Once you get your directory listings working for you, they will continue to work on your behalf even while you are focusing on other things.

Use All Your Email Contacts

Over the course of your career, you likely have accumulated a healthy list of email addresses. These contacts may consist of a combination of addresses belonging to former clients or employers, current customers, potential clients, past work colleagues, business connections, family members, and friends.

When you first start out to seek work online, send a quick email to everyone, explaining that you are now shifting to a career working online. If you have decided that you will pursue the second, third or fourth types of working online—contract work, self-employment, or starting your own business—share these plans with your email contacts. Tell them in specific terms what you will be doing, and how you potentially may be able help them within your new work arrangements. Be sure to point them to your website, your blog, your directory listings, your *LinkedIn* account, and any other convenient means for them to learn more and to access your products or services.

Continue to expand your email list. As any Internet marketer will attest, your email list is extremely valuable, and deserves focused attention. Harvest and harness it. Improve and supplement it. Invite and engage it. Each time you or your business has something new to offer that may be of potential value to the individuals on the list, send out a well-crafted message to your list. Recognize, too, that each individual on your growing email list has a network of her own. And each person on her list also has a network. And so forth. News will have a way of rippling outward, particularly if it is of potential value to the individuals receiving it.

In part because your email list is so valuable, but also to retain your reputation as a considerate colleague, friend, or family member, be discreet and discerning in your use of your email list. Do not abuse it. If you have an announcement that mainly serves you, but that may not be of particular use to everyone on your list, restrain yourself. The so-called "punishment" for over-broadcasting yourself "fits the crime." People on your list will simply stop reading what you send them.

But if your announcement is of potential professional or commercial value to the individuals on your list, make it a point to communicate and spread the word. It may be best at some point to segment your list according to what may be of particular interest to each set of individuals. This makes it possible to customize your messages, rendering them more relevant to your recipients. This also accomplishes the purpose of holding each sublist to a reasonable size so that your communication will not be rejected as "spam."

Later, as you continue to grow your online career or business, your email connections will be important ones to include when you send out a monthly newsletter. Or when you announce a website, a product, or a service. Or even when you just post a note to update people on how your business is progressing and growing.

As an added benefit of connecting with everyone on your email contacts list, you'll be pleasantly surprised to hear from past acquaintances who had dropped off your communications radar, but with whom you now find a new reason to re-establish contact!

Establish Your Own Web Presence

Since you eventually will want and need a website, you might as well take steps now to establish a presence on the World Wide Web. What better place to showcase who you are (your résumé) and what you can do (your portfolio)?

Whether you elect to create your website yourself or to hire a professional, creating a website is basically a two-step process:

- Create and launch your website.
- Generate "traffic" to visit your website.

Create and Launch Your Website

First you must purchase a web domain (URL), design your site and populate it with information. To launch your site, you will need to locate a place where your site will be "hosted"—an Internet-connected "server" where the files for your website will "live."

There are tools available, including some that are free, that will enable you, with "a little help from your friends," to establish your own simple, but attractive and functional website. Four key tools to get you started are:

- *GoDaddy* (*www.godaddy.com*);
- *Weebly* (http://www.weebly.com/);
- *Wix* (http://www.wix.com/); and
- *WordPress* (https://wordpress.com/)

Go with GoDaddy

GoDaddy (*www.godaddy.com*) is one of the well-known sites to research and purchase a web domain (URL). *GoDaddy* offers an entire array of services, ranging from helping you find and purchase your own unique domain, to helping you build your site, to providing marketing tools such as website visibility, or even assisting you in designing a logo. Another key service of *GoDaddy* is to act as host for your site, and also to provide regular website backups and security.

These additional services incur additional, but relatively reasonable, fees. The *GoDaddy* customer service reps are competent and eager to assist you in getting what you need, and no more, depending upon the level of service you want or require.

Create and Host Your Site on Weebly.com

Named one of Time Magazine' s *50 Best Websites*, *Weebly.com* is another user-friendly hosting service for creating your own Website. Its drag & drop *Website Builder* makes it simple to create a powerful, professional web presence, regardless of your limited technical skills. Over 6 million people and small businesses have joined *Weebly* to build their online presence.

When building a website, you start by choosing a theme, then adding content elements (like text, photos, maps, and videos) by simply dragging & dropping them into place. You are able to edit text just as you would with a word processor. Building your website is done in real time, right from within your web browser. There's nothing to install and no upgrades to worry about.

Through its *Help Center*, *Weebly* offers tremendous user support by providing an entire range of information under such topics as:

- Beginner's Guide to *Weebly*
- Common Questions
- Live Training Webcasts
- Text and Images
- Pages & Navigation
- Tablet & Mobile
- Blogging
- Domain Names
- Email & Google Apps
- Video & Audio
- Commerce
- Custom HTML & Embeddable Widgets
- Stats & Search Engines

The *Beginner's Guide* hand-holds you as a new user, offering a step-by-step process for establishing your own site.

Additionally, *Weebly* has some neat ancillary features. For example, it allows educators to create a classroom website and blog, manage student accounts, assign and accept homework assignments online, and keep parents informed about student assignments and activities.

Use WIX.com

Another option is *www.WIX.com*, a site that allows anyone to design and launch a basic website for free, or a more dynamic website for a monthly fee. Its user-friendly interface guides even the most technology-challenged user through the process of designing and maintaining a website that is not only aesthetically pleasing, but informative and easily navigated.

WIX features an almost limitless variety of templates, arranged by category. By using predesigned templates, you will not need to know the advanced html language used by professional webpage designers.

Create and host with WordPress.com

WordPress is reputedly one of the easiest ways to create a beautiful and powerful website or blog. At present *WordPress* powers 23% of the top 10 million websites on the Internet. It is the most popular blogging system in use on the web, supporting more than 60 million blogging sites.

Based on open source code, the core software for *WordPress* was built by hundreds of community volunteers. As you create your own website using *WordPress*, you will be working in a drag-and-drop visual environment, building a site that is based on your choice of "theme."

Pick a theme, any theme. You will be able to change the theme at will, without needing to reenter the content. When you change themes, the entire appearance and look of your site will be transformed. So your main concern will be to focus on developing and adding content. Visit the *WordPress* site (https://wordpress.com) to view examples of themes available for use with *WordPress*.

When you use *WordPress*, the functionality of your website can include some very sophisticated and impressive options, added through your choice from among over 30,000 available "plug-ins." Plug-ins offer programming features, but without the need to hire and pay a programmer. Contact forms, e-commerce support, mobile device support, search engine optimization, Google analytics, site maps, buttons, blogs, forums... The list goes on and on.

Or Hire a Professional

If you elect instead to hire a professional web designer to create your website, you will find many potential designers eager to take on your project. Return to some of the online contract work websites (like http://www.guru.com) from earlier chapters, this time as an employer seeking services. Or list your needed web design work in an ad on Craigslist.

Generate Web Traffic to Your Site

Once your website is launched, your next task will be to learn more about the mechanics of generating Internet traffic so that people will find your website (and you) on the Web. Understanding how to gain Web "traffic"—how to ensure that people who need you and your services will be able to find you and your website in the vastness of cyberspace —is a challenge in itself. There are excellent sources of training on this topic, as well as professionals for hire.

For now, understand that, as we have previously discussed, the essential concept to comprehend is that *Google* and other search engines are programmed to seek out *substance and relevance,* based on the actual words—called *keywords*—found on the billions of webpages available on the Web. And, yes, the search engines are actually able to view and analyze each and every word.

Keywords are those words that web searchers may be expected to type into the search box of a search engine, like *Google* or *Bing* or *Yahoo,* when they are searching for a specific topic, item or service. You use "*keywords*" yourself whenever you conduct a web search with some question or goal in mind.

Search engines automatically analyze websites and webpages based on four essential elements:

1. **URL** name,

2. **Metatags** (Titles, keywords and descriptions. Metatags are not visible on the webpage, but communicate to the browser what each website and webpage is about),
3. **Headings** and subheadings on the page, and
4. **Text** written on the page.

The key to getting visitors to your website, so that they have the opportunity to see what you have to offer, is to assist *Google* (and the other search engines) in matching your site with the search terms (keywords) that your potential visitors and clients can be expected to use when they are searching for the types of products or services you provide.

Pause for a moment and think about all this. In a word, it all seems absolutely and positively amazing—almost beyond credibility—that this level of matching up of questions with answers, information with information seekers, service providers with potential clients, workers with employers, and consumers with merchants, is even possible. But given that it is possible, you must understand how to work with it, and use it to your advantage.

Essentially, you must learn to identify and make use of the set of actual and literal *words* for which your potential clients will be searching. You then will enter these exact words on your website, in each of the four locations cited above.

If the thought of doing this yourself makes your head hurt, you will need to hire someone else to do this for you. The consequence of neglecting this all-essential task is that the search engines will not know that your website is relevant and important to the people who are looking for your services or products. *In the end, there is no magic wizard behind the curtain. There are only words—keywords—after all.*

If you are positioning yourself as an expert ghostwriter or editor, for example, you will need your site to "rank" for any keywords that your potential ghostwriting or editing customers might use in their searches.

This anticipating of their search terms will lead them directly to you. To repeat an earlier point, your goal is for your site to appear on the first page of the list of search results, preferably near the top, since this is the only page that most searchers actually read.

Tutorials about how to generate Web traffic through "Search Engine Optimization" (SEO, are readily available in the form of short videos on *YouTube* (*www.youtube.com*).

Additional tutorials are to be found at:

Tizag.com   *http://www.tizag.com/SEOTutorial*
Blog.hubspot.com   Article: *Shortest Tutorial Ever on SEO*   *http://blog.hubspot.com/blog/tabid/6307/bid/1436/Shortest-Tutorial-Ever-on-SEO-Search-Engine-Optimization.aspx*

Write & Publish Articles to Establish Your Expertise

Article directories throughout the Web continuously seek good quality articles, written by knowledgeable authors. By consistently submitting well-written, informative articles, you will develop a level of credibility and authority in your field. This is one of the prime ways to build your reputation online, and thereby to promote yourself and your services, your products, and your business.

As we have already discussed, at the end of each article you publish online, you will be allowed to include what is known as a *Resource Box*, with information about yourself as well as an active link that connects directly to your website. As readers come to recognize what you have to offer, they will click on your link and visit your site. This is a powerful way to generate traffic to your site, to build your reputation, and to gain the trust of potential employers and clients.

Another added benefit—having "external links" from article directory sites that point to your own website will increase the page rank of your site, moving it higher up on search engine results pages where more potential clients will view it.

Article marketing is proven to be extremely effective, with reliable results. And it is not difficult to do. But you need to be aware of several basic, necessary principles about article marketing in order to be successful.

First, this effort is critical to your launching your talents, services and products. Second, articles must be submitted on a regular basis and not in fits and starts, preferably every month. Third, the power of article marketing is cumulative. Its impact builds over time.

So now your mind is filled with questions. *What* should the articles be about? *How* should you write them? And once you have the written them, *where* do you submit them?

What Articles to Write?

Write articles about topics and issues that pertain directly to both your expertise and what it is you are trying to promote about yourself and your services or products. If you are offering editing services, write about the *"10 Top Grammar and Style Errors That Diminish the Credibility of Otherwise Capable Professionals."*

If you sell leather coats and products, write about *"How to Determine the Quality of Leather"* or *"How to Avoid Substandard Leather Products"* or *"How and Where to Find Excellence in Custom Leather Goods."* If you are entering the field of Internet marketing (SEO) as a contractor, employee or service company, write about *"The Top 10 Needed Actions to Make Your Site Rise to the Top of the List."*

How to Write Your Articles?

The *how* of writing articles is to make them valuable and interesting, clear and direct. Articles should demonstrate your capabilities and knowledge. They should be *relevant* to the types of keywords your potential employers and clients would be using as search terms when they are looking for services, products, or talent that match up with you and your business.

Again, the task is to connect what you have to offer with your potential clients' needs, and to use the actual *words* that people will type when they search the Web to meet that need. Through this, people who are searching for these words will be led to your article, and from your article to your website.

Where to Submit Your Articles?

Once your articles are written, they will be potentially useful on a variety of different channels that together will help you reach your target audience. Three types of channels are: 1) those that you *own* and control, 2) those where you will need to *"earn"* placement, and 3) those that you purchase. Marketing experts suggest using a balance of all three.

Owned media channels include your own website, your blog, and your social media accounts. These channels are beneficial because they are free, you are guaranteed placement of your content, and you have full control over your marketing message. Also, content on your own website has the highest likelihood of producing results, since experts report that consumers who are exposed to your website purchase almost three times more than those who see your advertisements.

Examples of *earned* media channels include any impartial third-party that accepts or selects your articles for publication on their own websites or in their own journals or newspapers. These channels include leading periodicals and publications in your industry, prominent industry commentators, and the wider media of ezines, off-line magazines and newspapers, radio and television. These channels extend the reach of your content to a wider market that is also a "warm" audience—individuals who already are showing clear signs of interest in your type of product or service.

Publication of your content by an impartial third-party adds to your credibility. According to experts, 92% of global consumers trust *earned* media above other forms of marketing. The benefits of earned media channels are that they are free, they enhance your credibility and reach, they extend brand awareness, and they increase the perception that you are a "thought leader" in your niche.

Paid media channels are ones that you purchase, with a guarantee of placement across a number of different marketing venues. The advantage is that they can target your specific audience with greater accuracy.

Create Your Own Blog and/or Join Forums

To review... The term "*blog*" is a short version of "*Weblog*," which, according to Google, is: "a personal website or webpage on which an individual records opinions and links to other sites on a regular basis." The person who posts to a "blog" is called a "blogger." Blogger posts are frequently updated pieces that are arranged chronologically, often featuring a "*What's New*" segment.

Simply put, a *blog* is an online forum that acts as a vehicle for you to establish your personal and professional presence on the Internet. Here you can showcase and share your mission and message.

Did you ever think that you would see the day when you would even consider establishing your own blog? It might be a good idea to give it some thought and to give it a try! Blogs can constitute an effective way to publicize your name to the Web community and to call attention to what you have to offer. If you decide to try your hand at blogging, consider your efforts as an investment of time to reach new clients or potential employers.

For the best return on your blogging efforts, base what you write on what you anticipate your potential clients will want to read about or learn. The point is to engage your potential readers and clients and to gain their confidence, not so much to satisfy whatever needs you may have to hold forth and express your point of view.

Be generous and responsive in sharing your knowledge. As people read what you write, learn about what you do, and begin to appreciate your level of expertise, potential clients will be eager to consider you for work.

Google and other search engines rate *blog* content to be *highly relevant.* Thus *blog* posts are likely to appear high on lists of search results. As always, remember that search engines seek *substance and relevance*. If you focus your writing efforts on these, anticipate the interests and needs of readers, and are responsive in your replies, blogging can become an important means for making yourself *visible* online to the people and markets who need and want to find you.

Blogs versus Forums

Actively posting to a "*forum*" is similar to creating a *blog* in that, again, you will have an opportunity to showcase your expertise and thoughts. The difference is that a *blog* is uniquely yours to post to and control, whereas a *forum* is a public online discussion venue where participants with like interests gather together *virtually* to contribute their opinions and knowledge about a topic.

By participating in a *forum*, you can communicate with others who have questions in your area of expertise, and even point them to a similar topic that you have covered in your *blog*, eBook or website.

Your goal in investing your time participating in *forum* discussions is to become a publicly known entity, an authority in your particular field—a "thought leader." This is a proven pathway to becoming a sought-after resource upon whom potential clients and employers will come to rely for expertise, guidance, and, ultimately, for paid work.

How Do You Juggle It All?

"How," you say, "can I maintain all these various connections— *LinkedIn*, emails, websites, articles, blog and forum posts—in an effective, current way?" This is the challenge you must assume. To meet this challenge, you will need to make multiple uses of each element you create, thus using one medium to fuel the other.

Let's say you write an article on some recent trend or innovative product you have created or an unusual (or unusually excellent) service that you now provide. You could multipurpose this information by simultaneously posting it on your website, your blog, and your chosen forums.

As an example of how this multi-purposing concept can work, the co-authors of this book, who also wrote the award-winning book "*Shifting Gears to Your Life and Work after Retirement,*" take turns writing a monthly article on a chosen topic. They publish each article on www.eZine.com, a well-regarded online journal, with demanding publication standards. Also, they provide the article for publication on several appropriate websites and blogs where their potential reading audience may be expected to visit. And they upload it to the book's website, www.ShiftingGearstoYourLifeandWorkAfterRetirement.com.

They carry the same messages into requested interviews with *USA Today* and other reporters, as well as television and radio programs. And they post on *LinkedIn*, and occasionally to their email lists, any new articles by or about them, their book, and any upcoming TV or radio interviews.

Since different audiences rely on different sources for their information, they know that, through this multi-purposing of their written work, they are reaching a variety of groups and individuals. This strategy becomes a win-win situation—multi-purposing work to achieve maximum exposure, while also providing other forums and bloggers substantive material for their own websites.

Conduct a *Google Adwords* Campaign

Who me? Conduct a *Google Adwords* campaign advertising myself? Are you serious? Yes, this is exactly what I mean. And, yes, you *can* do this! What's more, now that you are a "Web worker," you will no longer even need to limit your advertisements to a particular location. Think about it! The whole world has become your workplace... your client base... your "immediate location."

Adwords is one of the most popular advertising tools on the Web today. If you are offering a service or product, and have an established website, investing in an *Adwords* campaign is another excellent way to gain attention—and clicks—immediately.

When establishing an *Adwords* campaign, you will be able to design multiple ads, and to specify when you want your ads to be shown, based on what *keywords* you anticipate your targeted customers will use when they do a web search. *Google* will show your ads, at or near the top of the search result pages, following your specifications. You will pay for an ad only when someone actually clicks on it.

One important feature of setting up an *Adwords* campaign—you can establish a budget that limits your "ad spend" to the daily amount you are able or willing to allot.

Google will provide you with ongoing feedback, showing all essential details, such as how many clicks you have received for each ad or keyword, the average position where your ads have appeared on search results pages, and your average *"cost per click."* Additionally, you will be able to activate and run a campaign for a limited period of time in order to gather clients or business, then "pause" it temporarily until you need it again.

How or where can you go to learn more about how to use Adwords? A quick *Google* search, using the term, "Learn to Use Google AdWords," will yield a helpful list of websites that offer highly useful training modules on this topic, ranging from free to fee-based, beginners to advanced. As you have by now come to expect, the Web offers a virtual potpourri selection of training on almost any topic, designed to accommodate any and all levels of user interest and ability.

And So...

Until now, you have persevered in learning about the universal maze of online work opportunities available. You have *analyzed* an enormous amount of data, much of which might have been foreign to you until now. You have taken considerable time and expended the necessary energy to explore and to *summarize* the whole range of these online career options. Finally, you have *synthesized* and drilled down to those professional work areas that best align with your experience, your talent, your interests.

Your reward awaits you in the form of your readiness to act. The bottom line—whatever it is you confidently know you're good at, however you think you might want to start earning a living online, you are now armed with all the essential tools you need to launch your new online career.

Consider these chapters as your driving force, your launching pad. They have mapped out the process, the connections, the strategies you need to pursue. The next step is yours to take. If you are persistent, confident, open to new ideas, and self-disciplined enough to do the necessary legwork, you, too, can and will become a productive and well-compensated 21st century webworker.

Chapter 12:
Here's to Happy Beginnings

SO, can you make money working online at home? Absolutely! Can you shift to an online career? Certainly. Shifting to an online career, working from an office in your home, and making your full living that way, is absolutely possible, given the resources and interconnections of the Internet.

This doesn't guarantee that the jobs will come flowing to you on their own, like a steady spring stream. In fact, you may need to work harder than you ever have before. But you will be doing work that you chose. You will be doing what you love and loving what you do. And you will be doing it from home, with minimal travel back and forth to work sites.

When you shift to your career online, gone will be the days of working like Wally in the Dilbert cartoon, wandering around holding a cup of coffee and complaining, but doing little or no actual work (not that you ever would want to do that, anyway!).

As a web worker, you, in all your glory, capability and competence, will be fully exposed. There will be no one to take up the slack, except you. There will be no one to defer to, stand behind, or blame, if and when you come up short. Your charm and good looks will not buy you another chance or gain you forgiveness for a substandard product or a subpar service, or for either being submitted late.

On the other hand, what you've always wanted will be yours for the taking. You will stand (or fall) based on your own self-presentation, abilities, attentiveness, professionalism, responsiveness, capability, reliability, promptness, accuracy and results. You will be recognized for what you can and do contribute. You will control your work style, as it balances with your lifestyle. And you will learn more and more each day as you proceed along this path.

There is a passage from the movie, *A League of Their Own,* that embodies the essence of work versus reward. This quote bears remembering if and when you embark on a cyber-career. At one point, Geena Davis, who portrays a key member of a women's baseball team during World War II, decides to leave the team because, as she laments, "It's just too hard." Tom Hanks, the acerbic, sometimes obnoxious, seemingly unsympathetic coach, responds—"Too hard? *Too hard?* It's supposed to be hard! Hard is what makes it great! If it weren't hard, everyone would do it!"

You may not be destined to make millions of dollars through this new adventure of working online. But you certainly *can* make the shift to an online career and work from home... And you definitely *can* make money doing so.

From online tutoring to SEO writing to developing visual images. From being a *virtual assistant* to serving as a *virtual concierge* to creating information products. Who would have thought there would be so many different ways to earn money online?

The truth of the matter is that if you choose something that interests you, or an activity you enjoy, and you have the talent for it, you can earn a substantial income. Will it be enough to leave your day job? Many people—millions of people—already have done just that, and those numbers continue to increase.

Moreover, your level of income will depend on you and, to a degree, be determined by you, more than it ever was within a 9-to-5 job in the brick-and-mortar work world. How financially successful you are as a webworker will be based on *your* efforts, *your* talents, *your* determination and *your* hard work. You will be the one in charge of your work and work life. And you will be the one to gain the credit and reap the rewards.

Most certainly you will need to prepare both your work environment and yourself to make this shift online. But even those seeming hurdles can be rewarding and enjoyable—learning more, designing your physical space, determining your time parameters, and reassessing yourself and what you can and want to do, now and into the future.

What lies ahead after your transformation to webworker? Satisfaction and fulfillment in knowing that you are earning money in a meaningful career, even while you continue to enjoy all other aspects of your family, social, and professional life. And that's no small thing.

Here's to happy beginnings in cyberspace and beyond!

INDEX

Also Available

Through Amazon.com and other online booksellers,
in print and eBook versions.

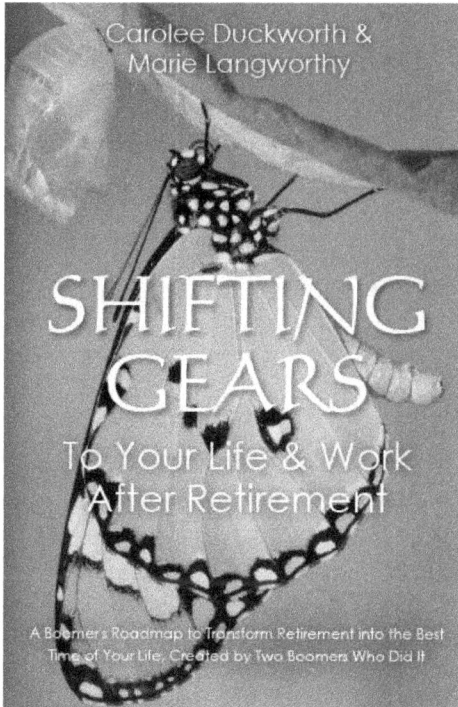

Carolee Duckworth &
Marie Langworthy

SHIFTING
GEARS
To Your Life & Work
After Retirement

A Boomer's Roadmap to Transform Retirement into the Best
Time of Your Life, Created by Two Boomers Who Did It

What Others Are Saying

"This is the most encompassing, yet practical book on transitioning career/life paths you will ever read. Carolee and Marie have provided an amazing action guide to assist in making this "Shift" an exciting and well thought through process. A must have!"

Dr. Ed Bice, III. Peak Performance Consultant.

Author of: "Journey to Peak Experience" & "The Wisdom."

"Drs. Duckworth and Langworthy have written a tour de force that is a "must read" for members of the Boomer generation who face a myriad of issues that transcend all previous generations in the United States. "Shifting Gears" is a gold mine of hard data, anecdotal stories, and invaluable sources of information for those of us who must make critical decisions in the immediate future regarding how we will spend this last phase of our lives."

Dr. Alan Hadad, Physics Professor, Associate Vice President, Dean of University Magnet Schools, University of Hartford

"The road to retirement is filled with high hopes and good intentions, but all too often, those on that highway find only potholes and detours. For many, that important life decision triggers anxiety, self-doubt and indecision. In "Shifting Gears," Langworthy and Duckworth provide a common sense pathway to a confident retirement decision."

George M. Reilly, Ed.D.

A great book and a new way of framing retirement, especially for those, who have never given thought to what they would best be suited for. A great "get off the couch and get moving" incentive. Fantastic!"

Marion DiGiammo, Retired Math Teacher & Guidance Counselor

A must read. An extraordinary, mind-opening story of life and work after retirement. Possibilities are unlimited.

Jeanne Hawver, Retired Teacher & Business Owner

www.ingramcontent.com/pod-product-compliance
Lightning Source LLC
Chambersburg PA
CBHW060324200326
41519CB00011BA/1831